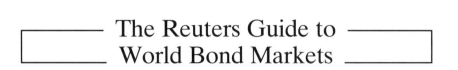

The Reuters Guide to World Bond Markets

The Reuters Guide to World Bond Markets

Martin Essex
Reuters

Ruth Pitchford
Reuters

JOHN WILEY & SONS
Chichester · New York · Brisbane · Toronto · Singapore

Published by John Wiley & Sons Ltd,
     Baffins Lane, Chichester,
     West Sussex PO19 1UD, England

     National   01243 779777
     International   (+44) 1243 779777
     e-mail (for orders and customer service enquiries): cs-books@wiley.co.uk
     Visit our Home Page on http://www.wiley.co.uk
            or http://www.wiley.com

Other Wiley Editorial Offices

John Wiley & Sons, Inc., 605 Third Avenue,
New York, NY 10158-0012, USA

Jacaranda Wiley Ltd, 33 Park Road, Milton,
Queensland 4064, Australia

John Wiley & Sons (Canada) Ltd, 22 Worcester Road,
Rexdale, Ontario M9W 1L1, Canada

John Wiley & Sons (Asia) Pte Ltd, 2 Clementi Loop #02-01,
Jin Xing Distripark, Singapore 0512

British Library Cataloguing in Publication Data

A catalogue record for this book is available from the British Library

ISBN 0-471-96046-2

Typeset in 11/13pt Times by Dorwyn Ltd, Rowlands Castle, Hants
Printed and bound in Great Britain by Biddles Ltd, Guildford, Surrey
This book is printed on acid-free paper responsibly manufactured from sustainable
forestation, for which at least two trees are planted for each one used for paper
production.

To Maureen, Katherine and Jonathan

And to Rob and Mary

With love

Contents

Preface

A few years ago it became clear to us that the conventional way of reporting on bond markets was no longer satisfactory. The kind of story that began: 'Bonds were slightly firmer in light trading' was of no use to the professional trader or salesman, analyst or economist who would be reading it on his or her terminal. They wanted a more forward-looking product: 'I don't want you to tell me why I lost money today but how I'm going to make it tomorrow' was one comment we all took to heart. Our stories began to incorporate market views on what was likely to happen as well as what had happened already; we added technical analysis and sentiment as well as fundamentals, despite some people's view that 'charting' was no different from voodoo. Others told us that technical analysis was widely used, both in its own right and to give entry and exit prices once economics had been used to determine the trend. And our writing became more sophisticated. We introduced reports on derivatives as well as the cash market and, in particular, we introduced a daily World Bonds report. This took a medium-term view of the international bond markets, giving analysts' views of which were likely to outperform or underperform and noting strategists' views on where on the curve to invest, along with concepts such as duration to give a more complex analysis than had been attempted before.

This book extends that concept by attempting to look ahead to how the major world government bond markets might perform in 1996. It is not another textbook on bond analytics; we are not qualified to write such a book and many exist already. Nor does it contain merely simple descriptions of how each market works, though we have incorporated some of that too. Instead, we have tried to look at the economics, the politics, the technical aspects and all the other factors likely to have an impact. We have pitched the book at the professional, though it is certainly not an academic textbook, but we hope it will be of interest to the serious amateur as well. We have only included the most important bond markets—the G7 countries plus Australia—and only government bonds rather than the corporate or municipal markets. We have not incorporated the emerging debt markets either. Though it is clear they are becoming increasingly important, none comes close to the eight key markets we have described in detail in this book.

Looking ahead, there is little doubt that the coming years will see enormous change, particularly if parts of Western Europe adopt a single currency. For now, though, this is how the markets look.

Introduction

Nineteen ninety five was a year when you had to be clever to make money in the world's major government bond markets, and the signs are that the rest of 1996 and 1997 will be the same. In both 1993 and 1994, making money was relatively easy. You just had to make the right decision as the year began and plough a straight furrow for the following 12 months. In 1993, the right decision on 1 January was to buy. You had to decide that the worldwide surge higher in government bond prices would continue, and whichever bonds you bought in any market, there was a fair chance of coming out on top. Similarly, in 1994 the right decision was to sell. You had to decide that the time had come for a correction; and as long as you kept selling as the year progressed, the chances were that on 31 December you crossed the line a winner.

Now, of course, life is never that simple. Thinking back to the early days of 1994, the impression is that more economists, bond analysts and strategists were expecting the advance in prices to continue than to end. Making the right decision was by no means easy. Take Robert Citron, for example. The Treasurer of Orange County in California was convinced that US interest rates would continue to fall. By February they were rising and, by December, Orange County was seeking bankruptcy court protection from its creditors, its $7.57 billion investment portfolio having lost some $1.69 billion of its value.

Moreover, despite the sophistication of the world's financial markets today, it is still easier to make money in a rising market than a falling one. A bull, who expects a market to rise, takes a long position—buys some bonds and puts them in the cupboard and forgets about them. A bear, who expects a market to fall, has to take a short position—sell something he or she does not own and prepare to buy it back later at a lower price to complete the transaction.

That sounds complicated, and it is. For one thing, in some countries the futures and options, swaps and repurchase markets necessary to take a short position are rudimentary or do not exist at all. For another, many operators in the financial markets are automatically long. A bank, for example, is likely to keep bonds in the cupboard (metaphorically of course) to sell to customers who want them.

None the less, if you had been a bull in 1993 or a bear in 1994 you could hardly have gone wrong. The trouble with 1995 was that as the year began, most of those economists, analysts and strategists expected the world's government bond markets to trade broadly sideways. That was why you had to be clever to make money in 1995. Our purpose is not to forecast what will happen in 1996 or 1997. That is best left to clairvoyants and astrologers. But it is possible to point out some of the pitfalls and some of the stepping stones that investors are likely to encounter in the world's major bond markets in coming months, for those times when you need to be clever again.

That means providing factual information on how each of the world's major government bond markets works. It means describing the economic and political position in each country: the so-called 'fundamentals'. It means looking at the technical situation in each market, for charts can tell you much about the future by describing the past. And it means spending some time on sentiment, perhaps the most important factor of all in determining whether a price is likely to rise or fall. It could even be suggested that institutional investors should employ behavioural psychologists along with their economists and statisticians.

As 1995 began, sentiment was bluntly dreadful: those without the foresight to sell in 1994 were nursing heavy losses. Investors who on 1 January 1994 put their money in a range of large, liquid government bond issues in each of the major world markets would have lost more than 3 per cent in local-currency terms by 31 December, even after offsetting the interest received from the bonds against the falls in the bonds' prices. Every single major market gave a negative return, measured in the local currency; the first year of the 1990s in which that was the case. In some markets the losses were much greater than 3 per cent: almost seven per cent in the United Kingdom in sterling terms, for example.

Data from Salomon Brothers in New York showed that of the markets the US investment bank included in its World Government Bond Index (WGBI), only Austrian government bonds made a profit in 1994, and there the annual return was a mere 0.02 per cent in local currency terms. The Salomon Brothers WGBI posted an annual loss for the first time since it was launched in 1986, reflecting a decision by the US central bank, the Federal Reserve, to start raising interest rates as a pre-emptive strike against inflation which analysts decided was too little too late. Political problems from elections to scandals made matters worse, and the index ended the year down 3.27 per cent in local currency terms. British gilts gave up 6.89 per cent of their value in sterling terms, and other large local currency losses included Australian bonds, which lost 6.47 per cent, French bonds, which gave up 5.67 per cent, and Swedish bonds, which registered a negative 4.74 per cent return.

Mind you, the picture was transformed for dollar-based investors overseas who benefited from a sinking dollar. A US-based investor in bond markets abroad would have made a perfectly acceptable return of 8.88 per cent in Japanese government bonds (JGBs), for example, while a yen-based investor would have lost 2.67 per cent. Other large returns for dollar-based investors included 12.22 per cent from Belgian bonds, 11.80 per cent from Austrian bonds and 9.98 per cent from German Bunds. In contrast Canadian government bonds would have lost an investor from south of the border 9.86 per cent as the Canadian dollar lost even more ground than its US counterpart.

The Salomon indices are calculated using all government bonds with a maturity of more than one year, weighted for market capitalisation. Only bonds which are freely available to institutional investors and with a certain minimum issue size outstanding are included in the index. Returns are calculated to take account of both price movements and accrued interest over the period.

This overall decline in world government bond values was reflected, among other places, at the hedge funds, the large mostly US-based investment funds managing the wealth of private individuals and using the derivatives markets to boost their earnings. Derivatives are products such as futures and options, swaps and warrants, the value of which is 'derived' from an underlying product such as a bond, a share, a currency or a commodity.

Figures released early in 1995 by Micropal, a UK-based performance measurement firm, showed the average performance of the 151 derivatives-related funds it tracked was an 8.25 per cent loss in 1994; in 1993 the sector offered a 21.34 per cent gain. Just 44 of the funds gave a positive return, and six of those were under one per cent. The Quantum Fund, made famous by its high-profile manager George Soros, lost 15.64 per cent in 1994 after a positive return of more than 50 per cent in 1993, according to Micropal.

Hedge funds often use derivatives because derivatives allow them to take a large stake in an underlying market for a relatively small outlay, boosting potential returns but also increasing potential losses. Some did do well in 1994, especially those that went short for example. However, the vast majority lost money, and many tacticians began 1995 recommending defensive strategies and tipping the large, liquid, so-called 'core' markets like the United States, Germany and Japan, while turning their backs on the rather rudely named 'peripheral' markets like Spain and Sweden.

There is an argument used by some chartists that says economic strategists' opinions reflect not what is likely to happen but what has happened already. When we as financial journalists ask traders if German Bunds are about to rise in value and they say 'yes', they are almost certainly telling us not that they are about to buy Bunds but that they already have. No problem with that— they would not have bought had they not expected prices to go up. The problem comes when there is a strong consensus that Bund prices are due to rise.

That means almost certainly that everyone around has already bought and is now hoping to sell at a profit once prices have risen. It means that all those wanting to buy have already done so. Thus potential sellers abound, buyers are nowhere to be found and prices have only one direction to go—downwards. It is a scenario the contrarian exploits by taking the opposite position from the consensus. And the contrarian is always on the look out for signs a move has gone too far: the hairdresser asking if she should have a dabble in bonds, the trader on the radio saying he's a raging bull or perhaps the television programme where the pundits are all arguing for the same market.

Still, it is the case that core markets have provided a relatively safe haven in the past when markets have fallen, while high-yielding markets have tended to outperform on the way back up. Early in 1995 many strategists suggested investing in markets with high liquidity where bonds can be bought and sold fast, and with low transaction costs, so it is cheap and easy to move out if you want to.

Investors seemed to agree, with low volumes as the year began suggesting that they were unwilling to throw good money after bad in the government bond markets. Corporate bond issuers and their investment bankers appeared to agree too, bringing new issues in the opening days of the year only in the currencies of countries with sophisticated financial markets, so that they could hedge their risks effectively.

The proponents of a defensive, core-only policy were soon given extra backing in the new year by a financial crisis in Mexico which knocked emerging markets around the world. Those are not the subject of this book. But Mexico's problems may well have persuaded some investment funds to shift their money from high-risk regions such as Central and South America, Eastern Europe and the less-developed Asian markets into the relative safety of North America, Western Europe, Japan and Australia.

If so, some analysts think that from a long-term perspective such a move would be against the trend, for there is a widespread feeling that funds will be committed increasingly to the developing world, attracted by high potential returns and prepared to put up with a bumpy ride along the way. Indeed, the argument runs that countries like the United States, Japan and Germany may have to pay far more for their funds in future as they compete for investment with countries like China, Russia and Brazil.

Be that as it may, in early 1995 those strategists backing core-developed markets were also given fresh ammunition by huge political problems in Italy and Spain, currency turmoil and the dreadful earthquake in Kobe, which led to talk of Japanese investors bringing their money back home to help pay for reconstruction after the devastation. Evidence suggests that even before that, in 1994, the Japanese investors who were so crucial to the US Treasury market in previous years repatriated funds on a huge scale. As the dollar sank against the yen in early 1995, it was hard to think of any logical reason why a Japanese investor should want to commit funds to the United States.

Yet such a strategy would have been completely wrong. The Salomon Brothers figures for 1995 show that in local currency terms the top performing market was Sweden, which gave a return of 20.20 per cent. That was followed by Canada, giving 20.03 per cent, and Australia, offering a return of 19.85 per cent. In contrast, the core markets were among the worst performers, with the US giving investors a healthy 18.30 per cent but Germany offering just 16.27 per cent and Japan giving a meagre 13.29 per cent, the worst return of any major market. In dollar terms, Sweden offered a stunning return to investors of 34.83 per cent, compared with a paltry 9.57 per cent return from an investment in Japanese government bonds.

As for 1996, the Reuters quarterly interest rate poll conducted in December 1995 gave the following results:

Table 0.1   Reuters Quarterly Interest Rate Poll—December 1995

It features forecasts from 21 London-based economists, surveyed on where interest rates and bond yields would be in the Group of Seven industrialised countries at year end, and the end of the first and second quarters.

Respondents' forecasts were updated to take account of interest rate moves last week in three of the countries, Britain, France and Germany.

The rates covered are the key rates according to the current monetary policy in each of the countries listed.

Figures listed are averages of the forecasts.

	End Q4 95 (pct)	End Q1 96 (pct)	End Q2 96 (pct)
US FEDERAL FUNDS	5.62	5.38	5.25
Low/High	5.25/5.75	5.00/6.00	4.50/6.25
US 30-YEAR YIELD	6.05	6.14	6.28
Low/High	6.00/6.25	5.60/7.10	4.50/6.25
GERMAN DISCOUNT RATE	3.00	3.00	2.93
Low/High	3.00/3.00	3.00/3.00	2.50/3.00
GERMAN 10-YEAR YIELD	6.06	5.95	6.00
Low/High	6.00/6.20	5.75/6.50	5.50/6.75
JAPAN DISCOUNT RATE	0.50	0.50	0.49
Low/High	0.50/0.50	0.50/0.50	0.25/0.50
JAPAN 10-YEAR YIELD	2.77	3.01	3.21
Low/High	2.50/3.00	2.30/3.50	2.10/3.80

UK BASE RATE	6.50	6.24	6.11
Low/High	6.50/6.50	5.75/6.50	5.50/6.75
UK 10-YEAR YIELD	7.52	7.49	7.55
Low/High	7.35/7.90	6.80/8.25	6.75/8.62
FRENCH INTERVENTION RATE	4.45	4.26	4.11
Low/High	4.45/4.45	3.80/4.75	3.40/4.75
FRENCH 10-YEAR YIELD	6.80	6.69	6.76
Low/High	6.65/6.95	6.25/7.45	6.10/7.75
CANADA BANK RATE	6.06	5.90	5.74
Low/High	5.90/6.25	5.60/6.15	5.50/6.30
CANADA 10-YEAR YIELD	7.32	7.37	7.33
Low/High	7.00/8.00	6.60/8.40	6.50/8.50
ITALY DISCOUNT RATE	9.00	8.73	8.55
Low/High	9.00/9.00	8.50/9.00	8.00/9.00
ITALY 10-YEAR YIELD	11.12	11.00	10.94
Low/High	10.50/11.25	10.40/11.50	10.00/11.87

Of course, there are many different kinds of investment funds and they do not all act in the same way. Speculative and short-term accounts might be more nimble, but they are also less likely to risk a near-term loss than a long-term investor such as a pension fund, which can afford to take on a position for the long haul and ignore relatively minor portfolio losses in the mean time.

Flows from hedge funds can dry up as their wealthy individual clients decide to buy paintings or Ferraris instead. Even the dealing community may well decide to restrict itself to what one analyst has called a 'baby steps' strategy, taking out a succession of small positions that are closed very quickly to avoid suffering the feeling of having a huge position under water and sinking fast.

In the last few years currency traders have made fortunes from selling the dollar. But when there are threats of US rate rises to support the currency, or rate cuts elsewhere to make other currencies less attractive, or even concerted intervention by the major central banks, having an exchange rate 'target' makes little sense. It is much better, surely, to sell a few dollars, buy them back at a profit and go home at night able to sleep soundly without having to worry that the market might have moved against you while you've been having 40 winks.

If the old adage is true that bond markets are only a good investment in a recession, 1996 may not fit the bill and may be a year for caution too. But the arguments are far more complex than that and the purpose of this book is to map a path through the maze, put up signposts and just possibly lead the determined investor to the point where if money does not grow on trees at least it does not disappear into a hole in the ground.

Deciding which country to invest in is clearly an important part of any international investment strategy, but questioning whether to put money into fixed-income securities, stocks and shares, commodities, property or anything else is also clearly crucial. Even if some of those funds are to be put into the debt markets, the decision still has to be made as to where on the yield curve best value may be found.

To take the asset class question first, fixed-income securities are often seen as the best place to invest in a recession because long-term bond yields reflect inflation expectations, and inflation is likely to rise during a period of economic growth and fall during a period of economic contraction. In contrast, stocks and shares are likely to be favoured during a period of economic expansion, as companies find it easier to raise prices, sell more and grow, increasing the value of their shareholders' equity. Similarly, commodity prices, property values and prices of 'collectibles' such as fine art are all likely to gain more ground in a recovery than a recession. If 1996 is another year of world growth, as some economists believe, bonds are only moderately attractive. If the recovery in the United States and a few other countries is over and their economies are turning down, as other economists believe, then bonds are more attractive compared with other assets.

A Reuters asset allocation poll in late February 1996, asking US-based investors about their intentions, showed a significant six per cent allocation increase into the Asian markets, excluding Japan, at the expense of US holdings over the first two months of 1996. On average, portfolio managers decreased their US holdings by five per cent over the time period. A similar poll collated in London showed fund managers reducing their weighting in US equities while holding their US bond allocations steady. And the equivalent poll in Japan showed investors there turning slightly cautious of possible dips in major share markets. In the debt markets a defensive strategy implies opting for short-dated securities rather than long-dated ones because bonds with short maturities and high coupons have a lower duration than bonds with long maturities and low coupons, meaning their value drops by less when the general level of yields rises.

Figure 0.1 gives a snapshot of the US and German yield curves out to 10 years as they were on one day in March 1996. The US curve is very flat, with the two-year yield at 6.1 per cent and the 10-year yield at 7.0 per cent, a difference of just 0.9 percentage points or 90 basis points. That shows investors at the time believed there was little chance of strong economic growth in the United States because the recovery was by then mature, suggesting little chance of a surge in inflation in the foreseeable future.

The German curve is much steeper, with the two-year yield at 4.2 per cent and the 10-year yield close to 7.1 per cent, a spread between twos and tens of almost three percentage points or 290 basis points. That reflected a belief that as Germany was well behind in the business cycle, its recovery less mature, there was more of a chance of bond-negative inflation in Germany than in the United States.

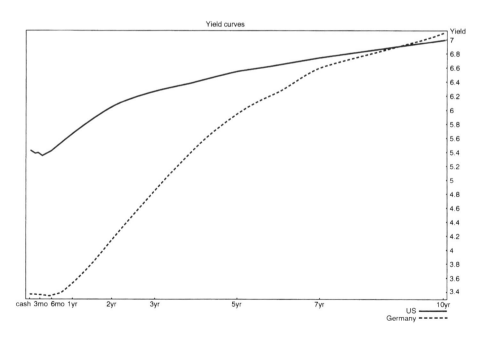

Figure 0.1

Unfortunately for those adopting a defensive strategy, if the US economy does turn down in late 1996, perhaps with the UK and some of the other economies that are well advanced in the business cycle, it is long-dated bonds that are likely to benefit most. In early 1996, some yield curves were relatively flat, with long-dated bond yields only a little higher than the yields of short-dated securities. And that would remain the case, with curves flattening even more or perhaps even inverting, with long yields moving lower than short yields.

Evidence of economic slowdown, in an environment where inflation is relatively subdued, tends to trigger buying interest at the long end. Bond markets can also react positively when authorities take fast, effective action to control inflation by raising interest rates at the first sign of unsustainable growth. On the other hand, if the US economy keeps on growing, as suggested by some early 1996 data, or Germany is not seen to be reacting correctly to expansion, the short-duration proponents would be vindicated as yield curves would steepen and the short end would be the right place to be positioned.

These then are the arguments that will be analysed in this book, with the intention of giving the professional fund manager, investment banker or corporate treasurer enough information to develop a coherent investment strategy in the fixed-income markets in the year ahead. The first chapter looks at the world economic position, and the next at the technical, or chart, situation. There are still economists who regard technical analysis as voodoo research and chartists who think economics a total waste of time. But there are also researchers who think that any serious investor should look at both types of analysis, and that is the approach taken here.

Chart 0.1 is a monthly bar chart of the front-month US Treasury bond future on the Chicago Board of Trade, showing 10 years of prices. The bars show the high, low and close each month, and the fact that leaps out from the chart is that the downturn that began late in 1993 and continued for most of 1994 may have felt savage at the time but was relatively mild in an historical context.

The trend for most of those 10 years has been upwards, and it is still too early to say whether the 1993 highs above 120 marked the end of the bull run and the beginning of a bear market or whether the losses will be seen in due course to have been just a steep

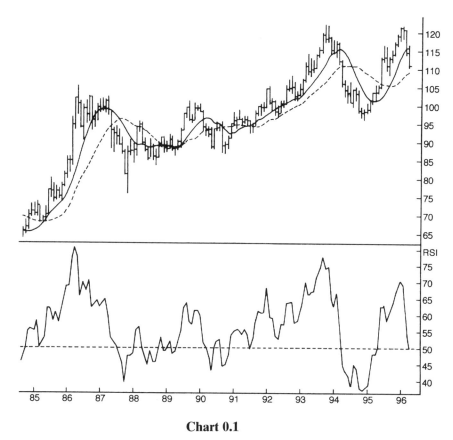

Chart 0.1

correction. The fact that the subsequent recovery ran out of steam at almost exactly the same level, forming what technical analysts call a 'double top' is certainly a bearish signal. However, at the moment Chart 0.1 was printed, the price was above the 10-month moving average, which was itself above the 20-month moving average; meaning the market was still technically in a bull trend. The 14-month relative strength indicator, charted below the main chart, gives sell signals when it dips to 30 and buy signals when it climbs to 70. That was in neutral territory and not yet giving a signal.

Incidentally, having noted that many economists failed to predict the bond market rally in early 1995, it is perhaps only fair to note that it caught some technical analysts by surprise as well. In January many were saying that a new bull run was still some way away and that the general trend still appeared to be downwards.

Even some who were relatively optimistic were talking of just a period of consolidation and predicting range-trading at best.

These arguments are discussed in more detail in Chapter 2 and individual country sections follow, with plenty of information, as well as advice, on topics such as how the bond market is structured in each country, the political outlook, the role of the central bank and what the rating agencies think.

Structure, as mentioned earlier, is important because fund managers need to know they can move in and out quickly and cheaply, hedge their holdings and not be caught out by unexpected changes in taxes, say, or exchange controls. It is important to know that Italy, for instance, has a large and stable base of private, domestic 'retail' investors in its bond market who are perhaps less likely to shift their funds away than overseas institutional investors.

Politics, like sentiment, can be crucial, not just because politicians make important decisions on fiscal and sometimes monetary policy but also because markets hate uncertainty and few events cause more uncertainty than an election. France, for example, chose a new president back in April and May of 1995. First the then prime minister Edouard Balladur appeared to be the front runner; then he was overtaken in the opinion polls by his Gaullist ally, the then mayor of Paris Jacques Chirac; then came the first round of elections ending with socialist Lionel Jospin in the lead. Not until the second round two weeks later was Chirac finally elected president.

That sort of uncertainty is detested by investors, who other things being equal would much rather send their funds to a country where no elections are due for a while and the political outlook seems stable. This is how NatWest Securities of the United Kingdom summarised the importance of politics in its *European Political Handbook*, published in March 1995, under the heading 'Weakness is the enemy':

> Everywhere there is agreement on the need to cut budget deficits and bring down inflation to acceptably low levels. What matters to markets is the ability of governments to carry out these policies successfully.

The currency outlook can be crucial too; as mentioned earlier currency losses can more than offset bond market profits, so that element is woven into our analysis. Also included is a look at the central bank in each country. An independent central bank can maintain monetary stability in a country like Italy, providing a counter-weight to swings in fiscal policy that can follow rapid changes of government. Equally, where a central bank is not independent, as in the United Kingdom, it is important for investors to realise that a change of government can bring simultaneous changes to fiscal and monetary policies.

Research by French investment bank unit Paribas Capital Markets summarised the degree of central bank independence in early 1995 as shown in Table 0.2.

Changes to a country's debt rating, particularly by the two leading US rating agencies, Moody's Investors Service and Standard & Poor's Corporation, can bring investors windfall profits or unexpected losses because the rules of some investment funds only allow them to put their money in 'investment grade' debt.

We have also included a look at how the principal countries in the European Union are bringing their national accounts into line with the Maastricht Treaty guidelines. This treaty, signed to pave

Table 0.2 Central Bank Independence, early 1995

Country	Changing key interest rates	Exchange rate regime	Setting monetary targets	Execution of monetary policy
Austria	*	*	*n	*
Belgium	*		*n	*
Denmark	*		*	*
Finland	Joint	Joint		*
France	*		*	*
Germany	*		*	*
Ireland	*		*n	*
Italy	*		Joint	*
Netherlands	*		*n	*
Norway				*
Portugal	*			*
Spain	*		*	*
Sweden	*	*	*	*
Switzerland	*		*	*
United Kingdom				*

Key: *   central bank has responsibility for this function
        n   no target set at present
        Joint   government and central bank have responsibility for this function

the way to eventual European Economic and Monetary Union, or EMU, lays down five principal 'convergence criteria' which analysts in Europe have come to look at ever more closely to determine whether a country's markets look like a good investment or a poor one.

The key criteria have been laid out lucidly by US investment bank Merrill Lynch as follows:

1. Consumer price inflation must not exceed by more than 1.5 percentage points that of the three countries with the lowest inflation.
2. Yields on long-term government debt must not be more than two percentage points higher than that of the three countries identified in the inflation criterion.
3. The currency must have been held within the normal fluctuation band of the ERM (Exchange Rate Mechanism) without severe tensions and without devaluation on own initiative against another EU (European Union) country for at least two years.
4. A general government deficit no greater than three per cent of GDP (Gross Domestic Product), unless either (a) the ratio has declined substantially and continuously and reached a level that comes close to 3 per cent or, alternatively, (b) the excess over 3 per cent is only exceptional and temporary and the ratio remains close to 3 per cent.
5. A ratio of government debt to GDP not in excess of 60 per cent, unless the ratio is sufficiently diminishing and approaching the reference value at a satisfactory pace.

Merrill Lynch calculated in early 1995 that the candidates for 'Inner Circle' membership were Germany, the Netherlands, Austria, Luxembourg, France, Ireland, Belgium and Denmark. The countries it described as candidates for the periphery were Italy, Spain, Sweden, Portugal, Finland, Greece and the United Kingdom.

However, its analysis was accompanied by a European Commission graph showing that a mere three countries, Luxembourg, Ireland and Germany, achieved the Maastricht deficit/GDP target of three per cent in 1994. A second European Commission graph showed just four countries, Luxembourg, France, the United Kingdom and Germany, were in line with the Maastricht debt/GDP target of 60 per cent.

These, then, are the issues addressed. Much of the information is from the central banks and government departments concerned—and we are grateful to the central banks, ministries of finance and treasury departments that sent us so much useful information. We are also grateful to the many economists and analysts, brokers and traders who provide us with information day in and day out. The opinions expressed are theirs rather than ours—as reporters not columnists we try to keep our own opinions out of our writing as much as possible and simply write down what we are told. We are grateful as well to our colleagues at Reuters who follow the markets' ups and downs with us day after day, and in particular to Tiziana Barghini and Sharman Esarey for their help with the Italian and German chapters respectively and to Cheryl Juckes and Mariam Isa for their help with the UK chapter.

1
The global economy

Long-term bond yields reflect inflation expectations, at least according to one theory that is widely accepted. The higher the level of inflation predicted, the higher bond yields must be to compensate holders for its likely ravages. Inflation tends to rise as an economy expands and fall as an economy contracts, again in theory. In practice many other factors, such as political uncertainty and currency weakness, may be just as important to bond investors, but the economy still provides a good starting point. Moreover, since the United States' economy is the one that drives the others, that is where this book begins.

Since 1970, the US economy has suffered four recessions, according to Citibank analysis of data from the National Bureau of Economic Research. The first was from November 1973 to March 1975, the second from January to July 1980, the third from July 1981 to November 1982 and the fourth from July 1990 to March 1991. The definition of recession is hotly disputed by economists in different countries, but during each of those four periods there was a decline in real GDP, the economy's output. Put simply—the economy shrank.

The most recent of those four recessions was followed by a strong recovery in most of 1991 and 1992, a minor pullback in 1993 and then a further advance that started in 1994 but was showing distinct signs of faltering by the first quarter of 1995. It was that pullback that gave the world government bond markets such a good year in 1993. It was the feeling that it might be only a temporary setback in a solid climb out of recession that gave bonds such a tough time in 1994; and it was the renewed signs of a slowing economy that allowed bond markets to recover so well in 1995.

The US recovery pulled the rest of the world behind it. As the United States staggered to its feet, Europe struggled onto its knees and Japan tried not to be left flat on its back after its first major recession since 1974. The US authorities' response to the recovery was to begin raising official interest rates in February 1994 and then to continue raising them as the economy steamed ahead so as to avoid consumer prices being forced up by the economic expansion. The market reaction was unusual. Instead of bond yields rising with short-term interest rates, the authorities discovered that the more they raised rates the more the bond markets liked it; analysts arguing that the climb in rates represented a positive response to the inflation threat.

The yield curve flattened dramatically, with the gap between higher long-term and lower short-term rates steadily reducing, as inflation expectations were scaled down. Other countries with fairly advanced recoveries, such as the United Kingdom, Australia and some Nordic countries, began to raise rates too. Much of the rest of Europe, well behind in the economic cycle, delayed the process of rate cutting. The Japanese, still further behind in the cycle, were left to ponder the wisdom of rate cutting on their own. Thus it was that so many analysts went into 1995 neutral on the bond markets, arguing that although yields should rise to compensate for economic growth and rising inflation expectations, bond prices were likely to benefit from the increases in interest rates that would keep economic growth slow and inflation in check.

In fact, 1995 turned out to be a very good year for bond investors, who could have received a return of about 17 per cent from a geographically-spread portfolio of government bonds. However, the picture painted by the Paris-based Organisation for Economic Co-operation and Development (OECD) at the end of 1995 was essentially a negative one for bonds. It noted that world growth had been disappointing in 1995 but predicted a pick-up in 1996, helped by a recovery in Japan and a continued moderate upswing in the United States.

It said growth was slowing in Europe but still forecast growth for its 25 members as a whole of 2.6 per cent in 1996 and 2.8 per cent in 1997, compared with about 2.4 per cent in 1995.

There were few signs of the cyclical downturn that would lead to lower inflation and a continued bull trend in bonds, even in the leading United States. Citibank's analysis of the National Bureau of Economic Research data put the average length of US recoveries since 1945 at 52 months, implying that this one, which began in March 1991, would end in July 1995 if it proved to be a typical recovery. Moreover, the average length of recoveries since 1958 has been only 37 months, implying an even earlier economic downturn.

However, this recovery started off weakly, so it would not be a surprise if it lasted longer than average. And after some signs of economic weakness in late 1995, by early 1996 there were distinct signs of economic expansion again.

The view in the financial markets at the beginning of 1995 was that interest rates in most of the major industrialised economies worldwide would climb in both 1995 and 1996 as the authorities reacted to the risk of inflation prompted by economic growth. Economic expansion tends to force commodity prices up, leading producers to put up their prices if they can. Wholesalers and retailers follow suit, employees demand higher wages, industry faces rising costs and comes up against capacity restraints as it struggles to meet demand for its products. Finally, the authorities either push up interest rates or increase taxes or both in an attempt to dampen the fire.

In the United States, though, some analysts were even saying that inflation might be less of a problem than in previous cycles, reflecting the relatively subdued nature of the recovery in many of the advanced economies. The US Federal Reserve agreed and cut rates. And throughout 1995 and into early 1996 Germany surprised almost everyone by cutting rates rather than increasing them, showing that the Bundesbankers at least did not see inflation as a problem.

Mind you, in looking at fixed-income investments, other factors are just as important as inflation and the economic cycle: supply for example, the behaviour of currencies and the attractions of alternative investments such as shares and commodities.

Supply tends to fall as an economy emerges from recession because growth raises tax revenues and reduces the need for spending on social benefits, allowing governments to cut their borrowing. Those governments also try not to borrow when rates are rising, to minimise their borrowing costs, and the resulting drop in supply is positive for bond markets.

In early 1995, for example, when global growth was well established, it was clear from a look at the Eurobond market that sovereign borrowers were simply not interested in issuing bonds. They knew they could arrange cheaper finance from their banks in the form of enormous syndicated loans. Similarly, supply tends to climb as an economy contracts, offsetting the benefits of increased demand prompted by the squeeze on inflation. In truth, though, many economists believe supply considerations are far less important than demand in setting government bond prices.

As 1996 began, many European nations, struggling to achieve monetary union, expected to reduce their budget deficits over the course of the year but were making little progress in reducing their overall debt funding needs. A Reuters survey in January, compiled from official figures, showed forecasts for smaller deficits in 10 of 12 European nations in 1966. But gross funding was seen rising in several countries and few expected big falls in debt supply. Table 1.1 shows the findings from the survey.

Table 1.1 The 1996 Reuters Government Debt Survey

The survey, compiled from official sources, covers the gross funding requirements for 12 major European economies in 1996, indicating redemptions and net funding needs where possible.

It compares the latest 1996 official funding and deficit forecasts with last year's funding forecasts and the amount of debt actually issued last year.

	1996 funding breakdown (top figures gross unless indicated)	1995 actual totals or latest govt estimates	1995 official est (listed by or before June 95) SEE NOTE (1)
BELGIUM	819 bln BEF includes 579.1 bln redemptions, 239.9 bln govt debt requirement	714.6 bln inc 424.5 bln redemptions, 290.1 bln debt requirement	562 bln 265 bln net
DENMARK	102.7 bln DKR Net 24.5 bln	141.5 bln Net 39.3 bln	141.2 bln 40.9 bln
FRANCE	540 bln FFR inc net 250 bln redemptions, 290 bln govt debt requirement	503 bln	495 bln 322 bln net SEE NOTE (2)
GERMANY SEE NOTE (3)	194.9 bln DEM inc net 60.0 bln	196.3 bln net 50.2 bln	48.7 bln

IRELAND	2235 mln IEP inc 1506 mln redemptions, 729 mln net	1737.0 mln inc 1062.0 mln redemptions, 675 mln net	1875 bln
ITALY SEE NOTE (4)	303 trln lire inc 109 trln PSBR 194 trln redemptions	320 trln 130 trln PSBR	130 trln PSBR
NETHERLANDS	39.1 bln NLG inc 19.7 bln redemptions, 19.4 bln budget deficit	54.3 bln inc 29.0 bln redemptions, 26.2 bln budget deficit	56.9 bln 26.7 bln budget deficit
SPAIN	16.5 trln pesetas inc 13.5 trln redemptions	19.1 trln 16.2 trln redemptions	
SWEDEN SEE NOTE (5)	N/A 60–70 bln net	354 bln crowns 138.5 bln net	165 bln net
SWITZERLAND	5.0 bln SFR 2.6 bln net	4.1 bln 3.0 bln net	4.5 bln 3.0 bln net
BRITAIN SEE NOTE (6)	35.3 bln stg inc 22.4 bln PSBR, 12.9 bln redemptions	33.1 bln 29.0 bln PSBR	21.5 bln PSBR
AUSTRIA	200 bln schillings 90 bln net (estimated)	240.8 bln 115–120 bln net (final figures due by end-Jan)	120 bln deficit

Notes:

1. Where possible Reuters gives the government's 1995 forecasts as of early 1995 for comparative purposes. In some cases forecasts were as recent as July 1995.

2. France revised up its 1995 issuance programme last July, to 495 billion francs from 470 billion to take account of the fact that receipts from privatisations were used to repay national debt rather than finance current spending.

3. The 1996 funding breakdown, from the German Finance Ministry, is as follows—131.9 billion marks of four years or more, 13.0 billion of one to four year debt and 50.0 billion of debt of shorter than one year.

4. BOTs are excluded from Italian issuance figures.

5. The Swedish debt office does not publish a gross funding forecast for the year. Only a two-month forecast is available. It has said it will borrow treasury bonds for 10 billion crowns and bills for 20 billion in January and bonds for 9 billion and bills for 11 billion in February.

The Swedish fiscal year runs from July 1, 1995 to December 31, 1996. Thereafter it will match the calendar year.

6. The British fiscal year runs from the beginning of April to the end of March. As a result, fiscal 1995–96 totals are provisional. Of the 33.1 billion stg funding estimate for that year, 10.8 billion stg remains to be funded before March 31, 1996.

On the deficit side, the most notable offender was Germany. Its net budget deficit, which authorities believe totalled 50 billion marks in 1995, was forecast to jump to 60 billion marks in 1996. A larger budget deficit was also expected in Ireland. However, some countries were making progress; Belgium, Denmark and the Netherlands among them.

Crucially for the bond markets, both Britain and France were expecting to raise more from the markets in 1996 than in 1995, but Italy was forecasting both a drop in its gross funding requirements and a smaller public sector borrowing requirement.

While supply often has only a limited impact on bond markets, exchange rate gyrations can have a formidable effect. Quite simply, no overseas investor wants to commit funds to a country where the currency is 'falling out of bed'. This means that in times of currency turbulence, so-called 'safe-haven' countries such as Germany tend to benefit at the expense of countries like Spain and Italy with traditionally weak currencies. Often a modest rise in bond prices can be turned into a dramatic return by currency strength, and the results can be stunning.

In just one week in March 1995, for instance, a period when the foreign exchanges were going through one of their periodic convulsions, a US-dollar-based investor in Japanese government bonds would have seen the value of his or her portfolio climb by some 7 per cent, partly because of Japan's safe-haven status but mostly because the yen was soaring in value against the dollar at the time.

Investment intentions are not the only influence either. A currency speculator such as a hedge fund exchanging pesetas or lire for marks can keep those marks in cash but may well want to put them to work in German securities, be they shares, bills, bonds or anything else. Investors burnt badly by a drop in bond prices in Spain or Italy may be unwilling to have their fingers burnt again buying bonds in Germany and may think very seriously about the rival attractions of shares, commodities, property or even cash as a defensive investment.

But in March 1995 there was little doubt where the yen-buyers were putting their money. The Japanese stock market was crumbling, so Japanese government bonds were the obvious place to be. Meanwhile the central banks that were buying dollars in a vain attempt to stem the yen's advance were putting them in short-dated US securities, mostly bills and short-dated notes, so both the Japanese and the US debt markets benefited even though the dollar was weak.

Economists say that a falling currency is bad for bonds because it is inflationary, raising the price of imported goods and of products priced in another currency. A weakening lira means Italian industry must pay more for its imports from Germany and also more for its imported oil, which is priced internationally in dollars. That means imported bond-negative inflation.

But as noted above with the example of currency intervention, there can be offsetting factors. The main impact on bonds of a weakening currency comes via its psychological impact on overseas investors. A Japanese investment fund's board, meeting in April at the start of the new fiscal year in Japan, is bound to be influenced by the knowledge that an investment in Italy in March would have been disastrous because of the lira's slump against the yen. Italian investors might still fancy their own fixed-income markets, but the Japanese are highly unlikely to. Even the Italians themselves might prefer something other than inflation-sensitive bonds, particularly if the political scene is turbulent and there are fears that a weak government will fail to tackle inflation. That brings us to the all-important question of politics.

If there is one thing guaranteed to scare away an international investor, it is the prospect of a change in government, with the handover of power likely to create, at the very least, considerable uncertainty in the financial markets. France's two-round presidential election in 1995 was a good example. First there was the uncertainty of the election itself, then the uncertainty as President Chirac appointed a government, then the uncertainty as the markets waited to see if his election pledge to make unemployment his top priority would mean extra borrowing and a less 'responsible' fiscal policy.

Of course, the spotlight can easily turn elsewhere, to elections in another country perhaps, and that can allow the country that has just had its upheaval time to recover outside the glare of publicity. In some countries, like Italy, political uncertainty is so commonplace that sometimes it barely seems to matter any more. But like it or not, politics are a major influence on sentiment. And the effects can be long-lasting. It is arguable, for example, that the United Kingdom government's hostility towards EMU has discouraged investment in Britain, along with the idiosyncratic nature of the gilt market (now being reformed), even though its economy is in better shape than many others.

That said, judging whether an economy is in 'good shape' is very hard to do. The Maastricht criteria for EMU were mentioned in the introduction to this book, but it is difficult to avoid the conclusion that there are fashions in economic analysis. One year it is the trade figures that everyone watches. Then it is the weekly money supply data, then inflation, then capacity utilisation, then trade again. Certainly, the point in the economic cycle has an influence, but it is arguable that fashion is a more important factor.

So what of 1996/97? From the middle of 1995 to the early weeks of 1996, the evidence in favour of that 'soft-landing' grew, with analysts saying there was a fair chance the US economy, instead of swinging violently from boom to bust, would simply slow down gently to near the 2.5 per cent which the authorities are widely believed to regard as a sustainable non-inflationary growth rate.

Few economists were ruling out the possibility that the slow-down would prove temporary—just like the earlier setback in 1993—and that growth would take off again, particularly after the Federal Open Market Committee, defying many analysts' predictions, lowered its target for the Federal funds rate on 6 July 1995 and brought its previous steady 16-month tightening of monetary policy to an abrupt end. A few days earlier, a Reuters poll of 25 economists had shown just nine predicting an easing of monetary policy, with 15 opting for no change. The Federal funds rate had doubled to 6 per cent between February 1994 and July 1995.

There was talk of a boom in house sales giving a boost to consumer spending, and there was speculation that a weak dollar would give a fillip to exports. But other economists were warning that the United States would only just avoid a recession, with weak consumer demand and warehouses full of unsold goods cutting the growth rate to between 1 and 2 per cent. Fed Chairman Alan Greenspan, for one, told the Economic Club of New York on 20 June that economic reports suggested a 'risk of a modest near-term recession', sending shudders through the financial markets. Economists noted that business inventories remained high, with cars and furniture produced in 1994 when the economy was expanding remaining unsold and filtering out only slowly. Some suggested that Fed rate cuts take at least six months to work through into the real economy.

The reason the 6 July rate cut was such a surprise was that although the economy had clearly slowed by then, recent data had been contradictory, with some figures pointing to recession but others implying the first-quarter slowdown might already be over. Growth in the first quarter had slowed to an annual rate of just 2.7 per cent from 5.1 per cent in the fourth quarter of 1994, but it was unclear that second-quarter growth would be equally slow. In the end, some insiders said, the desire of Fed Vice-chairman Alan Blinder to act pre-emptively against the possibility of recession had swung the day in favour of a monetary easing.

A few weeks earlier, the OECD had added fuel to the fire by revising down the world growth forecasts in its end-1994 outlook. Figures released by the think-tank in May suggested that the Japanese economy would grow by just half as much as previously estimated, denting growth forecasts for the industrialised world as a whole. Japan's GDP growth in 1995 was estimated at just 1.3 per cent, compared with the 2.5 per cent forecast made six months earlier, and 1996 growth was put at 2.3 per cent rather than 3.4 per cent, incidentally provoking an argument with the Japanese Economic Planning Agency which said the OECD had under-estimated the impact of the government's latest budget.

Anyway, as a result, growth in the whole 25-nation bloc was likely to be 2.7 per cent rather than 3 per cent in 1995 and 2.7 per cent again rather than 2.9 per cent in 1996 OECD chief economist Kumiharu Shigehara told reporters in Paris. The US economy would grow faster than foreseen, at 3.2 per cent in 1995 and 2.3 per cent in 1996. European growth rates would be largely as previously predicted the OECD added. The key forecasts in its May 1995 report, showing annual percentage changes with December's projections in brackets are shown in Table 1.2.

The OECD also gave a forecast for world trade, measured by the arithmetic average of world import volumes and export volumes, in annual percentage changes.

World Trade:

1994	1995	1996
9.8 (8.9)	8.9 (8.2)	7.8 (7.8)

The OECD gave the following forecasts for short-term interest rates (for the United States, three-month Treasury bills; for

Table 1.2   OECD Key Forecasts, May 1995 (%)

	1994	1995	1996
Real GDP:			
United States	4.1[1] (3.9)[2]	3.2 (3.1)	2.3 (2.0)
Japan	0.6 (1.0)	1.3 (2.5)	2.3 (3.4)
Germany	2.9 (2.8)	2.9 (2.8)	2.7 (3.5)
OECD Europe	2.4 (2.3)	3.0 (3.0)	3.0 (3.2)
Total OECD	2.9 (2.8)	2.7 (3.0)	2.7 (2.9)
Real Total Domestic Demand:			
United States	4.7 (4.6)	3.3 (2.8)	1.8 (1.6)
Japan	1.0 (1.7)	2.4 (3.2)	3.1 (4.0)
Germany	2.6 (2.7)	2.5 (2.4)	3.3 (3.6)
OECD Europe	1.9 (1.6)	2.8 (2.6)	3.2 (3.2)
Total OECD	3.0 (2.9)	2.5 (2.9)	2.6 (2.8)
Inflation (GDP Deflator):			
United States	2.1 (2.0)	2.0 (2.5)	2.7 (3.2)
Japan	0.1 (0.6)	−0.3 (0.6)	0.2 (0.6)
Germany	2.2 (2.3)	2.1 (2.0)	2.3 (2.2)
OECD Europe*	2.6 (2.5)	2.8 (2.5)	2.9 (2.6)
Total OECD	3.9 (4.1)	4.1 (3.1)	3.7 (3.0)
Unemployment:			
United States	6.1 (6.1)	5.6 (5.6)	5.7 (5.6)
Japan	2.9 (2.9)	3.1 (3.0)	3.1 (2.9)
Germany	9.6 (9.6)	9.2 (9.1)	8.7 (8.6)
OECD Europe	11.3 (11.6)	11.0 (11.3)	10.6 (10.9)
Total OECD	8.1 (8.2)	7.8 (7.9)	7.6 (7.7)
Current Account Balances:			
United States	−2.3 (−2.3)	−2.7 (−2.4)	−2.5 (−2.3)
Japan	2.8 (3.0)	2.5 (2.8)	2.2 (2.6)
Germany	−1.1 (−1.2)	−0.7 (−0.6)	−1.2 (−0.5)
OECD Europe	0.7 (0.5)	0.9 (0.8)	0.8 (1.0)
Total OECD	−0.2 (−0.2)	−0.1 (−0.1)	−0.1 (0.0)

[1] Annual percentage changes
[2] Bracketed items are the projections for December
* Excluding Turkey

Japan, three- to six-month CDs; for Germany, three-month inter-bank rates; and for the four European countries, the unweighted average of three-month inter-bank rates in Germany, France, Italy and the United Kingdom):

	1994	1995	1996
United States	4.3 (4.2)	5.9 (6.5)	6.4 (6.7)
Japan	2.3 (2.2)	1.7 (2.6)	1.6 (2.9)
Germany	5.4 (5.3)	4.8 (5.0)	5.2 (5.6)
'Major 4' European countries	6.3 (6.3)	6.9 (6.3)	6.9 (7.0)

That forecast of a 5.9 per cent interest rate in the United States at the end of 1995 almost exactly matched the result of the Reuters quarterly interest-rate poll conducted at the start of June. That month, 22 economists were asked where key interest rates and benchmark bond yields in the Group of Seven industrialised countries would lie at the year-end, and their mean forecasts are shown in Table 1.3.

Interestingly, just eight of the 22 economists correctly forecast a rate cut in the United States before the end of 1995 and the overwhelming mood was one of caution, with the long bond yield in the US seen at close to 7 per cent by the end of 1995, up from about 6.5 per cent when the analysts were polled.

A month later—just before the two-day policy-setting meeting in Washington of the Federal Open Market Committee that cut the Federal funds rate—a Reuters poll of New York analysts was less bearish. A majority of the economists there reckoned that

Table 1.3   Results of Reuters Poll: Forecast for End-1995, June 1995 (%)

US Federal funds	5.86
30-year yield	6.90
German discount rate	3.90
10-year yield	6.74
Japan discount rate	0.83
10-year yield	3.40
UK bank base rates	7.23
10-year yield	8.12
France intervention	4.94
10-year yield	7.38
Canada bank rate	7.71
10-year yield	8.31
Italy discount rate	9.74
10-year yield	12.22

short-term US interest rates were likely to be about a half percentage point lower by late 1995 and would remain lower through the first half of 1996.

In the poll of 30 economists, the Fed funds rate was seen averaging 5.52 per cent at the year-end and 5.50 per cent in June 1996. Longer-term rates were seen close to the levels at the time. The average forecasts were as follows:

Fed funds		Two-year note		10-year note		30-year bond	
6-month	Year	6-month	Year	6-month	Year	6-month	Year
5.52	5.50	5.74	5.90	6.26	6.34	6.63	6.69

The forecast of almost 6.75 per cent for the 10-year Bund yield (see Table 1.3) compared with a level around 6.5 per cent when the poll was taken. That caution was perhaps surprising given that world government bonds enjoyed a bonanza in May, the month before the poll was conducted. The Salomon Brothers World Government Bond Index showed its strongest one-month advance since June 1987, gaining 3.44 per cent in local currency terms. Australian bonds led the way, giving a return of 4.63 per cent in Australian dollars, and US Treasuries performed almost as well, returning 4.07 per cent in US dollars and helping bond markets across the world upwards. 'A series of economic reports confirming a slowing [of the US economy], pushed Treasuries to their best one-month return since March 1986,' the Salomon report said. Looking at returns for dollar-based investors, some even juicier amounts were on offer, given May was a month which saw concerted central bank intervention to support the dollar. Italian BTPs, for example, gave a 5.57 per cent return to US investors.

Anyway, the economists arguing that the US economy was growing only moderately appeared to be winning the argument right up to 8 March 1996 when the financial markets were stunned by news of a surge of 705 000 in non-farm payrolls in February, compared with a drop in January of 188 000 and expectations of an increase of 326 000. The figures stunned traders, few of whom had been expecting a strengthening economy as implied by the data. And the economists arguing for a recession were put on the defensive. A strong economy would be bad news for US Treasuries, and the markets also have a major political event to contend with in 1996 that could badly damage sentiment. Bill Clinton faces a presidential election in November. Already Clinton, a Democrat, is faced with Republican majorities in both houses of the US Congress, restricting his ability to enact fiscal policy. While markets might be expected to welcome the election of a more right-wing Republican president, they would certainly not welcome a prolonged period of political uncertainty before and after the election.

Perhaps the economic and political background favours the short end of the US yield curve rather than the long, an investment in two-year Treasury notes rather than 30-year bonds to reduce duration and benefit from a yield curve that might steepen in the face of renewed economic growth. Even if growth remains subdued, the political background might suggest underweighting US Treasuries. Stronger growth would reinforce the argument against them. Alan Greenspan was certainly very upbeat in his semi-annual testimony to Congress in July 1995. He called the US economic outlook encouraging and said the economy seemed to have skirted a recession. He predicted further growth ahead, saying he expected the period of economic expansion to last at least until the end of 1996; and yet he thought inflation pressures would ease.

He gave no clear indication of where he thought rates were heading and he said the risk of a near-term recession could not be ruled out. But, the Fed chief said, the worst may be over. 'We may have passed the point of maximum risk. The economic outlook . . . is encouraging . . . the most probable [outlook] is for an upturn . . . over the rest of this year [1995] and a moderate pace of expansion next year.'

He urged Congress and the Clinton administration to take advantage of this scenario and eliminate the $200 billion annual Federal government budget deficit. He played down fears that budget cuts could hurt the economy by reducing government spending, arguing the impact would be cushioned by a drop in long-term interest rates that was likely to accompany any move to end the deficit. He made clear the Fed would be ready to help prop up the economy in the unlikely event that the long-term budget cuts reduced growth.

One private-sector economist, speaking at a conference in September, suggested that after a pause in the first half of 1995, the

US economy was growing again in the second half. Europe, he added, was about six months behind and was pausing in the second half. It would resume its growth path in the first half of 1996.

If the United States is not the best place to invest, where is? One obvious alternative is Germany, where the economy contracted in 1993, grew by just 2.5 per cent or so in 1994 and is only likely to grow at around the same pace in 1995 and 1996, a sufficiently subdued growth rate to allow the independent Bundesbank to cut its discount rate by 50 basis points to four per cent in March 1995 after the United States had been increasing rates for more than a year to combat 'excessive' economic expansion and four months before the US decided to cut rates in turn. Moreover, Bundesbank president Hans Tietmeyer's six-year term does not end until 1999, ensuring stability in Bundesbank policy.

The main reasons given by the Bundesbank for cutting the discount rate that time were the strength of the German mark—which had effectively tightened monetary policy—and below-target growth in the M3 measure of money supply, which contracted in each of the first five months of 1995. It could also have mentioned falling unit labour costs and weak domestic demand.

Since then the Bundesbank has continued to lower German interest rates gradually and many economists expect the discount rate to be reduced until it reaches the 2.75 or 2.50 per cent level where it has bottomed out in previous business cycles.

To be sure, the Bundesbank may well begin to raise interest rates at some point. But if the US experience is anything to go by, that will bring a flattening of the yield curve that will benefit investors in long-dated Bunds. If the German mark remains as strong as it has been in recent years, that will continue to stifle inflation. It is hard to think of any good reason for underweighting the assets of Germany and its hard-core European neighbours such as the Netherlands, where bond prices follow Bunds slavishly.

Germany's Ifo institute forecast in early August 1995 that pan-German GDP growth would be 2.5 per cent in 1995 and the same in 1996, with growth at just 2 per cent in western Germany but 8 per cent in the eastern states. It urged the Bundesbank to cut the discount rate again while it had the chance—a chance the central bank soon took—and urged the Bundesbank not to make any deep changes in its monetary policy.

The Bundesbank had earlier received much the same advice from elsewhere. In July, the President of the Federation of German Industry, Hans-Olaf Henkel, told Reuters Financial Television he also predicted a 2.5 per cent growth rate in 1996 and he warned that the strong mark was having an impact on the competitiveness of German industry. Deutsche Morgan Grenfell, the research unit of Deutsche Bank, wrote of 'a west German economy that still exhibits considerable weaknesses, a dampened inflation trend and the prospect that monetary growth will very likely remain below the Bundesbank's target corridor'. On the face of it, that would suggest higher bond prices, but Deutsche Morgan Grenfell thought not, saying it believed German bond yields were near their low point of this cycle and would probably start to rise slightly in the first half of 1996.

How about Japan then as an alternative place for the bond investor? That was certainly not looking a bright idea in September 1995, when the official discount rate had just been halved to 0.5 per cent, 10-year yields were at a mere three per cent and most extraordinary of all the yen had actually stopped strengthening and had weakened beyond the 100 level to the dollar. That reflected at least in part what seemed to be a determined effort by the Japanese government to promote overseas investment by Japanese institutions and thereby curb the yen, boost the competitiveness of Japanese industry and inject some life into a struggling economy showing every sign of slipping back into recession.

The measures to boost overseas investment were announced the month before, in August, by Finance Minister Masayoshi Takemura and included elements such as the removal of limits on insurance companies' participation in syndicated loans and on their foreign-currency loans. 'We believe these measures are very likely to become a good opportunity for investors to give more attention to investment overseas,' Takemura told a news conference. About time too, said some economists, noting that after nearly four years of zero growth, Japan's tentative economic recovery had stalled and that repeated government stimulus packages had done little more than keep the economy from faltering further.

In the event, though, Japan's GDP rose a real 0.9 per cent in 1995 after a revised figure of 0.5 per cent growth in 1994, according to preliminary figures from the country's Economic Planning

Agency. In particular, growth was better than expected in the final quarter, with real GDP up 0.9 per cent from the previous quarter, or an annualised 3.6 per cent. The numbers bolstered hopes that the fragile economic recovery might have more strength than first thought, suggesting little reason to invest in Japanese government bonds.

If not the United States, Germany or Japan, how about the United Kingdom as a good place to invest? Not a bad idea, perhaps, given the weakness of the economy and a reshaping of the gilt market designed to make it less quirky and therefore perhaps more attractive to overseas investors. On the economic front, the Chancellor of the Exchequer Kenneth Clarke and the Governor of the Bank of England Eddie George seemed to spend much of 1995 squabbling semi-publicly about whether to raise British interest rates with George saying they should be increased to ensure inflation did not become a problem and Clarke saying there was no need because the economy was slowing anyway. Minutes of their June monetary meeting, for example, showed that George said 'the Bank could only repeat their advice of last month that monetary policy needed to be tightened sooner rather than later'. Clarke responded that 'the arguments against a tightening of policy had if anything strengthened slightly and his inclination was that rates should not be raised that month'. In the end, insiders said, George backed down when signs of economic slowdown did indeed emerge when the summer data were released in the early Autumn.

Three interest rate cuts followed, taking UK base lending rates to 6 per cent by March 1996, at which point many economists were arguing that the bottom of the rate cutting cycle had been reached, though others were talking of more cuts to come for essentially political reasons; to bolster the government's popularity ahead of a general election.

Earlier, independent economists had mostly taken George's side. A Reuters poll in July 1995 of 31 securities houses and banks showed the vast majority, 22 or roughly two-thirds, thought the next move in British interest rates would be up rather than down. No fewer than eight predicted that rates would rise to a peak of 8 per cent or more in this cycle, and one even predicted a peak of nine per cent. At the time, UK bank base rates were just 6.75 per cent.

Yet those same economists were predicting neither a surge in growth nor soaring inflation. Their GDP forecasts for 1996 ranged from 1.9 per cent to 3.7 per cent, with an arithmetic mean of 2.8 per cent. Their forecasts for underlying retail price inflation, which excludes mortgage interest payments, in 1996 ranged from 1.9 to 4.3 per cent, with an arithmetic mean of 3.2 per cent. Britain's official aim is for underlying retail price inflation to be 2.5 per cent or lower by the time of the next general election, which must be held by mid-1997, with a wider tolerance band of 1–4 per cent.

Since Clarke rather than George is the man who takes interest rate decisions in Britain, cynics were saying that he would have resisted George's pressure to raise rates anyway, given that many of his Conservative Party colleagues were calling for lower rates and lower taxes to boost the party's prospects ahead of the election.

If that makes the United Kingdom sound unattractive, at least the reforms of the gilt market could be an offsetting factor. The UK Treasury said in July 1995 that it was going to introduce a new funding policy in 1996–7 and that it was considering uniform price gilt auctions, with prices pre-set. Previously buyers bid for gilts so prices depended on the strength of demand. It added that gilt 'tap' sales would not exceed 10 per cent of total issuance and that it was considering reforming index-linked gilts and perhaps auctioning them. Index-linked gilts have their value tied to the rate of inflation.

'Beginning in 1996/97, the government has decided to introduce a new framework for financing which will continue to provide the necessary discipline to ensure a prudent maturity structure for debt issuance,' the Treasury said. It listed several changes which had already been announced, including tax reforms and plans for gilt strip and open repo markets. Eddie George said the reforms should help cut the cost of funding the UK government deficit. Economists gave the package a warm welcome, saying it would simplify and modernise the gilt market, bring it more into line with other international bond markets and reduce uncertainty, that great hate of bond investors worldwide. The index-linked proposals were welcomed particularly.

If the United Kingdom does not appeal as an investment, how about Europe's high-yielding trio of Italy, Spain and Sweden?

Just as UK investors spent much of 1995 watching the Chancellor of the Exchequer and the Governor of the Bank of England squabbling about interest rates, so investors in Italy had to watch a seemingly endless debate about politics and the budget. Yet confidence seeped back into the market so steadily that many commentators began backing Italy as the best market of all for investment.

Lamberto Dini, often described as a grey technocrat, was drafted in to head a stop-gap Italian government in January 1995. Yet within a few months he had achieved far more than most post-war governments, pushing through a tight budget, masterminding a reform of pensions and laying down new rules for local government elections. That helped the lira, stocks and bonds to recover and had international investors dreading the day he might have to leave.

Almost every statement from his government seemed designed to attract those fund managers. Budget Minister Rainer Masera, for example, said in a speech in September that inflation-bashing was his government's key target given that the economy was growing at a less explosive rate and showing signs of sustainable growth. 'The macro economic picture is positive, the struggle against inflation can't be anything but the main goal of the government and its budget to bring it back to and then stabilise it at the level of other major European countries.' At the time, Italian inflation was 5.8 per cent, compared with a European Union average of 3.1 per cent. The same minister had earlier boosted confidence by saying that the lira could be ripe for a return to the European exchange rate mechanism. Yet some analysts remained wary, noting that Dini had only a limited mandate and would have to face an election before long.

His government finally collapsed in January 1996 and a general election was set for April, with Dini allying his party to the centre-left 'Olive Tree' coalition.

As for Spain, politics and budget worries overshadowed the financial markets there too for much of 1995, with the ruling Socialists battered by allegations that they organised death squads against the Basque separatists in the 1980s. This was a particular problem for Prime Minister Felipe Gonzalez because he needed the support of the Catalan nationalist party, the Catalan Convergencia i Unio, for the 1996 budget. As Economy Minister

Pedro Solbes said in September: 'It would be disastrous for political pressures to prevent agreement, because it would bring a serious risk of 1996 being a lost year for economic recovery.'

In the event, the 1996 budget was rejected, and soon after the Socialists presented their 1997 budget predicting three per cent growth they lost office in the general election held on 3 March. Yet Spanish government bonds still found plenty of support from international investors.

Sweden had its proponents too, perhaps due to rather than in spite of an economy seen widely as having serious financial problems. These were spelt out succinctly by the OECD in early September. Although Sweden is climbing out of a recession, a weak domestic sector and a depressed labour market will continue to haunt the country said the OECD.

> Overall, output expansion may not exceed 2.5 per cent a year, which is unlikely to permit a significant reduction in joblessness, and 12 per cent of the labour force could still be without regular jobs in 1996. Economic development since the last . . . review has been relatively favourable in so far as the recovery is continuing at a moderate pace. The economy is, however, still in a serious imbalance, with a booming export sector contrasting starkly with weak domestically-oriented sectors.

The Paris-based think-tank said Sweden's most urgent priority was to reduce its debt to GDP ratio, which was 20 points above the 60 per cent ceiling stipulated by the Maastricht Treaty. It praised the government for its efforts to reign in spending. 'However, even if debt stabilisation is achieved in the near-term, public finances would still be vulnerable to a downturn in the economy thereafter,' said the OECD. And due to the immensity of the state's debts, even harsher measures would be necessary in the early years of consolidation, it added. As mentioned earlier, this kind of scenario attracts bond investors, and Sweden's bond market proved to be the best investment of all in 1995, according to the Salomon Brothers data.

Finally on this quick jog round some of the world's major bond markets to France, where investors looking for economic weakness needed to look no further. France's GDP fell by 0.3 per cent in the final quarter of 1995 from the previous quarter, hit partly by a paralysing public sector strike. Full-year growth was just 2.4 per cent, down from 2.9 per cent in 1994. However, economists said there were signs of strength going forward that might allow Prime Minister Alain Juppe to achieve his twin goals of curbing the budget deficit and reducing mass unemployment.

Moreover, some economists said the slowdown reflected weaker growth worldwide rather than specifically French problems, and that was certainly backed by the United Nations Conference on Trade and Development (UNCTAD) when it released its annual report in September. Its forecast for 1995 world growth was just 2.9 per cent, affected by the weakness of the United States and spillover effects from Mexico's currency crisis. Western economies should maintain their expansion of 2.8 per cent, it said, while recession was likely to continue in Japan, with growth contracting slightly to 0.5 per cent. 'The world economy has been losing steam in 1995. The biggest slowdowns in growth are in the United States and Latin America.'

A similar picture was painted by the London Business School in its Economic Outlook released a few days earlier. It predicted growth in the major industrial economies of 2.6 per cent in 1995 and the same in 1996, a sufficiently strong growth rate to require interest rates to rise again. The LBS forecast inflation at some 2.5 per cent, said the 'soft landing' scenario was still in place and noted the Mexican financial crisis had been of less importance than had been feared at the time.

The US economy 'appears set for a long, steady upswing lasting for several years,' LBS said, with growth predicted at 3 per cent in 1995 and 2.7 per cent in 1996. Europe was also expected to grow at 3 per cent in 1995, with France and Italy posting the strongest growth. The prospects for Japan were described as weakest of any of the industrial nations, and its economy was expected to grow by only 1.4 per cent in 1995, held back by the high yen and financial and banking problems.

This was the economic background, then, for the world bond markets. In the next chapter we look at the technical factors likely to affect bonds in the months ahead and then at each market individually.

2

The technical outlook

Any doubts that bonds have been a good investment over the last 10 years or so should be dispelled by the charts in this chapter. All are monthly or weekly front-month continuation charts of bond futures and their related interest-rate futures. They are included because technical analysts, once known as chartists, believe that by studying historical information it is possible to tell what is likely to happen in the future.

Technical analysis is now widely used in the futures markets and, as the futures markets are a key influence on the cash markets, they are crucial there too. Moreover, while traders will look at daily, hourly and even five-minute charts, any reputable technical analyst will tell you that your first stop on a technical tour of the markets should be the long-term charts to put the short-term information in perspective.

Charts, of course, can be read many ways, and there are dozens of technical indicators that can be used, as well as applications of the work of past gurus such as W.D. Gann and R.N.Elliott. But in essence the idea is simple: if a trader knows that selling has occurred before at a particular level, he or she is unlikely to buy there and the level will become resistance. Similarly, if a level has been a good point to buy at in the past, traders are likely to buy there again and the level will act as support. The charts are therefore a pictorial representation of market psychology.

Chart 2.1 is a monthly bar chart of the US Treasury bond future traded at the Chicago Board of Trade. The bars show the highest, the lowest and the closing price each month for the last 14 years or so, and the most obvious point to note is that the price has been

Chart 2.1 US Treasury Bond (30-year) Future Monthly Bar Chart, Chicago Board of Trade

in an uptrend for most of that time. This is shown by the support line drawn under the rising lows recorded from mid-1984 to late 1993. As mentioned earlier in this book, that uptrend gave way in late 1993 to a downtrend that lasted for most of 1994 and is marked by the downward sloping resistance line joining the falling highs recorded throughout that period. By 1995, prices were rising again and that uptrend is marked by the support line on the right-hand side of the chart. In early 1996 they were falling.

Perhaps the best-known expression in technical analysis is 'the trend is your friend', so the first conclusion to make from Chart 2.1 is that while an uptrend is in place the best position to be in is

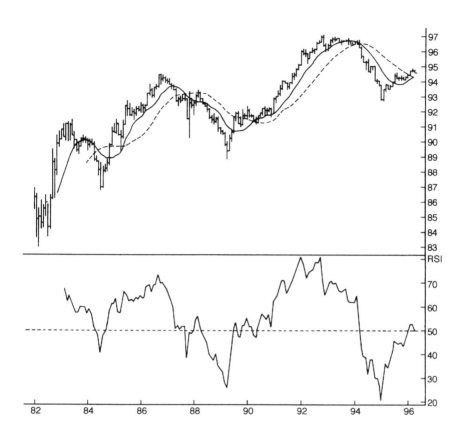

Chart 2.2   Eurodollar (3-month) Future Monthly Bar Chart, Chicago
Mercantile Exchange

long. It is quite possible to lose money being long in an uptrend;
imagine buying in early 1987 around 103 and selling late the same
year around 77, having lost about a quarter of your funds, for
example, but you are still more likely to make money than lose it
in an uptrend.

The next most obvious point to make is that while the 1994
downtrend was steep and savage, the lost ground was made up
very quickly. To add a degree of sophistication to the picture,
note the two moving averages weaving their way through the bars.
The shorter one, which clings more closely to the bars, is a 12-
month moving average which takes the 12 previous closes, divides

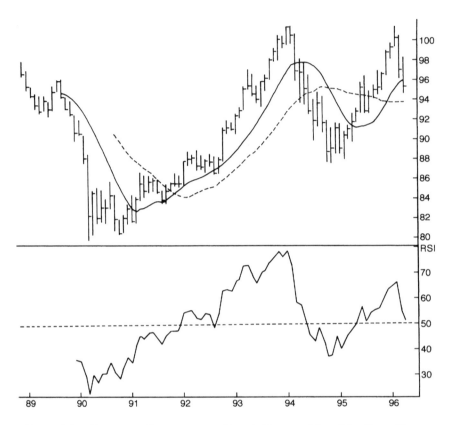

Chart 2.3 German Government Bond Future Monthly Bar Chart, London International Financial Futures and Options Exchange (LIFFE)

the total by 12 and plots the resulting numbers as a line. The longer one is a 24-month moving average which takes the 24 previous closes, divides the total by 24 and plots the resulting numbers as another line. One definition of an uptrend is a chart pattern where the price is above the shorter moving average which is in turn above the longer moving average. That was true for most of the period from mid-1985 to mid-1987, for example, again from late 1991 to late 1993, and from 1993 to early 1996.

Some technical analysts believe it is important to note when moving averages cross because the cross can give a buy or a sell signal. The cross in early 1985 certainly gave a good buy signal, as

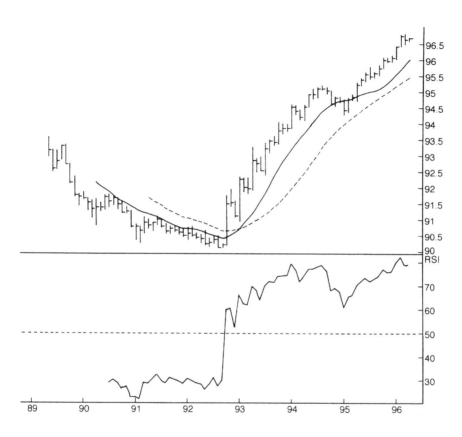

Chart 2.4 Eurodeutschmark (3-month) Future Monthly Bar Chart (LIFFE)

did the cross in late 1991. Others were less useful and much depends on which two moving averages are chosen. Some analysts try to find the 'best' two for a given market, others use the 'Fibonacci' numbers such as five, eight and 13. At the end of the day, numbers that look right intuitively—such as one-year and two-year moving averages on a monthly chart—are probably as good as any other.

By early 1996, the uptrend had been broken and the 'double top' just above 120 was leading many technical analysts to turn bearish. For some, a drop to the 1994 low just over 96 was a real possibility.

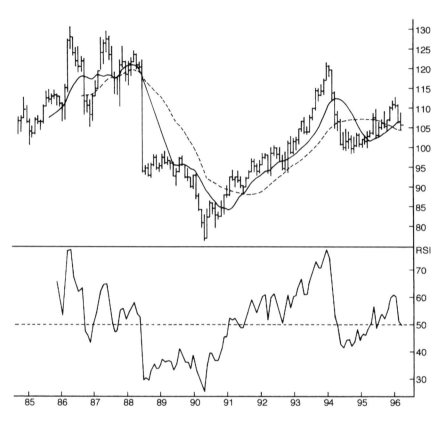

Chart 2.5   UK Long Gilt Future Monthly Bar Chart (LIFFE)

The line below the main bar chart and its moving averages is an RSI or relative strength indicator, in this case a 14-month RSI. This is an oscillator or momentum indicator. The mathematics are neither here nor there. What matters is that when the line rises above 70, it gives an overbought signal and when it drops below 30 it gives an oversold signal. There are many alternative indicators that can be used and their value is clear. In 1993 the RSI shot above 70 to around 77. An investor who had sold when it passed 70 would have sold almost at the top of the market. Unfortunately, as some of the other charts in this chapter show, RSI signals are rarely that good and a market can stay overbought or

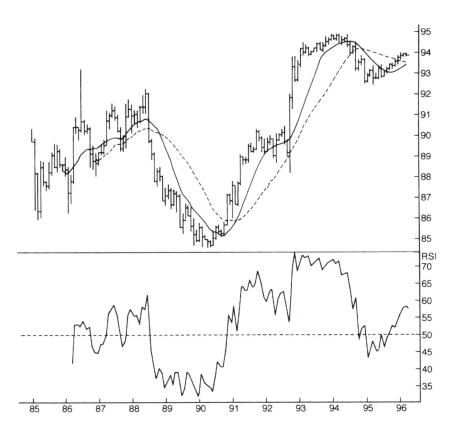

Chart 2.6 Short Sterling Deposit Rate (90-day) Future Monthly Bar
Chart (LIFFE)

oversold for long periods. None the less, the move above 70 in
December 1995 gave another good feel signal.

Turning from the long end of the US debt market to the short,
Chart 2.2 shows the Eurodollar future on the Chicago Mercantile
Exchange. This is a three-month interest-rate future and as with
all interest-rate futures you take the latest figure from 100.00 to
give the implied level of three-month interest rates at a specified
time in the future. A price of 94.56, for example, implies an interest rate of 5.44 per cent.

There are very strong similarities with the T-bond future, but
there are also some clear differences. Note that while the T-bond

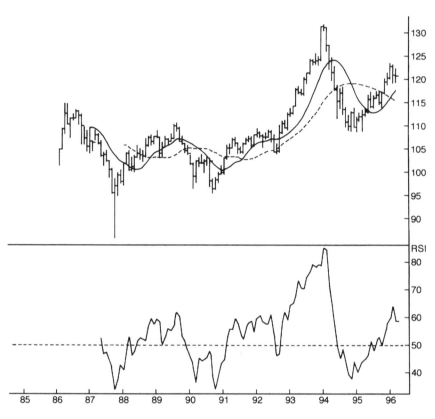

Chart 2.7 French Notionnel Bond Future Monthly Bar Chart
(MATIF)

had recovered all of the 1994 move down by the end of 1995, the
Eurodollar future was slower to regain the ground lost. However
the price was still climbing in early 1996, the moving averages had
crossed over and the RSI had nipped above the 50 mark.

Chart 2.3, a monthly bar chart of the German Bund future
traded on the London International Financial Futures and Options Exchange (LIFFE) also has its similarities with the T-bond
future, showing how highly correlated the world's two major bond
markets are. In particular, the 'double top' in early 1996 coincided
almost exactly with the 'double top' in the T-bond. Note the lag,
though, between the T-bond peaking in late 1993 and the Bund

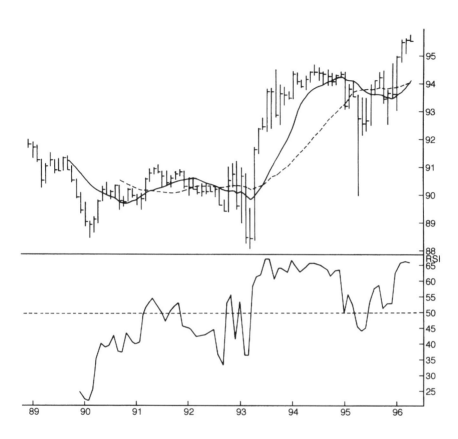

Chart 2.8 3-month Paris Inter-bank Offered Rate (PIBOR) Future Monthly Bar Chart (MATIF)

peaking in early 1994, showing the advantages of following old adages like the one that says 'when America sneezes, Europe catches a cold'.

Chart 2.4, showing German interest rate futures on LIFFE, paints a different picture entirely, though. The first three contracts all show prices well below their old highs. Euromarks, in contrast, took out the old high in early 1995 and have been in a strong, solid uptrend ever since. In early 1996, the price was above the shorter moving average, which was in turn above the longer moving average, a classic uptrend. The support line was working well and the only warning sign was the RSI. This was over 70,

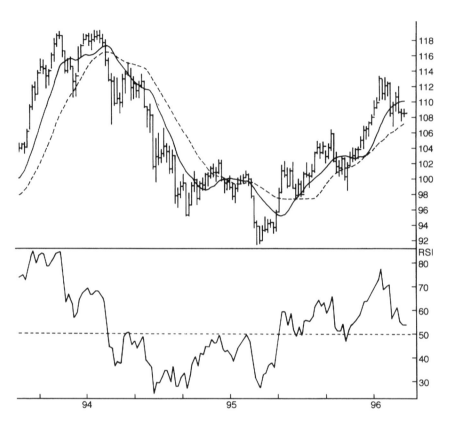

Chart 2.9 Italian Government Bond Future Weekly Bar Chart (LIFFE)

suggesting an overbought market. However, the new highs for the price were accompanied by new highs for the RSI—reinforcing the bullish picture.

The UK gilt chart, Chart 2.5, has much in common with the T-bond and Bund charts, again showing how the world's key bond markets tend to move together, but the short sterling chart, Chart 2.6, is fascinating. This shows UK interest rates and has a number of features to delight those technical analysts who look for patterns in the charts. First, note that the support line joining the 1990 and 1992 lows checks in not far from the support line joining the 1995 lows. Any break below those two lines would be highly bearish.

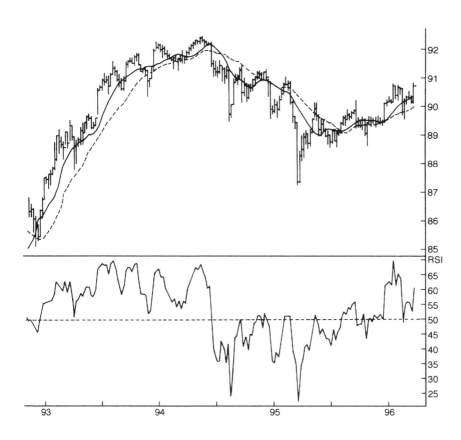

Chart 2.10 Eurolira Interest Rate Future Weekly Bar Chart (LIFFE)

Note though that the resistance line joining the 1994 and 1995 highs forms a symmetrical triangle with the long-term support line. With a symmetrical triangle, chartists say 'go with the break', be it up or down, and in this case the break is upwards. Overall, then, this is perhaps a more bullish chart than most seen so far, suggesting UK interest rates have further to fall.

Chart 2.7 shows the notionnel French government bond future traded on the MATIF in Paris and is again similar to the bond charts shown so far. But the French interest rate (Pibor, or Paris Inter-Bank Offered Rate) chart, Chart 2.8, is another curiosity. Two months on the chart have highs and lows more than three

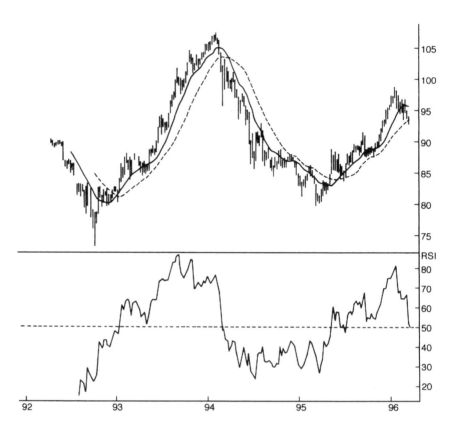

Chart 2.11 10-year Spanish Government Notional Bond Future
Weekly Bar Chart (Meff Renta Fija)

points apart, suggesting dramatic changes in market expectations
in each of those months. Like the Euromark chart, though, the
price is in an uptrend; reinforcing the close links between French
and German interest rates.

Chart 2.9 is the first weekly chart in this section and shows the
Italian government bond or BTP future traded on LIFFE. The
pattern in the bottom right-hand corner looks like a classic
inverse head-and-shoulders, an often reliable trend-reversal
pattern. If you look at the line drawn just above 102 (the 'neck-
line'), the bars below seem to form first a shoulder, then a head,
then another shoulder. When the neckline is finally broken, the

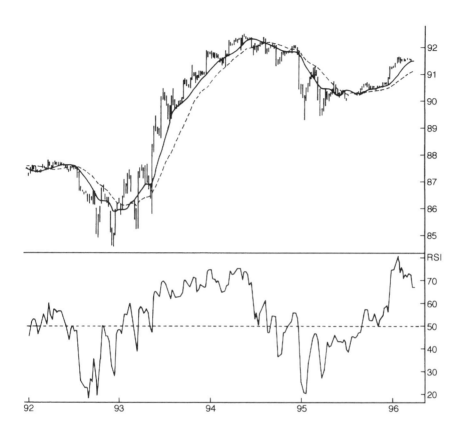

Chart 2.12 Mibor (90-day) Future Weekly Bar Chart (Meff Renta Fija)

price returns to it and then rises strongly. The break of the neck-line gave a classic buy signal. That confirmed an earlier buy signal when the moving averages crossed over. By early 1996, the price was below the shorter moving average so the uptrend was over. But the chart appeared less negative than the T-bond or the Bund, with the 'double top' much less obvious.

The Italian interest rate (Eurolira) chart, Chart 2.10, has many similarities, but as with most of the charts so far the interest rate futures chart appears less bearish than the equivalent bond chart.

The Spanish bond (Bono) future on Meff Renta Fija, plotted on Chart 2.11, also has similarities, and while the pattern in early

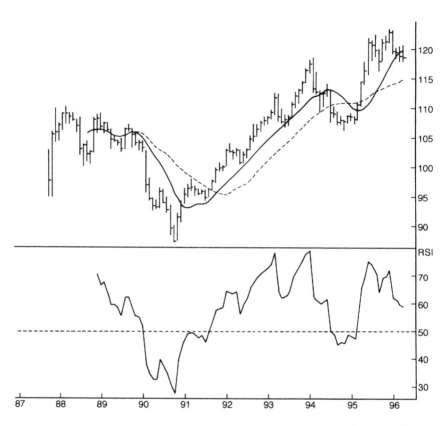

Chart 2.13   Japanese Government Bond Future Monthly Bar Chart
(Tokyo Stock Exchange)

1995 may not be obvious as an inverse head-and-shoulders, it
none the less looks like a reversal pattern of some sort, if not such
a classic one. This looked exceptionally bullish, with little major
resistance seemingly before the old high above 106 in early 1994
until the price began to turn down in late 1995. If you accept the
argument that Europe's high-yielding bonds are set to converge
with Germany's, the Italian and Spanish charts certainly lend
some support to your view.

Note too that the Spanish interest rate (Mibor) chart, Chart
2.12, is similar to the Eurolira Chart 2.10 but with one crucial
difference. The price has broken out of the symmetrical triangle

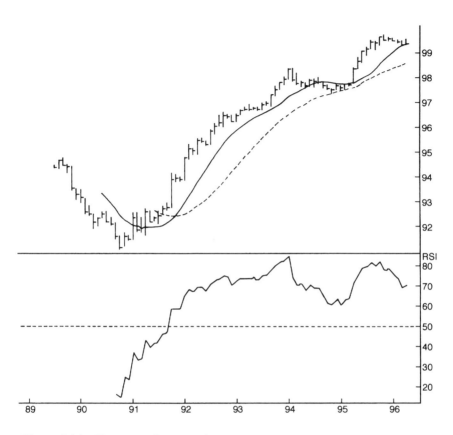

Chart 2.14   Euroyen (3-month) Future Monthly Bar Chart (Tokyo International Financial Futures Exchange)

marked by the trend lines, and it has broken out to the upside, implying higher prices and lower interest rates.

Moving from Europe's key markets to Japan, we have another chart that has come off the boil in Chart 2.13, a monthly chart of the Japanese government bond future on the Tokyo Stock Exchange. An uptrend was well established, and the early 1994 pullback unwound the overbought reading on the RSI. The moving average crossover in mid-1995 was a 'golden' cross, with the shorter average climbing above the longer average while both were rising. But after an all-time high was recorded in late 1995 the market slipped back with the world's other major bond markets.

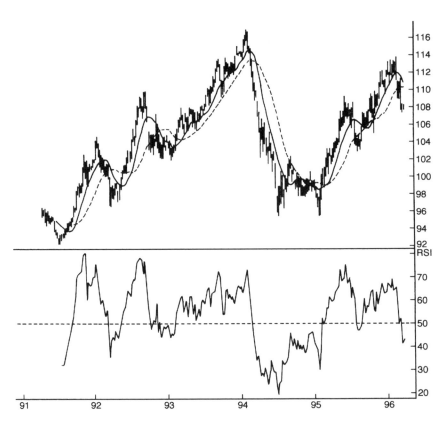

Chart 2.15 Canadian Government Bond (10-year) Future Weekly Bar Chart (Montreal Exchange)

Chart 2.14 shows Japanese interest rate (Euroyen) futures on the Tokyo International Financial Futures Exchange (TIFFE). There too an uptrend was clearly in place, and new highs were reached. But note at least three potential problems: the strongly overbought signal from the RSI (not just above 70 but above 80 in 1995), the failure of the RSI to take out its old high from late 1993 and, perhaps most important, the closeness of the price to the 100 level. Any climb above that would suggest negative interest rates in Japan, not impossible but clearly unusual.

Crossing continents again, Chart 2.15 is a weekly chart of Canadian bond futures in Montreal. The most obvious pattern on it is

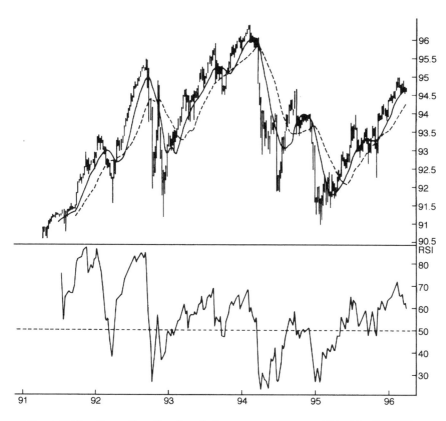

Chart 2.16 Canadian Bankers' Acceptance Future Weekly Bar Chart
(Montreal Exchange)

the double bottom, which signalled the 1995 rally. The subsequent pullback looks more modest than in most of the other bond markets looked at so far. And the Canadian interest rate futures in Chart 2.16 look well established on an upward path and seem to be heading for the old highs above 96 once the early 1996 pullback is concluded.

Crossing continents again, the Australian (Commonwealth) bond futures monthly bar chart, Chart 2.17, from Sydney has a familiar look to it. It is very similar to the bond charts seen earlier though with a less pronounced double top. And the Australian interest rate chart, Chart 2.18, similarly has much in common with the Eurodollar chart.

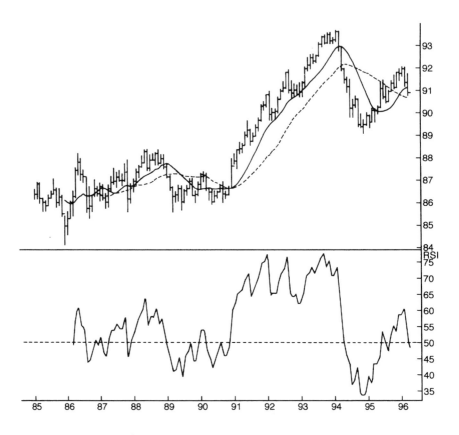

Chart 2.17   10-year Commonwealth Treasury Bond Future Monthly
Bar Chart (Sydney Futures Exchange)

Finally in this chapter, the Swiss interest rate weekly chart, Chart 2.19, is included more as a curiosity than anything else. Note how similar it is to the Euroyen Chart 2.14 but with at least two crucial differences. First, the uptrend has been so methodical that the RSI is at 60 rather than 70; second the price is at 98 rather than 99. While the Euroyen price has only one point to go before hitting key psychological resistance at 100, when the market would be looking for rates to turn negative, the Swiss future has two points to go before hitting the buffers.

To summarise then, most of the bond charts now look bearish thanks to 'double top' patterns, implying higher bond yields.

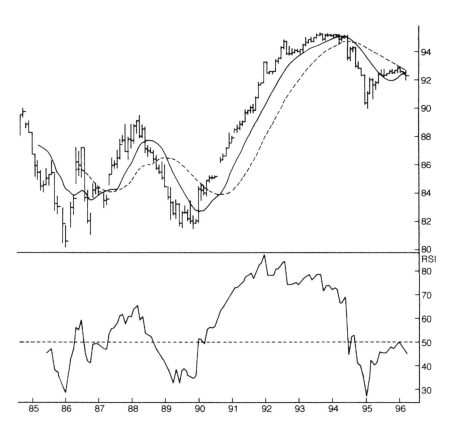

Chart 2.18 Australian Bank Accepted Bills (90-day) Future Monthly
Bar Chart (Sydney Futures Exchange)

However, the interest rate charts look less bearish, suggesting
scope for further falls in interest rates.

Practical traders rather than theoretical chartists often say that
charts are most useful when they say the same as the fundamentals and can then be used to provide entry and exit points. In this
case it is not hard to imagine bond yields rising on signs of economic strength in the major industrialised countries, while interest
rates continue to fall for a while before governments decide to
tighten monetary policy to reign in that growth.

As for the levels to aim at, many technical analysts look for
retracements of previous moves measured between major highs

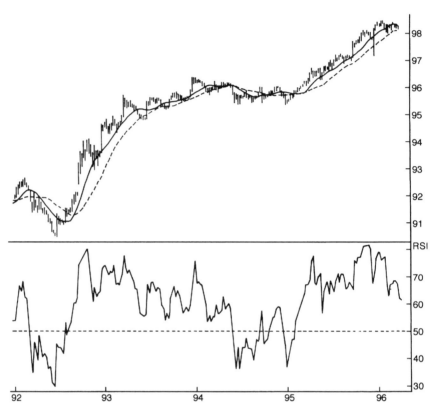

Chart 2.19 Euro Swiss Franc (3-month) Future Weekly Bar Chart
(LIFFE)

and lows. In particular they watch for 38.2 per cent, 50 per cent
and 61.8 per cent retracements, based on the work of the 13th-
century mathematician Leonardo Fibonacci of Pisa. But for many
technical traders, old highs and lows are all that matters. That
may be simplistic, but the beauty of it is that it seems to work.

3
The United States

OVERVIEW

The US debt market is no stranger to international investors but how many realise quite how awesome it is? Looking at Treasury securities, at marketable or tradeable public debt alone, new issue volume totalled $2.1 trillion ($2100 billion or $2 100 000 million) in 1994, up from $2.0 trillion in 1993, according to figures compiled by the Public Securities Association (PSA), an international organisation of banks and broking firms that underwrite, trade and sell US debt instruments. Add in municipal and mortgage-backed securities issued by the Government National Mortgage Association (GNMA), the Federal National Mortgage Association (FNMA) and the Federal Home Loan Mortgage Corporation (FHLMC) and the total new issue volume for public securities climbs to an extraordinary $2.7 trillion. Corporate bonds and stocks add a further $446.7 billion.

Daily trading volumes are stunning too. In Treasury securities the PSA estimates the 1994 figure at $192.5 billion and the total including municipal securities, mortgage-backed securities and money market instruments (commercial paper and bankers' acceptances) at $265.5 billion. The daily trading volume of corporate securities is estimated at $25 billion. As for the volume of securities outstanding in 1994, the PSA estimates the number for Treasury securities at $3.1 trillion, the total for public securities at $6.3 trillion and puts the corporate securities total at an additional $6.6 trillion. Is it any wonder that many American politicians are mesmerised by the size of the public debt?

As the figures show, US debt is enormous in every category: the municipal bonds issued by state and local governments to finance the construction of roads, bridges, airports, hospitals, public power projects, schools, water systems and so on; the US government bonds sold by the Treasury to finance its general borrowing; and the mortgage-backed bonds issued by Federal agencies to finance housing and homes. It is often described as the largest, most liquid government debt market in the world, with Treasuries providing the benchmarks against which all other US dollar-denominated debt is measured.

Long-term new capital and refunding issuance had been climbing inexorably from 1987, when it totalled $105.2 billion, to 1993, when it reached $291.7 billion, though it dipped to $162.9 billion in 1994. Similarly, short- and long-term municipal issuance climbed from $124.1 billion in 1987 to $338.8 billion in 1993 before dipping in 1994. Starting in 1980 the total of Treasury securities outstanding has climbed every single year from $616.4 billion to the $3.1 trillion reached in 1994. Average daily trading volume has been on a similar upward path, from $18.3 billion in 1980 to 1994's $192.5 billion. Within that, it has been broker/dealer transactions rather than customer transactions that has shown the more rapid growth: up from $11.4 billion a day in 1980 to $116.1 billion a day in 1994.

To put it another way, the United States has moved from being the world's biggest creditor until the early 1980s to being the world's biggest debtor after a decade of current account deficits. In 1996 it faces a big bulge in its borrowing needs as previously auctioned five-year notes begin to mature. Against this background, it is no wonder that the budget deficit is such a problem for US politicians and that the arguments about US borrowing and spending reached such a height in November 1995 that the government was actually shut down for a while; essential services excepted. It is also worth noting, though, that by the end of 1995, US debt had provided investors with a total rate of return of more than 18 per cent over the year, according to Salomon Brothers, even more than the 16.88 per cent gain for the firm's world government bond index calculated in local terms. There may be a lot of US debt, but clearly there are a lot of people who want to buy it despite the fight between the Congress and the White House over balancing the federal budget, holding up a permanent increase in the debt ceiling and raising the possibility of default.

POLITICS

Politics are perhaps less important for investors in the United States than for investors in any other country. As the (admittedly American but none the less independent) rating agency Standard & Poor's said in a report:

> The implied ratings of the United States are based on its pre-eminent international position, with the world's largest, most diversified economy, the key currency underpinning the global system of trade and finance, unmatched military power and diplomatic influence, and a long-standing stable political system.

S&P's implied long-term foreign currency rating of the United States is AAA, its implied long-term local currency debt rating is also AAA and its implied short-term debt rating is A1+. These ratings were assigned in 1941 and have never been changed since.

Bill Clinton, a Democrat, was elected president in November 1992 and faces his next battle for the presidency in November 1996. Until then he is both head of state and government, but the Congressional elections in November 1994 gave the Republicans a majority in Congress, effectively limiting his power. Therefore whether he hangs on in 1996 or is defeated by a rival, the changes in the political situation look set to be limited. The Republicans have, and will continue to have, control of both houses of Congress for the first time in 40 years. But their 'Contract with America', with its promises of tax and spending cuts, had at the time of writing had virtually no impact on the $250 billion budget deficit.

The management of the money resources of the United States is the primary function of the Department of the Treasury, which was formally established in 1789, though its roots go back even further and pre-date independence. Its head is the secretary of the Treasury, who since January 1995 has been Robert Rubin, a former co-chairman of the US investment bank Goldman Sachs and head of the National Economic Council. His immediate predecessors were Lloyd Bentsen (1993–4), Nicholas Brady (1988–93), James Baker (1985–8) and Donald Regan (1981–5).

The basic functions of the Department of the Treasury include:

- Economic and fiscal policy
- Government accounting, cash, and debt management

- Supervision of national banks and thrifts
- Production of coin and currency
- Assessment and collection of internal revenue
- International economic policy
- Promulgation and enforcement of tax and tariff laws
- Enforcement of customs and trade laws
- Anti-counterfeiting operations and executive protection

The secretary of the Treasury, according to his department

is responsible for formulating and recommending domestic and international financial, economic, and tax policy, participating in the formulation of broad fiscal policies that have general significance for the economy, and managing the public debt. The Secretary oversees the activities of the Department in carrying out its major law enforcement responsibilities; in serving as the financial agent for the U.S. Government; and in manufacturing coins and currencies.

The secretary is the chief financial officer of the government and serves on the President's National Economic Council as well as many other bodies both domestic and international. He is chairman of the boards and managing trustee of the Social Security and Medicare Trust Funds. He is chairman of the Resolution Trust Corporation Oversight Board, and he serves as US governor of the International Monetary Fund, the International Bank for Reconstruction and Development (the World Bank), the Inter-American Development Bank, the Asian Development Bank, the African Development Bank and the European Bank for Reconstruction and Development.

For the markets, the key section of the Treasury is the Bureau of the Public Debt, which borrows the money needed to operate the federal government and account for the resulting public debt. The treasurer, incidentally, is a relatively little-known official, currently Mary Ellen Withrow.

THE FEDERAL RESERVE

The key reason why investors, at home and overseas, regard politics as of relatively little importance in the US is that the country's central bank, the Federal Reserve, is largely independent. Note that word 'largely', though. MMS International, a consultancy and research group, noted in a report that while the Fed is nominally independent, its chairman and board are appointed by the government and must be ratified by Congress. In a controversial table ranking the world's leading central banks by their degree of independence, it put the Fed only in fifth place, with an independence index of 51 per cent. That compares with the 71 per cent rating given the Bundesbank in first place (and the 20 per cent given to the Bank of Japan, near the bottom of the list). The MMS rankings were based on a World Bank study which looked at the legal framework in which the central banks operate, the annual turnover of central bank governors and an international survey of monetary economists. MMS noted a debate in the United States on whether there should be more political influence on the Fed and whether it should be more accountable, in contrast to the trend elsewhere for more rather than less independence.

Certainly, investors see the Fed structure, signed into law on 23 December 1913, as a safeguard against political ineptitude. The Fed itself recognises that its reputation is crucial. 'Ultimately the only way central banks can achieve their goals is if their integrity is without question and people have confidence in the policies they pursue,' said William McDonough, president of the Federal Reserve Bank of New York, in a conference speech in Chicago in 1994. 'At the end of the day, it is public confidence that is a central bank's most precious commodity in a democracy,' he concluded.

MMS summarises the Fed's principal objectives as 'price stability and employment', in contrast with the Bundesbank's, which are 'to safeguard the value of the currency' and to 'support the general economic policies of the government'. The latter key objective was not included in the Federal Reserve Act signed by President Woodrow Wilson in 1913.

The Fed itself naturally sees its role as somewhat more complicated than MMS's four words: the eighth edition of its *Purposes and Functions*, dated December 1994, runs to 157 pages. The Fed is a federal system consisting of a central government agency, the Board of Governors, and 12 regional Federal Reserve Banks. The publication says the Fed's duties fall into four general areas:

1. Conducting the nation's monetary policy by influencing the money and credit conditions in the economy in pursuit of full employment and stable prices;

2. Supervising and regulating banking institutions to ensure the safety and soundness of the nation's banking and financial system and to protect the credit rights of consumers;
3. Maintaining the stability of the financial system and containing systemic risk that may arise in financial markets; and
4. Providing certain financial services to the US government, to the public, to financial institutions and to foreign official institutions, including playing a major role in operating the nation's payments system.

Of most importance to the bond market is the way it conducts monetary policy, which it does using three major tools:

1. Open market operations—the buying and selling of US government (mainly Treasury) securities in the open market to influence the level of reserves in the depository system. It targets the overnight Federal funds or inter-bank rate via these operations;
2. Reserve requirements—the amount of funds that commercial banks and other depository institutions must hold in reserve against deposits; and
3. The discount rate—the interest rate charged commercial banks and other depository institutions when they borrow reserves from a regional Federal Reserve Bank.

A major component of the system is the Federal Open Market Committee (FOMC), which is made up of the Board of Governors, the president of the Federal Reserve Bank of New York and presidents of four other Federal Reserve Banks, who serve on a rotating basis. The FOMC oversees open market operations, which are the main tools used by the Federal Reserve to influence money market conditions and the growth of money and credit. Policy regarding open market operations is established by the FOMC. However, the Board of Governors has sole authority over changes in reserve requirements, and it must also approve any change in the discount rate initiated by a Federal Reserve Bank.

Another key point for the financial markets is that members of the Board of Governors testify frequently before Congressional committees on the economy, monetary policy and other matters. In particular, under the Humphrey–Hawkins Act, the Board of Governors must submit reports on the economy and the conduct of monetary policy to Congress by 20 February and 20 July each year. The chairman of the Board of Governors, currently Alan Greenspan, is called to testify on the report before the Senate

Committee on Banking, Housing and Urban Affairs and the House Committee on Banking, Finance and Urban Affairs.

The markets therefore watch the Fed's actions, listen to its members speak and, perhaps most important of all, wait with bated breath for FOMC meetings to see if the Fed is raising rates, lowering them, leaving them unchanged or leaving them unchanged but changing its bias towards tightening or easing monetary policy. Formal FOMC meetings are held eight times each year in Washington, with telephone conversations and other meetings held when needed.

In February 1995 the Federal Reserve announced it was adopting a formal procedure for disclosing policy decisions made by the FOMC and for releasing transcripts of FOMC meetings. As it had done provisionally for the previous year, the Fed said it would announce each change in monetary policy on the day it was made. If no change was made, it would simply say the meeting had ended and that there were no further announcements. The Fed also said no change would be made in its practice of issuing FOMC minutes, with dissenting statements, at 16:30 New York time on the Friday following the next meeting.

Alan Greenspan was nominated for a third four-year term as Fed chairman in February 1996. He was appointed to the Fed in 1987 by President Ronald Reagan after serving in the mid-1970s as chairman of President Gerald Ford's Council of Economic Advisers. He is seen as a moderate Republican but at the Fed has built a reputation for what the *Financial Times* has called 'non-partisan professionalism'.

MARKET STRUCTURE

The US Treasury issues three types of marketable, or tradeable, securities: bills, notes and bonds, all of which are direct obligations of the US government and are therefore regarded as having in essence no credit risk. They are sold initially by auction and may then be bought and sold freely in the secondary (commercial) market at market prices through various financial institutions such as brokers and dealers. Treasuries are identified by the coupon—the interest paid as a percentage of the nominal or face value—and the maturity date.

Treasury bills are issued with a term to maturity of one year or less. Notes have an initial maturity of one to 10 years, and bonds are issued with a term greater than 10 years. Please note, incidentally, that these definitions are not universal; in virtually every other country a 10-year issue is regarded as a bond rather than a note. A key difference between bills and notes and bonds is that bills do not bear a stated rate of interest but are sold at a discount from par. The owner receives no rate of interest but benefits instead from a rising price as the bill nears maturity. Notes and bonds have stated interest rates and these interest payments are made semi-annually, in contrast with German Bunds, for example, which pay interest annually. This means that a comparison between the yield on a US T-note and the yield on a German Bund must be adjusted for the comparison to be valid. Interest on Treasuries is paid gross, without deduction of withholding tax, and Treasuries are registered securities.

Prices in the secondary market are quoted 'clean', no notice being taken of accrued interest, though this must be taken into account when settling a trade. Almost all trade in them is 'over-the-counter', and takes place 24 hours a day, with business conducted in New York, Tokyo and London, and to a lesser extent in other centres in Western Europe, Australia, Singapore and elsewhere. Treasuries are all listed on the New York Stock Exchange to satisfy those overseas investors which are only allowed to buy listed securities, and the market regulator is the Securities and Exchange Commission.

US Treasuries are not redeemable before maturity unless they are callable—the government having an option to redeem them early. New Treasuries do not exist in the form of paper certificates; they are now issued only in book-entry form, accounting entries maintained electronically on the records of the Treasury, a Federal Reserve Bank or Branch, or a financial institution. Previously, both bearer and registered definitive securities were issued as engraved certificates, and though these are no longer sold many have not yet matured and may still be bought in the secondary market.

The system operated by the Federal Reserve Banks, serving as fiscal agents of the Treasury, is the Treasury/Reserve Automated Debt-Entry System (TRADES), known as the commercial book-entry system. Book-entry securities may also be held on the

TREASURY DIRECT system, designed for investors planning to hold their securities from issue to maturity.

Treasury bills come in three varieties. Thirteen-week and 26-week bills are offered each week, the offering being announced on Tuesday with the bills auctioned the following Monday and issued on the Thursday following the auction. Bills with a 52-week maturity are usually offered every four weeks, the offering being announced on a Friday and the bills being auctioned the following Thursday and issued on the Thursday after the auction. These schedules can all change if public holidays intervene, and the Treasury also offers cash management bills from time to time with a $1 million minimum purchase requirement.

Notes and bonds are not issued as predictably as bills, but the Treasury generally issues two- and five-year notes towards the end of each month, and three- and 10-year notes in February, May, August and November, as part of the so-called 'quarterly refunding'. Thirty-year bonds were also issued at each quarterly refunding before May 1993 but are now issued only in February and August as part of a plan to shift issuance from the long and medium sectors of the yield curve to the short. The issuance of seven-year notes was abandoned at the same time as the issuance of 30-year bonds was reduced, and the issuance of four-year notes ended three years earlier. The logic behind the May 1993 changes was to reduce borrowing costs by taking advantage of the steep US yield curve at a time when short-term interest rates were at historically low levels. Whether that was wise, given the subsequent flattening of the yield curve, is open to question.

The minimum acceptable dollar amount for a tender (application) for bills is $10 000, and tenders above that level must be in multiples of $1000. Tenders may be submitted competitively, in which case the potential buyer risks putting in a bid which may not be accepted, or non-competitively, in which case the buyer is allocated all the bills wanted at the weighted average discount rate of accepted competitive tenders.

Treasury notes and bonds are sold at a minimum of $1000 and in multiples of $1000 except for notes with terms of less than five years which have a minimum of $5000 and are sold in multiples of $1000. The auctions are on a yield basis, and again potential buyers may send in competitive or non-competitive tenders. An advantage of buying Treasuries through Federal Reserve Banks and Branches or via the Bureau of the Public Debt is that these organisations charge no fees, as commercial banks, brokers and securities dealers are obviously entitled to do.

The most recently issued long (30-year) bond becomes the benchmark for the cash market and is the most actively traded US security, in contrast with most other debt markets, which have 10-year benchmarks. Treasury bond and three-month US interest-rate futures and options are also the most actively traded instruments in the derivatives markets. Trading is active too in STRIPs (Separate Trading of Registered Interest and Principal), which are created by stripping the coupon payments on 30-year bonds from the principal to form zero-coupon bonds. There is also plenty of business in the securities of the various agencies such as GNMA and FNMA, formed to provide credit to important sectors of the US economy. Non-marketable debt such as savings bonds exists too. Another major market is the repo market, where securities can be lent or borrowed.

A typical quarterly refunding announcement in August 1995 by the Treasury Department said it would sell $42.5 billion of notes and bonds the next week to raise $12.5 billion of new cash and to refund $30 billion of maturing securities. The refunding would consist of $18 billion of three-year notes to be auctioned the next Tuesday, $13 billion of 10-year notes to be auctioned the next Wednesday and $11.5 billion of 30-year bonds to be auctioned the next Thursday. The Treasury also said it might need to sell cash management bills in early September to cover a low point in the government's cash balance at that time.

At a news conference, Treasury Assistant Secretary Darcy Bradbury said the Treasury had been raising the size of its debt issues—the $42.5 billion total was a record, as was the $18 billion of three-year notes—to make a smooth transition to a big bulge in its borrowing needs in 1996 as previously auctioned five-year notes began to mature. She agreed that further increases were to be expected across the board over the next year in all the issue sizes but reiterated that the Treasury had no plans to sell foreign currency denominated securities.

As well as detailing the quarterly refunding, the Treasury said it would issue September's two- and five-year notes on 2 October to help meet the Treasury's fourth quarter borrowing needs and that December's two- and five-year notes would be issued on 2

January 1996. Bradbury said the Treasury planned to release a study of its experiment with single price bidding for two- and five-year notes, introduced in September 1992. Under this scheme, all allocations are made at one single yield, highest yield needed distribute the securities. But Bradbury said no decision had yet been reached on whether to issue new types of securities in 1996 to meet the bulge in borrowing requirements. The Treasury was focusing on new types of potential securities such as inflation-linked issues and variable rate notes tied to short-term Treasury bills.

That, then, is the format for one of the Treasury's quarterly refunding announcements, a key event for the debt markets worldwide. Most competitive bids are made by institutional investors, such as commercial banks or brokers, tendering for large quantities of the securities on offer. They must specify the percentage yield they are seeking to two decimal places, recognising that if they bid too high a yield they will not receive an allotment. The Treasury usually accepts the lowest bids (and therefore the highest prices). Most non-competitive bids are made by private individuals prepared to buy at the average yield determined by the accepted competitive tenders.

There is no limit on the size of competitive bids, but non-competitive bids are limited to $1 million for bills and $5 million for notes and bonds. Tenders must be submitted by mid-day on auction day, with the results announced late that afternoon. As mentioned earlier, bills are sold at a discount to par. New notes and bonds may be sold at either a premium or a discount, depending on the level of competitive bids. The Treasury may sell additional tranches of notes and bonds auctioned previously.

THE SECONDARY MARKET

Dealers trade new securities as soon as they are announced, and prior to their auction, in the 'when-issued' or 'grey' market, which allows them to short new issues or sell debt they intend to buy at auction. After launch, trading takes place in the secondary market, an over-the-telephone market with a huge number of participants. Until a decade ago, this was largely unregulated but the Government Securities Act of 1986 introduced rules designed to preserve the efficiency of the market while encouraging wider participation. Trading can take place anywhere in the world and prices are quoted in points and thirty-seconds of a point. The main participants include the Federal Reserve, which maintains a list of 'primary dealers' from which it selects its trading counterparties. Other secondary dealers also trade actively with each other and with their customers, while brokers exist to facilitate inter-dealer trading.

The Fed sells Treasuries to the primary dealers or buys Treasuries from them to drain or add reserves and thereby push market interest rates higher or lower. It does this at 11:30 New York time each morning using so-called 'open-market' operations. In particular it uses system repos and customer repos. System repos are the purchase by the Fed of securities from primary dealers, which agree to sell them back to the Fed either the following day or in a few days' time at a predetermined price. Customer repos are transactions conducted by the Fed using funds such as cash and Treasuries owned by its customers such as foreign central banks and international organisations. The Fed may also use a coupon pass, involving notes or bonds, or a bill pass, buying large quantities of securities to inject cash into the banking system on a more permanent basis.

The primary dealers are the major securities firms and they keep the market liquid by quoting firm and continuous bid and offer prices. In return they obtain many advantages such as being able to trade directly with the Fed and to make telephone bids at auctions. The secondary dealers account for a much smaller share of the market and may be there for a specific reason such as to hedge an active corporate bond trading book. The brokers allow the primary dealers to trade with each other anonymously, and by posting bid and offer (buy and sell) prices on their screens for trades up to a certain size they ensure the Treasuries market is transparent. Business in Treasury bills tends to be concentrated in the most recently issued (current) bills as liquidity is less in the older issues.

DEBT RATING

As mentioned earlier, US debt carries the highest possible ratings. Standard & Poor's Credit Analysis Service, in a November 1993 update, said the strengths mentioned earlier in this chapter 'continue to outweigh the adverse effects of the U.S.'s shift to a debtor from an external creditor nation, a development strongly influenced by high federal budget deficits over the past decade'. Those deficits, incidentally, are generally blamed on President Ronald Reagan, who introduced dramatic tax cuts while increasing spending on defence. However, by the end of President Reagan's period in office the deficits were reduced by strong economic growth and were cut further by the 1990 Budget Enforcement Act which helped constrain spending.

Standard & Poor's added that the ability of the Clinton administration to strengthen public finances is therefore important to maintaining the economic and political leadership of the United States over the long term. It noted the steps taken by the authorities to cut the federal deficit as a percentage of gross national product and concluded that the outlook was stable, reflecting the encouraging implications of government and Federal Reserve policies for growth and inflation as well as prospects for a stable overseas financial position.

Moody's Investors Service rates US long-term debt Aaa and its short-term debt P-1, while the European rating agency IBCA gives US long-term debt an AAA rating. Moody's notes that although the US government has no foreign currency debt rateable by it, the Aaa rating was established as a sovereign ceiling on the ratings of all issuers located in the US. The rating has remained in place in spite of budgetary pressures.

Moody's adds that financing sizeable nominal US current-account deficits 'has been relatively painless because foreigners continue to be willing to hold US dollars rather than demand that the US borrow in foreign currencies'. It indicates the size and depth of the economy, the underlying political consensus and the dominant role that the country continues to play in the world's economic and political forums. But it also points to challenges that lie ahead, including ever stiffening international economic competition.

As for the possibility of default, the major debt rating agencies held different views in early 1996. London-based IBCA put the entire US debt on watch for a possible downgrade on 13 November, 1995, and David Levy, managing director at Moody's Investors Service, said his firm put a small proportion of US debt on review for possible downgrade in February 1996. However,

Standard & Poor's president of the ratings division Leo O'Neill said his agency was not doing anything because of expectations that US government would pay its debt on a timely basis.

THE ECONOMY

As mentioned in Chapter One, the US economy has been growing at a respectable rate each year since the recession of 1990/91, giving Americans a long and undoubtedly welcome period of stable growth. The ideal growth rate for the US economy, giving the people a rising and sustainable standard of living without stoking the fires of inflation, is reckoned to be about 2.5 per cent. Since 1991 it has been well above that level at times—above 6 per cent at one stage in 1993 and above 4 per cent in 1994.

It has also been well below that level and by late 1995 many economists thought it might fall short in 1996. After the shock non-farm payrolls report in March 1996, suggesting stronger-than-expected growth, economists were revising their forecasts upwards again. Even ahead of that report there were signs of strength in the housing market and also in vehicle sales. However, employment growth was slowing and retail sales, excluding vehicles, were lacklustre. With the politicians wrangling over public spending, that element seemed unlikely to give the economy a boost and economists were predicting another fall in the size of the federal budget as a percentage of GDP, continuing the trend that started in 1993.

Inflation appeared to be coming under control, reversing a drift higher, wage inflation appeared to be subdued; unit labour costs were drifting downwards and commodity prices were benign. This rather sluggish picture suggested that the Federal Reserve was more likely to ease monetary policy than tighten it. In July 1995, the Federal Reserve had trimmed its short-term rates for the first time in nearly three years, and it cut again in December and January, bringing the Fed funds target rate to 5.25 per cent and the discount rate to 5 per cent.

Inevitably, reaction to the news that the rise in non-farm payrolls in February was 705 000 was mixed, particularly when subsequent data gave conflicting signals about the strength, or otherwise, of the economy. Federal Reserve governor Lawrence Lindsey took the middle line. He described the economy as 'soggy', as might be expected from a mature five-year old recovery, and said he did not expect either a takeoff or a recession any time soon. Economists also made the obvious point about not taking one figure in isolation and noted that such figures are always revised.

Lindsey, who was speaking to the National Association of Federal Credit Unions, later urged Congress and the Clinton administration to reassure the bond market by striking a balanced budget deal that reins in spending on entitlements. 'I would hope that Congress and the President would pass meaningful deficit reduction (measures) with long-term entitlement control,' he said. 'That would reassure the bond market and be the best form of insurance we could buy for this economy.'

Less than a week later his colleague Alan Greenspan appeared to be singing from the same hymn sheet, saying the economy was moving forward and that inflation was in check. He added, though, that inflation is never dead. 'You always have to be vigilant,' Greenspan said.

As for independent economists, they mostly took the view that further easing of US monetary policy could not be ruled out, given subdued inflation and the Fed's wish to pitch interest rates at a level where the economy would be neither stimulated nor reined in.

THE CURRENCY

A key advantage for export-oriented US businesses has been a seemingly endless depreciation of the US dollar. In the 14 months from February 1994 to April 1995 it fell, in round figures, from 1.77 German marks to 1.35, before stabilising as 1995 progressed (see Chart 3.1). Between January 1994 and April 1995 it crumbled from 113 Japanese yen to 81 before regaining its poise. Even an otherwise weak British pound managed to struggle up from $1.46 in February 1994 to $1.64 in November 1994. For some traders, shorting the dollar seemed like money for old rope.

A senior trader at a major UK bank explained to one of the authors of this book in 1994 that each month he would attend his bank's strategy meetings. Each month they would question whether they should continue selling the dollar; each month they would agree to do so. Each month they would set a profit target; each month they would achieve it by around the 20th of the

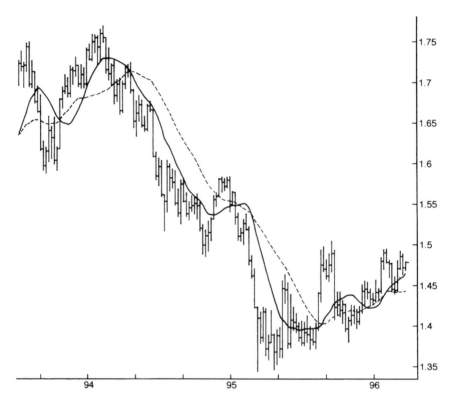

Chart 3.1 Dollar/Mark Monthly Bar Chart. Source: Reuters

month. Each month they would then close their positions and sit back satisfied their bonuses were safe; each month they would sleep easily at night.

According to HSBC Markets, the dollar's 1994 average of 1.62 marks is close to the five-year average of 1.60 but compares with a 10-year average of 1.78. Its 1994 average of 102 yen compares with a five-year average of 118 yen and a 10-year average of 136 yen, figures that illustrate vividly how far it has fallen. That may not matter to US investors in Treasuries, but for overseas investors such as the Japanese it is, of course, crucial. A sliding dollar can easily wipe out bond price gains. Where is the dollar heading now? It might be a triumph of hope over experience, but some economists think the dollar's climb from its 1995 lows may continue, especially against the yen, before the rally runs out of steam some time in 1996.

These economists point to the huge efforts made by the Japanese to try and boost their economy by improving the competitiveness of their exporters, to intervention in the foreign exchanges by both the Bank of Japan and the Federal Reserve, to official statements of support for the dollar by the Fed, and to buying of US securities by the Japanese. No one, however, seems to expect concerted multinational action of the kind seen in years gone by. In September 1985's Group of Five (G5) Plaza Agreement, for example, the United States, Japan, West Germany, France and the United Kingdom decided the dollar was overvalued and that central banks should stage a managed decline to cut the US trade gap and ease the strains on the world economy. By 1987 the authorities felt the dollar's fall had gone far enough and they agreed in the Louvre Accord in February of that year that central banks should try to stabilise it. Some observers were expecting something similar at the Group of Seven (G7) summit in Naples in July 1994, attended by the G5 nations plus Italy and Canada, and lamented that the G7's failure to act was a sign of waning international co-operation. Others said a further agreement was simply not necessary, a view perhaps vindicated by the dollar's eventual stabilisation.

Many, however, including officials of some major central banks noted the increasing ingenuity required by the authorities in timing their intervention to have any impact, given that global daily foreign exchange market turnover is now nearly double the total foreign exchange reserves of all the world's central banks.

Still less likely is the idea proposed by some monetary experts of 'target zones' to limit currency fluctuations. Many economists see such a concept as simply nostalgia for the monetary order established by the Bretton Woods conference in 1944 and argue that target zones only set up goals for speculators to aim at. As evidence, they cite the problems of the European Exchange Rate Mechanism (ERM), which has proved largely unsuccessful in limiting the fluctuations of the main European currencies against each other.

Other economists point to factors likely to ensure that the dollar's weakness persists. They agree it is hugely undervalued relative to its purchasing power parity—the theoretical exchange rate suggested by econometric models. But against this they note the US current-account deficit caused by Americans' buying of foreign goods and services. They note a relatively low level of savings by Americans and their appetite for foreign securities rather than the domestic variety such as Treasuries. They point also to a waning interest in US securities by foreigners.

DERIVATIVES MARKETS

Alongside the New York-based cash market in Treasuries is the Chicago-based futures market, another large and liquid trading centre. The key derivatives exchanges where US debt is traded are the Chicago Board of Trade (CBOT), where the principal contract is the Treasury bond future, and the Chicago Mercantile Exchange (CME), where Eurodollar (three-month US interest rate) futures are traded. These contracts are traded elsewhere too, though with varying degrees of success. For example, the Singapore International Monetary Exchange (SIMEX) has a flourishing Eurodollar futures contract, but the London International Financial Futures & Options Exchange (LIFFE) has abandoned both T-bond and Eurodollar contracts owing to lack of interest.

The trading unit of the T-bond future on the CBOT is one US Treasury bond having a face value at maturity of $100 000 or multiple thereof. Bonds that may be delivered are all US T-bonds that have a maturity of at least 15 years from the first day of the delivery month or, if callable, cannot be called for at least 15 years. The invoice price equals the futures' settlement price times a conversion factor plus accrued interest. The conversion factor adjusts the price of the delivered bond ($1 par value) to that of a bond with a coupon of eight per cent. Prices are quoted in points ($1000) and thirty-seconds of a point. The tick size/or minimum movement, is $\frac{1}{32}$ of a point ($31.25/contract); par is on the basis of 100 points. There is a daily price limit of three points ($3000/contract) above or below the previous day's settlement price (expandable to 4.5 points). Limits are lifted on the second business day preceding the first day of the delivery month.

Contract months are March, June, September and December. Delivery is by the Federal Reserve book-entry wire-transfer system. The last trading day is the seventh business day preceding the last business day of the delivery month, and the last delivery day is the last business day of the delivery month. Trading hours are 07:20 to 14:00 Chicago time, Monday to Friday. Evening trading hours are 17:20 to 20:05 Central Standard Time or 18:20 to 21:05 Central Daylight Time, Sunday to Thursday. Project A (the CBOT's electronic after-hours system) afternoon session hours are 14:30 to 16:30 Chicago time Monday to Thursday, and the Project A overnight session hours are from 22:30 to 06:00, Sunday to Thursday. Trading in expiring contracts closes at noon on the last trading day.

The CBOT also lists options and flexible options on T-bond futures; futures, options and flexible options on 10-year US Treasury notes, five-year US Treasury notes and two-year US Treasury notes; futures and options on a long-term municipal bond index; and futures on 30-day Fed funds as well as a variety of other products unrelated to the US bond market.

The trading unit of the three-month Eurodollar time deposit future on the CME is $1 million, and prices are quoted in IMM Index points. The IMM or International Monetary Market is a division of the CME. The minimum price fluctuation or tick is $25, equal to one IMM Index point or 0.01 or one basis point. There are no daily price limits and the contract months, as on the CBOT, are March, June, September and December. Trading hours are 07:20 to 14:00 Chicago time, except on the last trading day when the hours are 07:20 to 09:30. The last day of trading is the second London business day immediately preceding the third Wednesday of the contract month. The delivery date is the last day of trading, and the contracts are cash settled. Trading ends at noon on the business day before a CME holiday and on any US bank holiday that the CME is open. The contract is also traded on GLOBEX, the electronic after-hours trading system launched in June 1992.

Other relevant CME contracts include Eurodollar options, one-month LIBOR (London Inter-Bank Offered Rate) futures and options, 13-week Treasury bill futures and options, and one-year Treasury bill futures and options, all of which trade on GLOBEX. CME/GLOBEX trading takes place from Sunday night to Friday morning from 14:45 to 18:50 Chicago time, except that on Sundays it begins at 17:30; trading also takes place on some US holidays. There is additionally an enormous over-the-counter market in US debt derivatives.

USEFUL ADDRESSES

Mail inquiries to:

United States Treasury
Bureau of the Public Debt
Division of Customer Services
Washington, DC 20239–0001

Issues Division/Public Information
  Division
Federal Reserve Bank of New York
33 Liberty Street
New York, NY 10045

Division of Support Services
Board of Governors of the Federal
  Reserve System
Washington, DC 20551

Mail tenders to:

United States Treasury
Bureau of the Public Debt
Department N
Washington, DC 20239–1500

Public Securities Association
40 Broad Street, 12th Floor
New York, NY 10004–2373

Chicago Board of Trade
141 West Jackson Boulevard,
  Suite 2210
Chicago, Illinois 60604–2994

Chicago Mercantile Exchange
30 South Wacker Drive
Chicago, Illinois 60606–7499

4

Germany

Germany's Bund market has become Europe's safe haven for bond investors, just as the mark is the continent's anchor currency. The country owes much of this high credit status to the reputation which the Bundesbank has established since its creation in 1957 as the epitome of central bank independence. The market believes Bunds enjoy greater protection than any other government's bonds from the sort of political pressures which enable inflation to erode the real value of the paper.

The Bundesbank's crusade against inflation has also helped to propel the mark to reserve currency status, thus strengthening demand for Bunds as a core holding in any bond portfolio. The mark appreciated to 1.623 per dollar in 1994 from 2.427 in 1982.[1] Projections from the independent Oxford Economic Forecasting group suggest dollar-based investors face limited currency risk from Bund investments in 1996, when it expects the mark to average 1.44 to the dollar, little changed from 1995.

The Bundesbank is the highly successful agent of the mark's strength, but the foundations of the currency's reserve status lie, of course, in the real economy, the world's third largest measured by GDP after the United States and Japan. A diverse manufacturing sector, specialising in engineering, car and truck production, steel and chemicals, has built a reputation for high-quality output, enabling West Germany to run current account surpluses through most of the years since World War II. The disruption caused by the 1990 reunification of West Germany with the former Communist East Germany helped to provoke a severe recession. But most financial analysts believe united

Germany has the potential to generate economic growth with a new dynamism.

The mark and the Bund market benefited from the consistent policy-making of a steady succession of stable coalition governments in West Germany since World War II. The Bundesbank owes some of its success in containing inflation to the politicians, who have pursued conservative fiscal policies and economic consensus. So far reunification has had a relatively cosmetic effect on the political spectrum.

However, the end of the Cold War did raise two major potential threats to the Bundesbank's traditions. The bank fought in vain against a political decision to convert the east German Ostmark into its own Deutschmark at parity, a rate which put great strain on monetary policy. This one-for-one conversion also made east Germans' wages excessively uncompetitive, thus adding to the second inflationary threat—the cost of cushioning the east German transition to a market economy. Bund yields, once entrenched below those of US Treasuries, shot up above US yields as investors demanded higher premiums to cover the budget deficit and inflation risks incurred by the new Germany. Yet the mark ended 1995 buying more US cents than it did in 1989, while Bunds had largely closed their yield gap over US paper. The inflationary effects of German unity had been curbed by monetary rectitude.

After 1990, the Bundesbank needed its credibility more than ever because the new Germany needed foreign Bund purchasers to fund the reconstruction of the east. During the early 1990s, the German central bank not only refused to ease the pain of recession in west Germany and near economic collapse in east Germany; it also defied pressure to preserve Europe's Exchange Rate Mechanism (ERM), which had to be effectively suspended due to the tensions generated by high German interest rates.

The Bundesbank's evident insistence on putting its monetary credentials ahead of the country's European partnerships has not stopped Bund investors worrying about Europe's plans for Economic and Monetary Union (EMU). At best, EMU could cost Bunds their special identity and part of the price premium they now command over other European government bonds. At worst, EMU might drag Germany down to a lowest common denominator of UK-style inflation, a Belgian-scale debt to GDP ratio and Italian high-interest payments.

After all, say the Bund bears, the German political establishment has so far embraced European unity with passion, and the politicians have overruled the Bundesbank once before, by insisting on overvaluing the Ostmark in the rush for reunification. There is a risk that the Bundesbank will be overruled again: that German politicians will bend the rules to let debt-encumbered countries with unruly inflation rates merge their currencies with the mark. There is a bigger risk that even a restricted monetary union of Europe's fiscally correct hard core will generate the uncertainty that bond investors hate and thus increase Bund volatility, at least initially.

Such fears sent the German yield curve arching upwards in late 1995 as investors demanded a sharply higher risk premium to hold Bunds due to mature beyond the EMU target date of 1999.[2] The fears subsided somewhat—along with optimism over EMU's prospects—when leaked remarks by Finance Minister Theo Waigel suggested that German politicians shared the Bundesbank's reservations about alliances with more fiscally challenged countries.

It seems likely that the Bund market will remain exposed to similar scares for the rest of the decade, or as long as the European Union pursues the dream of EMU. Long-term investors therefore need to weigh the risk that German politicians, having rushed into reunification in defiance of Bundesbank advice, might let a long-held ideal override economics again when it comes to EMU. However, there is one big difference between reunification and EMU. In 1990, voters shared the politicians' dream of reunification, but in 1995, barely a third of Germans were willing to surrender the mark.

THE POLITICAL BACKGROUND

German unification in 1990 marked the first peaceful geographic expansion of Central Europe's main power. Fragmented for centuries after the breakup of a mediaeval German empire, Germany was reunited in the 19th century by a mixture of war and diplomacy. It promptly won continental hegemony on the back of a highly successful industrial revolution, only to have its territory truncated and its economy wrecked by defeat in World War I. Wartime government borrowing from the central bank combined with punitive war reparations to fuel catastrophic inflation, preparing the ground for Adolf Hitler to win power in 1933, establish his Nazi dictatorship and trigger World War II. In 1945, the Allied victors split Germany into four territorial sectors.

In 1949 the American, British and French sectors were formally reunited as West Germany (Federal Republic of Germany), while the Soviet sector became East Germany (German Democratic Republic). A year earlier each side had created its own currency to replace the Reichsmark, whose worth had been decimated by Nazi economics. West Germany's Deutschmark was protected by a two-tier central banking system, modelled on the US Federal Reserve. The system was under Allied control until 1951, but it was independent of German politicians and the German central bankers made sure it stayed that way when it was centralised to form the Bundesbank on 26 July 1957.

Whatever conclusions the rest of Germany drew from defeat in two World Wars, the designers of the post-war banking system drew two major lessons from the currency collapses that ensued from each conflict. The first was that politicians, exposed to the temptation to print money, are likely to do so. 'Right from its inception the Deutsche mark was a pure "paper currency",' the Bundesbank says in its own official history.[3] 'Behind this arrangement lay the generally accepted recognition that to maintain the value of a currency it is neither sufficient nor necessary to "cover" the notes issued with gold or foreign exchange, what ultimately matters is a tight money supply.' The second lesson was that independence in law is not enough: a central bank needs popular legitimacy. The Bundesbank has taken care to entrench its reputation at home, as well as abroad, as the guardian of the German citizen's money.

While Germany's central bankers were still under Allied supervision, West Germany had begun digging itself out from the financial and material debris of the war, ready to engineer the *Wirtschaftswunder* (economic miracle) which made the country the envy of many foreign observers—not least those in the east. During the 1950s and 1960s, manufacturing exports built persistent trade surpluses which, thanks to the Bretton Woods fixed exchange-rate system, forced the new Bundesbank to amass burgeoning reserves of dollars through obligatory intervention in the currency markets.

This economic renaissance was widely attributed to a post-war West German political framework which tempered free-market principles with a 'social partnership' between unions, industry and the state, with the emphasis on vocational training and co-operation to justify high wages in return for high-quality productivity. But growth slowed during the 1970s and much of the 1980s. Foreign economists became more critical of the West German model, saying the labour market had become too rigid and the taxation of business, to finance the welfare system, too onerous.

This period of slower growth was also the era when the Bundesbank was making its reputation as the guardian of price stability,[4] averting the double-digit inflation[5] which plagued its trading partners. The collapse of the Bretton Woods currency accord in March 1973 freed the Bundesbank from any formal compulsion to sell marks for dollars or to hold down the mark's value by holding down interest rates. Although it has had some obligations ever since then to support European currency agreements, it was not until the ERM crises of September 1992 and July 1993 that the Bundesbank was again forced to sell marks on such a grand scale.

Whatever the Western doubts about the West German model, it still looked irresistibly desirable to many East Germans as the credibility of the Communist authorities crumbled in 1989. Economic asylum-seekers flooded west, and monetary union, on 1 July 1990, preceded political reunification by three months. The re-unified Germany has a population of 80 million. Reunified Berlin is again the pan-German capital and the government and the Bundestag (lower house of parliament) are due to move there from Bonn by the year 2000. The Bundesrat (upper house) stays in Bonn; the Bundesbank stays in Frankfurt.

POLITICAL PARTIES

Two elections since reunification have done little to alter the post-war shape of German government. Chancellor Helmut Kohl's Christian Democrats (CDU) and their Bavarian ally, the Christian Social Union (CSU), continue to rule, as they have since 1982. The governing coalition is completed, as nearly every West German government has been since 1949, by the Free Democrat Party (FDP). The CDU's main rival is still the Social Democrats

(SPD); the two major parties advocate broadly similar policies, with the CDU tilted to the right of centre and the SPD to the left of centre. In the October 1994 election, the CDU/CSU won 41.5 per cent of the vote and the SPD 36.4 per cent.

Kohl, who launched Germany's head-first plunge into re-unification, turned 65 in 1995. He has vowed he will not stand for election again, although even his critics within his party have urged him to reconsider. His final decision could prove critical for monetary union. Kohl is widely viewed as one of the few politicians capable of infusing German voters with his own commitment to EMU. Meanwhile his government looks secure until his four-year term ends in 1998. Although the coalition has only a 10-seat majority in the 672-seat Bundestag, there are no by-elections in Germany: members who resign or die are replaced by another candidate from their party's election list. Although Kohl was re-elected Chancellor by a simple majority of just one seat, the opposition cannot unseat him by getting a majority to vote against him; they have to get a majority to vote for a replacement. However, the SPD has a majority in the Bundesrat, whose representatives are appointed by Germany's 16 *Länder* (federal states). The Bundesrat has limited powers, but it can delay and even block Bundestag decisions in some areas, including finance.

There is, of course, pressure for change, coming from two directions: the forces unleashed by reunification and the popularisation of the global environmentalist movement. The more immediate threat to the post-war status quo is probably posed by Germany's Green Party. Pragmatists won control of the party after a disastrous 1990 election showing and set about countering centre-right jibes that Greens were hopeless radicals intent on destroying German wealth. Making pollution a mainstream concern, they have attracted young educated voters and for the first time, in the October 1994 general election, the Greens won more votes (7.3 per cent) than the Free Democrats (6.9 per cent). Since then the Greens have consolidated their lead in local elections and were showing more than 10 per cent support in 1995 opinion polls. Political analysts say both the CDU and the SPD are having to consider the Greens as a more likely future coalition partner than the Free Democrats. This has implications for economic policy-making. The Free Democrats have been outspoken champions of free-market ideology, while the Greens are perceived as favouring higher taxes on business and as less committed to curbing the budget deficit.

The ultimate impact of unification on the German political scene is harder to quantify. The reformed East Germany Communist Party, the Party of Democratic Socialism (PDS), won only 4.4 per cent of the vote in 1994, below the normal five per cent threshhold for Bundestag membership. But it has up to 20 per cent support in the east and was awarded 30 seats under Germany's carefully balanced electoral system.

As for Germany's Nazi legacy, there was an upsurge of extreme right-wing violence, in which at least 30 people died, after unification and Bonn has since banned at least four neo-Nazi groups. The leading far-right group, the Republicans, enjoyed a surge of popularity, capitalising on anger at the flood of asylum-seekers from East Europe and the developing world during the late 1980s. But mainstream parties undercut Republican support by toughening the asylum law, and the party failed to win any seats in the 1994 election.

Within the European Union, Germany has sought a greater degree of political union than the other major partners. Both the CDU and the SDP, for instance, advocate a greater role for the European parliament and a switch from consensus to majority voting on foreign-policy issues. However, the parties seek greater political integration precisely because they doubt economic union can work without it. Both parties reflect voters' reluctance to give up the mark. The SPD, free of the diplomatic constraints placed on the ruling CDU, has been more vocal in demanding tough criteria for admission to monetary union and tough penalties for any indiscipline after the merger. It was the Social Democrats who ensured that the German parliament will have the final say on entering a monetary union.

THE BUNDESBANK

Every second Thursday and each Wednesday, European bond markets focus on the Bundesbank's Frankfurt headquarters. The Bundesbank Council meets fortnightly, usually on Thursday,[6] to set the monetary policy that influences and sometimes dictates the moves of other European central banks. On Wednesdays, the markets scrutinise the latest Bundesbank repo results for policy hints.

After each council meeting, the Bundesbank announces whether it has changed its discount and Lombard rates, the floor and ceiling of its desired 'interest rate tunnel'. No minutes are published, although the council sometimes holds a news conference straight after a meeting. In between meetings, the actions of the bank's executive directorate signal the nuances of monetary policy, especially through securities repurchase tenders.

Bids for these **repos** are usually invited on Tuesdays with the results announced on Wednesdays. The Bundesbank is effectively lending funds against deposits of securities, and the markets look for the lowest rate the central bank is willing to accept. Sometimes the council fixes the repo rate for several weeks ahead, or the Tuesday invitation to bid may state that the rate for that week's tender is fixed. In these cases, the policy significance of the repo lies largely in whether the Bundesbank buys or sells enough extra bills to increase or drain liquidity. Variable rate repos, when participating banks have to decide what rates to bid, offer more scope for speculation. Allotments are made US-style, starting with the highest rates bid. Lower bids may not be met in full, so sometimes, when commercial banks are short of funds and scared of bidding too little, the repo rate gets stuck when it is expected to ease. When this happens, a Bundesbank council member may suggest publicly that lower bids might prove acceptable next time. The markets, however, tend to credit the central bank with total control over the repo rate. Traders will sometimes read monetary policy implications into a change of just a couple of basis points, dashing Bundesbank hopes that repos would offer a discreet way of fine-tuning the money market.[3] The Bundesbank decides when the repurchase agreement will fall due, with two weeks a favoured maturity in recent years.

Banks can get cheaper funds by selling trade bills with less than three months to maturity to the central bank at its **discount rate**. The Bundesbank cut this rate to a record low of 2.5 per cent in December 1987, after the world stock market crash; the record high was 8.75 per cent in July 1992. Each bank has a rediscount quota, limiting its access to this source of refinancing and helping to ensure the rate is generally the floor for one- to three-month money market rates. Increasing the quotas will increase money market liquidity, and vice versa. Since the Bundesbank says it sometimes changes the quotas to counteract technical factors, such moves should not automatically be interpreted as monetary policy signals.

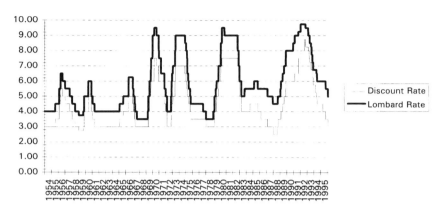

Chart 4.1 German Discount and Lombard Rates
Source: Deutsche Bundesbank

It also offers **Lombard** loans, backed by approved bills and securities of up to three months' maturity but intended to be very short term. The Lombard rate has sometimes been suspended altogether or offered on such restrictive terms that other money market rates have surged above it. However, the increased use of repos since 1985 has taken the pressure off the Lombard facility, enabling it to return to its intended role as emergency funding and thus the money market ceiling. The Bundesbank says[3] that while the discount and Lombard rates remain the cornerstone of its longer-term interest rate policy, these now tend to be changed only after sentiment is tested at the repos. In practice, when monetary policy is easing the market watches the gap between the repo and the discount rates, anticipating a discount rate cut as the difference narrows towards 25 basis points; when monetary policy is tightening, the focus turns to the gap between the repo and Lombard rates.

The Bundesbank wields extra control over the money supply through its power to require credit institutions to deposit certain percentages of their liabilities as **minimum reserves.** Raising or lowering these percentages can have a big impact in curbing or boosting the supply of credit. The requirement also has some day-to-day impact on money market rates. Each bank's reserve requirement is calculated as a monthly average. Towards the end of each calendar month, money market rates will tighten or ease depending on whether most banks have less or more than they need on deposit with the Bundesbank. Credit institutions dislike the requirement[7] and complain that it is one reason why 'Finanzplatz Deutschland', the German financial market, lags behind more liberal London.

The Bundesbank has taken some note of the argument by reducing the reserve ratios since the late 1980s. However, it shows no sign of surrendering its powers to exercise this powerful policy tool, albeit sparingly. It said the requirement 'underpins the effectiveness of monetary policy' because it compels credit institutions to deposit more money with the Bundesbank—and to borrow it back, on the Bundesbank's terms—whenever the volume of credit expands.[3]

The Bundesbank has developed several other instruments to fine-tune liquidity: notably 'fast tender' repos, which are held and settled on the same day; foreign exchange swaps, repos and reverse repos; and special Treasury paper. Injecting liquidity is usually done through the mark-denominated repos; through swaps in which the Bundesbank buys dollars and sells them forward; and through repos in which it buys US Treasury bills which the credit institutions must later repurchase. To withdraw liquidity it can sell Treasury paper issued solely for this purpose; or it can sell dollars and buy them forward; or it can sell US Treasury bills with a pledge to buy them back later in a reverse repo. All these transactions are set to mature after just a few days. So far the market has accepted that they have no monetary policy significance.

The credibility which the Bundesbank commands in the financial markets has its legal basis in the **Bundesbank Act**. This gives the central bank an unusually single-minded goal and an unusual degree of autonomy over how to achieve it. Although the Act says the Bundesbank should support general government economic policy, this obligation is overridden if government policies prejudice the central bank's main task, regulating 'the amount of money in circulation and of credit supplied to the economy . . . with the aim of safeguarding the currency'.[3]

The Act is less explicit in guaranteeing the independence of the Bundesbank president, who is nominated by the government. The government also nominates the vice-president and up to six other members to the executive directorate. However, the directors can only be sacked by the council and then only for gross misconduct. In practice directorate members can expect to serve at least an eight-year term before retiring on a comfortable pension—and they have proved ready to bite the hands that nominated them.[4] They are in any case outnumbered on the Council by the presidents of the nine central banks of Germany's *Länder*,[8] who owe their positions to the *Länder* governments and to the Bundesrat. The current Bundesbank president is Hans Tietmeyer, who took office in September 1993. His term is due to run until 1999.

The federal government has the right to delay a Council decision for up to two weeks, but it has never done so. The culture of monetary probity which deters the politicians from challenging the central bank is further underlined by the 1967 Act to Promote Economic Stability and Growth, which obliges the federal and *Länder* governments to avoid inflationary policies and which urges unions, industry and governments to co-operate to protect the economic equilibrium. The Bundesbank has been spared any ambiguities in its relations with commercial banks through the creation of a separate Federal Banking Supervisory Office.

The Bundesbank's **independence** has become part of market folklore. So too has its single-minded pursuit of price stability, in contrast with central banks like the US Federal Reserve which openly aspire to stabilise output growth over the economic cycle. However, many economists are mildly sceptical of the Bundesbank's assertion that it never tries to meddle with the cycle. In practice, the Bundesbank can ignore neither the government nor the markets.

The Bundesbank interprets its main goal of safeguarding the currency as meaning that the central bank should also aim to stabilise the mark's purchasing power parity with other currencies.[3] But although the Bundesbank owns Germany's substantial foreign-exchange reserves, the federal government has the final say on political **foreign-exchange** rate arrangements. This means, for instance, that the Bundesbank may have to distort the German money supply by selling marks to prop up other currencies in Europe's Exchange Rate Mechanism (ERM). The bank usually tries to 'sterilise' the intervention by draining the excess liquidity. But the foreign exchange market, with far more capital at its disposal than all the world's central banks combined, has sometimes forced the Bundesbank to hold down interest rates, notably in 1978 and in 1986–7, in order to limit the damage that a soaring mark was inflicting on West Germany's economy.

The **debt market**, too, often frustrates the Bundesbank in its efforts to attain its monetary policy targets, which are set annually in the form of a range for money supply growth. The range was set at 4 to 6 per cent in 1995 and 4 to 7 per cent in 1996. Since 1988 the Bundesbank has used the **M3 money supply** measure, which embraces currency held by individuals and non-bank enterprises and the relatively liquid deposits they hold at German credit institutions.[10] The purchase of longer-dated bonds takes money out of the M3 measure and is classified approvingly by the Bundesbank as capital formation. In 1994, when global bond market sentiment swung abruptly from greed to fear, investors inflated M3 by dumping German bonds and seeking refuge for their capital in liquid, short-term deposits. The market then added insult to injury by citing the Bundesbank's failure to meet its M3 target as another argument against buying longer-dated bonds.

The problems of measuring money supply growth also caused a standoff between the Bundesbank and the market over money market funds. These became legal in Germany in August 1994. However, they have had to operate without the benefit of true government benchmarks because the Bundesbank promptly discontinued issues of the most suitable candidate, liquidity discount paper called **Bulis**. It had begun issuing Bulis with three-, six- and nine-month maturities just 18 months earlier, aiming them at individuals and non-bank enterprises in the hope that this would extend its direct monetary control beyond the banking sector. But as far as the Bundesbank was concerned, Bulis attracted altogether the wrong sort of purchaser. 'The Bundesbank . . . prefers not to offer investment facilities for money market funds' said the central bank as it scrapped the Buli idea.

It dislikes money market funds partly because they attract money out of short-term bank deposits, artificially deflating M3 and escaping minimum reserve requirements. The funds also violate entrenched Bundesbank beliefs. Their short-term nature runs contrary to the Bundesbank's ideal of long-term monetary capital formation; and they tempt German governments to abandon the post-war discipline of eschewing the money market as a source of funding. The central bank's stance sets it at odds with German commercial bankers, who say the lack of short-dated paper handicaps the German market, and with some finance ministry officials. 'The federal government is entitled by law to issue short-term debt . . . there is no danger of negative effects for monetary policy,' said Juergen Stark, state secretary to the finance ministry,

in May 1995. He said short-term funding would help the market
and be cheaper for the government provided the yield curve was
normal. But the Bundesbank has so far blocked government plans
to issue three-month paper, based on FIBOR (the Frankfurt interbank offered rate) because it would be used for funding instead
of for controlling liquidity.

From 1995 the Bundesbank has included money market funds,
along with Euromark deposits held by German non-banks and
short-term bank bonds, in **extended M3**, and given this measure
more weight in its policy-making. It has also started publishing
two **headline rates for M3**. It still publishes the traditional
monthly figure, which compares the average level of M3 in the
latest month with the average level in the fourth quarter of the
previous year. Both figures are seasonally adjusted. The difference is then expressed as an annual percentage rate. This calculation tends to overstate changes early in the year and
understate them towards the end of the year and did so to spectacular effect in 1994 . The Bundesbank therefore added a second
comparison in 1995, using fourth quarter 1993 as the base: in 1996,
fourth quarter 1994 became the second comparative base.

The markets usually start anticipating the release of each
month's M3 data around the 20th of the following month.
However, no official time is set for its publication, and the Bundesbank rarely gives the market more than a few minutes' warning
that the figures are ready for publication. Although it publishes the
monthly figures, it is the final comparison of the fourth quarter with
the previous fourth quarter which determines whether the Bundesbank has met its **M3 target**. This is announced in December and
reviewed in July. In deciding the target, the Bundesbank aims to
allow enough liquidity for the economy to grow at the same pace as
its production potential. This was put at 2.75 per cent for 1995. The
target has been pan-German since 1991 and involves some 'guess-
timating' for east Germany, whose production potential has born
little relation to pre-unification assessments. The 1995 target also
made a 2 per cent allowance for unavoidable inflation and allowed
1 per cent for a long-term tendency for money to circulate more
slowly. This gave the 1995 target corridor of 4–6 per cent.

The Bundesbank has never suggested, as the US Federal Reserve has done in recent years, that it seeks to pre-empt inflation
by tightening before prices start to rise. It monitors M3 with the

long-term—some might say abstract—aim of setting ultimate limits on the scope for spending in the German economy. This is just as well, for the Bundesbank has achieved its money supply target in only 11 of the 21 years since it introduced the concept in 1975. The monthly figures are often distorted by what it calls 'special factors', such as domestic tax changes affecting investment decisions, turns in the global bond market cycle and central bank intervention in the foreign-exchange market. Above all, reunification has disrupted money supply calculations.

Initially the one-for-one conversion of Ostmarks for Deutschmarks sent M3 soaring by 15 per cent. Then money turned out to circulate more slowly in the east. But this pattern is set to change again as easterners use the much wider investment choices offered under capitalism. The inflation element in the M3 targets is subject to pressure as east Germans adapt to free market prices and seek west German wages. As for production potential, this will be hard to calculate for as long as east German industry is being rebuilt to western specifications, and that will take years.

Every so often the ability of M3 to short-circuit on special factors becomes too much for the markets. They question the wisdom of adopting a measure which is based on so many variables; they doubt the long-term domestic relevance of figures which can be bloated or shrunk by short-term swings in international asset allocation; and they deride the importance attached to a target which seems to be overridden as often as it is observed. The Bundesbank describes its use of money supply targets as 'pragmatic'[3] and cites Germany's inflation record in its defence.

THE ECONOMY

West Germany was the only OECD country apart from Switzerland which kept annual inflation rates in single digits throughout the four decades from 1950. West German inflation averaged under 1 per cent in 1948–60, 2.5 per cent in the 1960s, 5 per cent in the 1970s and 2.75 per cent in the 1980s.[11] In the mid-1980s, the Bundesbank achieved its ultimate goal of price stability.

Unification has marred this record. Although west German inflation peaked at less than 5 per cent in March 1992, this was during a period of such global recession that even veteran currency depreciators like the United Kingdom and Italy were able to better the German record at some point. In 1994, west as well as east German consumer prices lingered above the medium-term inflation limit of 2 per cent implied in the M3 target calculation. Only in 1995, with the help of an updated consumer price index, did pan-German inflation fall officially within target.

Although the Bundesbank stresses that it targets future inflation, in practice current cost-of-living data seems to have played as great a part in monetary policy as M3. Since the collapse of the Bretton Woods accord, the Bundesbank has started tightening only after consumer price inflation has started rising and easing only after inflation has peaked. Consumer prices are therefore watched particularly keenly by the markets. Financial analysts complain that, like most German statistics, the final figures tend to emerge slowly for such an important economy. The market therefore makes its moves on the basis of initial data released by four west German states. The most important of these is North Rhine-Westphalia, the old industrial heartland and Germany's most populous state; the others are Hesse (which includes Frankfurt), Baden-Württemberg and Bavaria. The data is released towards the end of the month to which it refers.[12]

In 1995 money supply growth kept sputtering, contracting and then growing only slowly, helping to justify a surprise half-point cut in the discount rate at the end of March. Further half-point cuts in both the discount and Lombard rates followed in August and again in December, taking them to 3 and 5 per cent respectively. In early 1996, a Reuter survey showed economists were confident that both the discount and Lombard rates would be cut further, probably by a quarter-point but possibly by a half-point, before the Bundesbank began tightening again. The mean forecasts were for the discount and Lombard rates to return to 3 and 5 per cent respectively by the end of 1996, rising to 3.5 and 5.5 per cent at the end of 1997.

Major factors which influence Bundesbank policy are the mark's external value and the annual wage round. The central bank was critical of early 1995 settlements of around 4 per cent in private west German industry, saying workers offered too little flexibility in return and risked adding to the price constraints imposed on exports by a strong mark. The Bundesbank has also expressed general concern that Germans have not trimmed their pay expectations to allow for the fact that the potential workforce has grown markedly in the past decade, especially since reunification. The independent Oxford Economic Forecasting group expected wage pressures to start pushing inflation back above two per cent during 1996. However, the Bundesbank's chief economist Otmar Issing said he saw no reason to expect inflation to rise during 1996. The Reuter survey's mean forecast was for annual inflation of 1.9 per cent in 1996 and 2.1 per cent in 1997.

Growth[11] in West Germany averaged 9 per cent annually in 1948–60, slowing to 4.5 per cent in the 1960s, 2.75 per cent in the 1970s and just over 2 per cent in the 1980s. The government forecast 3 per cent pan-German GDP growth for 1995, but, as the year wore on, the question became not so much what was happening in the real German economy as how and when anyone would find out. Official figures were released late, carrying warnings that they were likely to need major revision, as the Federal Statistics Office and the companies it surveys wrestled with European Union guidelines aimed at harmonising economic data in member states. The first reliable insights came only in September. The market was able to fall back on data from Ifo, a Munich-based economic research institute. Ifo, which gets about half its budget from the government but is politically independent, has been running a monthly survey of senior executives at around 10 000 companies since 1950. This is widely regarded as one of the best barometers of Germany's economy, even when in competition with official data.

In fact the German economy was growing slowly during 1995: the official pan-German figure was 1.9 per cent. There was a 0.5 per cent fall in GDP in the fourth quarter compared with the third, but many economists thought this would prove to be a mid-cycle blip. The German government forecast for 1996 was for 1.5 per cent GDP growth. Ifo thought it could be a little stronger, at 1.75 per cent. The Reuter survey produced a mean growth forecast of 1.6 per cent for 1996 and 2.4 per cent for 1997. Whatever the outcome, the implications for the Bund market were ambiguous. Faster growth would damage the prospects for further official rate cuts: slow growth would threaten efforts to rein in the budget deficit.

The eastern part of Germany was beginning to fall more into line with the west by late 1995. The Federal Statistics Office reported average 1994 consumer price rises of 3.4 per cent there, compared with 3 per cent in the west. 'Eastern Germany seems set to continue as the fastest-growing region in Europe,' said the OECD.[1] However, some economists challenge this description, given that the OECD itself calculates that net transfers from the west account for about 40 per cent of eastern Germany's GDP.[13] The Berlin-based German Institute for Economic Research (DIW), estimating that eastern unit wage costs were 20 per cent higher than in the west, said it would take at least 10 more years of transfers before the east became competitive enough for output growth to become self-sustaining.

PUBLIC-SECTOR DEBT

Since 1990, the federal government's budgets have been in deficit due almost entirely to transfer payments from west to east, estimated at a net DM150 billion in 1995.[13] The government, under repeated encouragement from the Bundesbank to pare back these subsidies, has set a target of gradually reducing the federal deficit to DM27 billion in 1998. Much will depend on cyclical tax revenue: economic growth of 2.9 per cent unexpectedly knocked DM19 billion off the 1994 federal deficit, reducing it to DM50 billion, but the 1995 federal deficit overshot the budgeted DM49 billion by DM1.2 billion as the economy slowed.

The 1996 budget deficit was set in June 1995 at DM60 billion (see Table 4.2) but at the time of writing a significant overshoot seemed inevitable, partly because of high unemployment and slow economic growth and partly because of tax reforms due to take effect in 1996. Some of these reforms are essential because of German court rulings, such as one compelling the government to raise income tax thresholds, while others are part of a programme to simplify the tax system and to encourage investment in east Germany. But there are political and legal problems over how the reforms should be financed and some economists believe the government will have to resort to indirect taxes, pushing up the cost of living.

The cost of reunification has been borne partly through taxes, notably the reintroduction in 1995 of a 7.5 per cent surcharge on standard income and corporation tax, first levied in 1991–2. This tax is needed to help finance interest payments.[1] The government says it plans to phase out the tax gradually, but this process is likely to take until the end of the century.

Although it would be anathema to the Bundesbank to finance the government in any way which involved increasing the money supply, the central bank does present Bonn, as its sole shareholder, with a generous dividend every April. The handout in April 1995 from the Bundesbank's 1994 profits was DM10.24 billion, three billion more than anticipated.

Meanwhile the federal government's debt burden had risen to over a trillion marks by the end of 1994, according to Bundesbank data.[14] Of this, 712.5 billion (compared with 685.3 billion at end-1993) was direct government debt. The rest was in off-budget 'special funds', of which the most important relate to unification. The federal government is responsible for all the liabilities of the special funds. These include a railways fund set up in 1994 and the ERP fund, which grants soft credits for small enterprises and infrastructure, mainly in the east. The federal government also guarantees debt which was issued by a post office fund before the post and telecommunications system was reformed in 1995.

As 1995 began, the Treuhandanstalt, the agency set up to privatise east German industry, was wound up and its remaining debts were allocated to a new Inherited Debt Redemption Fund (*Erblastentilgungsfonds*) to be repaid over 30 years. The new fund also took over the liabilities of the Debt Processing Fund (*Kreditabwicklungsfonds*) which handled the main debts of the former East German state. In addition, the debts of former East German housing enterprises were transferred to the redemption fund on 1 July 1995. The Bundesbank, replying to queries in September 1995, said the new fund took over debts including 233 billion marks in securities and loans against borrowers' notes at end-1994 and that so far it had financed itself in the market exclusively by means of loans against borrowers' notes. The OECD[13] estimated that at end-1995, the new fund's debt would total DM346 billion. For a breakdown of projected public-sector debt at end-1995, see Table 4.1. There is also a German Unity Fund (*Fonds Deutsche Einheit*) which remains separate but which now only services its existing debt.

Including the *Länder* and municipalities, the Bundesbank put total German public-sector debt at DM1.65 trillion at end-1994 against DM1.51 trillion at end-1993 and DM929 billion at end-1989. The OECD[1] calculates that in 1995 and 1996, Germany

Table 4.1 Public-Sector Debt by Government Level,
estimated, End-1995 (billion marks)

Federal government	761
Länder West	442
Länder East	64
Communities West	142
Communities East	35
Unity Fund	88
ERP Fund	35
Railways Fund	80
Inherited Debt Fund	346
Total	2015
as a share of GDP	57.6%

Source: *OECD Economic Surveys*, Germany, August 1995

Table 4.2 German Public-Sector Finances to 1999[1]

	1995	1996	1997	1998	1999
Public-sector Balance	−102.5	−104	−79.5	−55.5	−27
o/w Federal Government	−49	−60	−52	−43	−33
Western States	−22	−21.5	−16.5	−9	+0.5
Western Municipalities	−5	−4	−0.5	0	+1
Eastern States	−12.5	−11	−8	−6.5	−2.5
Eastern Municipalities	−4	−3.5	−2.5	−1.5	+1
Other Federal Items	−10	−4	−0.5	+4	+6.5

[1] These figures, in billions of marks, were released to Reuters in Bonn after a meeting of the financial planning committee in June 1995. Figures have been rounded. Figures for 1996 are subject to minor revision because of pending tax reforms.
[2] Include payments to and receipts from the European Union, off-budget items such as the German Unity Fund, other debts connected with unification and railway debts.

will be scraping the debt ceiling advocated by the Maastricht Treaty for joining EMU, with gross public debt hovering just below 60 per cent of nominal GDP. The OECD forecasts German debt, according to the treaty definition, at 58.6 per cent of GDP in 1995, and similar levels in 1996 and 1997. This compares with 50.2 per cent in 1994 and 43.8 per cent in 1990.

The German budget deficit has been breaching the Maastricht target of a maximum 3 per cent of GDP, reaching 4.5 per cent in 1993 and 3.5 per cent in 1994, including the Treuhand's deficits. Fiscal rectitude was meant to return in 1995, to reinforce

Germany's authority in demanding economic discipline from its potential partners in European monetary union. Instead, slow economic growth helped to push the 1995 budget deficit, including regional and local government spending, to 3.6 per cent of GDP. Worse, the government had to acknowledge that the 1996 deficit was also likely to swell to around 3.5 per cent of GDP.

STRUCTURE OF THE GERMAN BOND MARKET

The steady succession of current account deficits since 1991 has been a novel experience for west Germans. Germany, a capital exporter for much of the post-war era, is now importing capital to help pay for reunification. The German government has been able to raise funds from foreigners relatively cheaply, thanks to the country's immaculate post-war credit record for both public- and private-sector domestic mark bonds. The Bundesbank says non-residents held about DM478 billion of all German public-sector debt securities at the end of 1994. It does not give separate figures for foreign holdings of federal government securities.

The need to attract foreign buyers has accelerated reform of the government bond market, previously geared towards domestic investors and relying heavily on privately placed promissory notes called *Schuldscheine*. After reunification, the German authorities made a major shift towards issuing standard bonds with liquid benchmarks. According to economists at Merrill Lynch,[15] the value of publicly placed federal bonds outstanding, including paper issued to finance reunification, rose to DM865 billion in 1993 from DM375 billion in 1989, while the value of federal *Schuldscheine* outstanding remained relatively static at just over DM100 billion.

The German *Länder* and municipalities also issue publicly placed bonds, but foreign-investor interest focuses on the government-guaranteed issues which are linked to futures and op-tions contracts on London's LIFFE and Frankfurt's Deutsche Terminbörse (DTB). Deliverable paper has included bonds issued by the former Treuhand and those of the German Unity Fund.

The main types of government bond all pay an annual coupon and are book-entry securities listed on German stock exchanges.

There is no fixed issuance programme, but the Bundesbank, which acts as advisor and agent in issuing debt on behalf of the government and its special funds, publishes issuance calendars for each quarter. This gives the type, maturity, likely volume and approximate timing of issues. More details are announced about a week before each issue.

Europe's benchmark bond is the 10-year Bund, short for *Bundesanleihe*. Since July 1990, the first tranche of each Bund issue has been offered to a Federal Bond Consortium. This is managed by the Bundesbank and includes foreign-owned as well as German banks. The banks effectively underwrite their shares of the issue. The second tranche is then sold through a tender, but bids have to be submitted through a consortium member. Allotments are made US-style, with the highest-priced bids allotted first.

LIFFE and the DTB have rival futures and options contracts based on 10-year Bunds. Europe's benchmark yield spread is that between 10-year Bunds and US Treasuries. At one point during the 1980s, Bund yields fell to nearly six points below Treasuries. They surged as high as two points over Treasuries in the early 1990s, but by mid-1995 the spread was vacillating either side of zero. Since 1951, real 10-year Bund yields—taken as the nominal yield less the year-on-year rise in the cost-of-living index—have averaged 4.1 per cent.[11]

Some 30-year fixed-rate Bunds were issued in 1986 and again at the peak of the 1993 bond market rally, prompting the DTB to introduce a BUXL (extra-long Bund) futures contract on Bunds with more than 10 years to maturity. However, very long-dated bonds tend to be particularly volatile, especially if the coupons are relatively low which these were. Such bonds have long duration, a property which means their prices rise and fall more sharply than those of shorter-dated, higher-coupon bonds for a given change in yield. The 1994 bear market therefore put paid both to deliverable issuance and to demand for long positions in the BUXL contract, which was eventually suspended.

Until mid-1995, the German government made regular issues of five-year notes, called Bobls (*Bundesobligationen*), and four-year Schätze (*Bundesschätzanweisungen*). Schätze were sold at US-style tenders, but they slipped quickly below the 3.5 year maturity limit for delivery against the DTB's five-year BOBL contract. Meanwhile new BOBLs could be bought only on tap by private individuals and institutions such as churches and charities. Banks and foreign investors could not buy them until the tap closed, when they were introduced to official trading on stock exchanges. The five-year sector therefore became heavily dependent on the extra liquidity offered by the Treuhand's five-year TOBL issues. The Treuhand's demise led to chaos at the expiry of the DTB's March 1995 BOBL contract. Many participants were fined for late delivery, and in July the German authorities responded to market pressure to reform the sector. They said they would stop issuing four-year Schätze and start holding quarterly auctions of BOBLs.

The Bundesbank gave the following totals for federal government bonds, excluding special funds, outstanding at end-1994:

- Bunds DM369.5 billion
- Bobls DM186 billion
- Schätze DM71.84 billion
- Federal savings bonds (for resident retail investors) DM59.331 billion
- Treasury discount paper, including financing paper, DM16.99 billion.

It anticipated 1995 redemptions would total DM105.398 billion. The Bundesbank carries out market-smoothing operations in the German government bond market and very occasionally it buys or sells extensively to enhance or soak up bank liquidity.

During 1995, both LIFFE and the DTB launched a facility to help market participants to trade the basis, the difference between the price of an underlying bond and the futures' price. Basis trading enables investors to hedge against the risk that futures' price movements will not exactly offset the price movements of a specific bond. The trades involve exchanging futures contracts for cash bonds. The exchanges now offer to ensure that the futures leg of the deal is properly matched, so that the two parties can buy and sell the agreed number of contracts at the same price.

OUTLOOK

Bund investors need to be aware that when global bond markets are on a bull run, there are often bigger gains to be made outside Germany, in what London-based analysts have dubbed 'the

periphery'—a catch-all phrase for markets situated on the geographic, political or economic outskirts of the European Union.
Such phases often accompany periods of optimism about EMU,
with the bulls justifying their enthusiasm for markets like Italy,
Spain and Sweden by pointing to the scope for such governments
to enhance the quality of their debt by reducing its quantity,
together with the speed of their inflation rates, to meet the
Maastricht criteria.

But even when the prospects for EMU seem remote, the quest
for yield in a bull market will raise the attractions for investors of
the 'periphery' relative to the German 'core', just as highly
structured Eurobonds offering enhanced interest—at enhanced
risk—become more fashionable than straight bullet bonds as a
bull market matures. The converse is also true. When the bears
get their turn to run the market, capital losses prompt a flight to
quality and 'plain vanilla' bonds look reassuring rather than
boring. Bund prices tend to fall more slowly than those in other
markets, as the prevailing wisdom swings around to favour the
proven prudence of the Bundesbank—the role model for the
proposed European Central Bank—over the reform pledges of
politicians on the 'periphery'.

Bunds and the mark are still inclined to suffer on news of
instability in Russia, a legacy of the days when West Germany
formed the North Atlantic Treaty Organisation's front line
against communism. These reactions were never wholly rational
in a world whose geography has been shrunk by the range of
nuclear weapons. As economic and political reforms become
entrenched in Germany's immediate eastern neighbours, Poland
and the Czech Republic, the German markets should become less
vulnerable to events in Russia.

The low yields which Germany is paying to fund the high cost
of reunification are due largely to the Bundesbank's single-
minded pursuit of its uncluttered brief: price stability. The central
bank has enjoyed popular backing not just because of folk
memories of hyperinflation, but also because its policies have
underpinned a culture of considerable economic security in which
long-term investment could be planned and pay claims could be
moderated.

Unemployment is putting some pressure on that consensus. By
the time the Treuhandanstalt closed itself down at the end of

1994, only 1.5 million of the nearly four million people employed by the companies the agency took over in 1990 were still working. In early 1996, unemployment in the east remained above 16 per cent, compared with just under 9 per cent in the west. The west is itself suffering from an underlying trend towards higher unemployment.

These pressures ought to hold wages, and inflation, down for years to come. But that theory was being sorely tested by the implementation of deals to equalise eastern and western wages, involving pay rises over the course of 1995 of 15.5 per cent for eastern workers in the metal and engineering sectors, for instance.[14] The process is testing popular faith in the Bundesbank's creed that only sound money can create sound jobs. And however cheap the credit raised on the bond market, the cost of reunification has bred tensions between rich western and poor eastern *Länder*. Resentment in the west erupted into acrimony in 1995 over reports that some of the public funds poured into east Germany had been abused. Easterners accused western profiteers of taking advantage of their inexperience of free markets.

But all this bears little resemblance to some of the more apocalyptic visions of what reunification would do to German society. As for the German economy, in early 1996 it was still the only country in the European Union (apart from tiny Luxembourg) that came close to meeting all the Maastricht Treaty criteria for membership of Economic and Monetary Union in 1995 and 1996.

The significance of this lies mainly in the fact that the criteria are those of a safe-haven investment. As far as EMU is concerned, the Bundesbank has not concealed its reluctance to surrender its monetary sovereignty to the whims of less 'stability-oriented' European nations. 'The history of German central banking shows that the value of money can be durably safeguarded only on the foundation of a "stability culture" shared by all social groups,' the Bundesbank said[3] in a typically ambivalent note on EMU's prospects. It has warned repeatedly against relaxing the rules on admission to monetary union and has dropped strong hints about the need to close Maastricht's loopholes.

Individual Bundesbank Council members have been more explicit. 'If the road leads to a less homogenous, less stability-oriented currency union, then one must expect turmoil in the capital markets,' said Deputy President Johann Wilhelm Gaddum in September 1995. A few days earlier, Bundesbank board member Gerd Häusler agonised aloud about how much German savers had to lose.

> All of us preparing monetary union have to do the utmost so that at the end of the day we will be able to say to a holder of a 10-year Bund, 'Yes, you can buy that bond and you will have it exchanged, not against the mark . . . but you will get something in return that is at least of the same value.'

This is a lot to ask of a common European currency. If the Bundesbank means what Häusler said, then European monetary union is a very long way off. Besides, the German parliament has to approve the final stage of EMU: the politicians are unlikely to do so without their voters' backing; and turning around German public opinion to that extent could prove a lengthy process. There are also safeguards for Bund investors in a ruling which the German constitutional court delivered in 1993, giving qualified approval to the Maastricht Treaty. This left open the possibility that, at the last minute, the court could still declare German accession to EMU to be unconstitutional on the grounds that the entry criteria had not been enforced strictly enough.

However, European unity is a potent political ideal, and even the Bundesbank is not immune to occasional onslaughts of market scepticism. Consequently, Bunds could have a rough ride during 1996, when EU governments are due to hold a series of negotiations to clarify their plans for unity. These negotiations will offer plenty of scope for speculation that Germany's desire for Europe's political integration might finally overcome its terror of inflation. The long end of the Bund market is likely to prove more volatile than in the past as investors seek to assess whether monetary union would in any way diminish the high status of German government paper.

NOTES

1. *OECD Economic Outlook 58*, December 1995.
2. Yields on 10-year Bunds rose to just over two full points over two-year notes, the steepest since January 1988.

3. Monetary policy of the Bundesbank, Deutsche Bundesbank, March 1994.
4. *The Bundesbank: the bank that rules Europe*, David Marsh, Mandarin, London, 1992.
5. West German inflation peaked at 7 per cent and fell to 2.7 in 1978.
6. The council observes a summer recess from mid-July to mid-August. Once a year it meets in an east German town.
7. The Bundesbank pays no interest on reserves. It charges interest, up to 3 per cent above the Lombard rate, if minimum reserve requirement is not met.
8. Five of the *Länder* central banks cover two or three of the 16 *Länder*.
9. M3 includes sight deposits, time deposits for less than four years and regulated savings deposits. An alternative definition is Bundesbank lending, bank lending and Germany's net external assets, less monetary capital formation and other more minor factors.
10. From 1975 to 1987 its target measure was the central bank money stock, which comprises currency in the hands of non-banks and required minimum reserves on domestic deposits.
11. IBJ International Research.
12. For further details, see *Market Movers, Understanding and Using Economic Indicators from the Big Five Economies*, Mark Jones and Ken Ferris, McGraw-Hill International (UJ) Ltd, London, 1993.
13. OECD Economic Surveys, Germany, August 1995.
14. Deutsche Bundesbank monthly report June 1995, Vol. 47 No. 6.
15. *Size and Structure of the World Bond Market, October 1994.* Merrill Lynch and Co. Global Securities Research & Economics Group, International Fixed Income Research.

APPENDICES

Box 1—Credit ratings

Both Moody's and Standard & Poor's award Germany their highest ratings, implied Aaa/AAA for long-term and P-1/A1+ for short-term foreign currency debt. Germany has never used any of these ratings. The Bundesbank says it is inappropriate for a country with a reserve currency to issue public-sector debt in foreign currencies—and that includes the Ecu, the prototype currency of European Economic and Monetary Union.

S&P says Germany's ratings reflect

> the size, diversity and strength of its economy, the country's long-standing political stability and its increasing international political influence and leadership following geopolitical changes in the late 1980s . . . the government's commitments to fiscal consolidation and structural reforms as well as the Bundesbank's commitment to low inflation . . . [reunification has] extracted substantial costs in terms of deteriorating public finances, a growing tax burden, and tight monetary policies.

S&P said the ratings' stable outlook 'reflects the expectation that government and Bundesbank policies will remain conservative, ensuring further fiscal consolidation, low inflation and a strong external position'.

Moody's says its ratings remain

> stable in spite of the pressures put on the German economy by the unification process. While Germany's external position has temporarily weakened, the underlying economic parameters remain solid . . . Germany's total foreign debt remains small . . . Most of the credit needs of the public sector were satisfied by the domestic market. Thus total external debt, which stood at 13.3 per cent of GDP at the end of 1994, consists mainly of borrowings by the banking sector.

Box 2—Futures contracts

Bund: DTB, LIFFE Contract nominal value: DM250 000.
Residual maturity 8.5–10 years, 6 per cent
coupon
Monthly volume: DTB 1.42 million; LIFFE
3.33 million
Trading hours: DTB 08:00–17:30, LIFFE 07:30–16:15,
APT 16:20–17:55

Bobl: DTB only Contract nominal value: DM250 000
Residual maturity: 3.5–5.25 years, 6 per cent
coupon
Minimum deliverable bond issue size:
DM4 billion
Monthly volume: 0.77 million
Trading hours: DTB 08:00–17:30

Three-month: DTB contracts based on FIBOR; LIFFE's
on Euromark
Contract size: DM1.0 million; Cash settled
Quoted as 100 minus the interest rate
Monthly volume: DTB 1325; LIFFE
2.16 million
Trading hours: DTB 08:45–17:15, LIFFE 08:00–16:10, APT
16:25–17:59

Futures delivery months: March, June, September, December
Basis trading facility available on both DTB and LIFFE

American-style options on futures

Monthly volumes: DTB Bund 7801 Bobl 20 678
LIFFE Bund 708 546 Euromark 290 978
Trading hours: LIFFE Bund 07:32–16:15, Euromark
08:02–16:10
DTB Bund and Bobl 08:00–17:30

Expire: DTB February, May, August, November
LIFFE March, June, September, December,
plus extra nearby months

All futures and options minimum price movements 0.01
Volume figures for September 1995, compiled by Reuters.

APT is LIFFE's Automated Pit Trading. All DTB trading is electronic. Regular LIFFE trading is by open outcry. All trading hours local time.

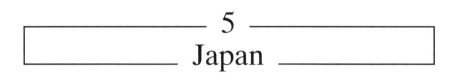

5
Japan

OVERVIEW

In a fact book on Japan's securities markets, the Japan Institute for Securities Information and Public Relations has this to say:

> As an economic superpower, Japan has to meet the needs arising from the maturation of its economy and contribute to the progress of the world economy by ensuring a sustainable growth of its economy. In particular, Japan has to improve the functions of its securities market as an important support for its economy.

It adds that the securities industry 'is determined to enhance the trust of investors and market players, do its utmost to structure a fair, transparent and vital market and meet the expectations of all.' The remarkably frank and hard-hitting message seems to be not just that Japan's economy has matured in recent years and that the high growth rates seen in previous decades are unlikely to be seen again but also that foreign understanding of Japan's markets is not as widespread as the Japanese would like and that there is still plenty of work to be done to improve the markets to the best international standards.

The Institute, whose members are the Japan Securities Dealers Association, the country's stock exchanges, the various associations of stock exchange regular members, the Investment Trusts Association and the Bond Underwriters Association of Japan, talks of 'a host of problems in the securities market' and suggests that the primary market in bonds should be made broader and more efficient, while the secondary market should be improved as well. It calls for new products, improved marketability of existing ones and a streamlining of the securities tax system.

The need is vividly illustrated by accompanying charts showing Japanese portfolio investment abroad, both on the buy side and the sell side, declining year by year through the 1990s and, more importantly for the Japanese government bond (JGB) market, non-residents' investments in Japan falling too and from a very much lower base. Economic stagnation in Japan over the period may well be a factor, but the Institute also calls the revitalisation of the securities markets 'an urgent task'.

In reality, at the time of writing, the JGB market was widely regarded as illiquid by overseas investors, other than in the current 10-year issue. That is only true to a limited extent. Any bonds deliverable into the Tokyo Stock Exchange's JGB futures contract—that is listed seven- to 11-year JGBs—are reasonably liquid too. Certainly, in Japan, benchmarks seem to dominate more than in many other markets and there is little liquidity in new two-, four- and six-year issues or in the 20-year area of the curve. But old 10-year bonds with, say, two, four or six years left to maturity are still liquid and could therefore be of serious interest to investors outside Japan's shores. In late 1995 Japan was offering 10-year bonds by price-competitive auction in volumes of a trillion yen per auction. But a Reuters survey of 22 top bond analysts in September 1995 found that the JGB market was the least liked of all the world's major government bond markets despite the recession in Japan then and a rate of inflation as close to zero as makes no difference.

The analysts polled suggested that 10-year JGB yields would climb steadily from 2.98 per cent when the poll was taken to 3.14 per cent by the end of 1995 and 3.25 per cent by 31 March 1996, the end of the Japanese fiscal year. To put this in context, 10-year JGB yields were almost at 8 per cent in 1990 but then fell steadily to around 2.6 per cent in mid-1995. Over the same period, the US 10-year note yield fell from almost 9 per cent to about 6 per cent. Some words of caution here: the market convention on yields in the JGB market is the Japan simple yield, which takes no account of reinvestment income, although international investors are often quoted the semi-annual yield instead—the one that is comparable with US and UK yields (though not continental European annual yields). That can make quite a difference; a Japan simple yield of 2.83 per cent on the benchmark 174th JGB issue in September 1995 equates to a semi-annual yield of 2.98 per cent.

Indeed JGBs proved to be a poor investment in 1995. They returned 13.29 per cent in local currency terms and only 9.57 per cent in dollar terms, making them the worst investment of all the major bond markets over the year, according to data from the US investment bank Salomon Brothers. Those figures compared with gains of 16.88 and 19.04 per cent respectively for Salomon's world government bond index.

Anyway, the analysts polled in September attributed their JGB pessimism to the government's resort to deficit financing to shift the economy up a gear (explained in the economy sector later in this chapter) and a succession of pump-priming government spending packages that would result, inevitably, in the increased issuance of JGBs. Further cuts in the half per cent official discount rate were also regarded as unlikely, adding to the general gloom surrounding JGBs' prospects. There was also talk of a sharp steepening of the Japanese yield curve as long-dated bond yields rose at a time when short-term rates were anchored to the ground. Economists noted too that if the yen's reversal of fortunes in the spring of 1995, when it began weakening against both the US dollar and the German mark, proved to be more than a temporary blip, that too would reduce the attractions of Japanese assets to overseas investors.

MARKET STRUCTURE

The Japanese may be most important in the world government debt markets as buyers rather than sellers but, despite the comments above, the JGB market is of major importance in its own right. According to figures produced by the Bank of Japan, the country's central bank, issues of so-called 'ordinary' government bonds floated domestically totalled Y55 855 billion in 1994. At 100 yen to the US dollar, that equates to $558.55 billion, or roughly a quarter of the $2.1 trillion volume of new US Treasury securities issued the same year.

In Japan, the volume of new issues has been rising too as it has elsewhere; 1994's Y55 855 billion comparing with Y54 801 billion in 1993 and Y46 146 billion in 1992. With redemptions totalling Y39 263 billion in 1994, that left the outstanding total at Y201 459 billion at the year-end, up from Y184 867 billion at the end of 1993 and Y178 368 billion at the end of 1992. The outstanding total at the end of 1994 of Y201 459 billion equates to approximately $2014 billion or around two-thirds of the $3126 billion of US Treasury securities outstanding at the same time. The JGB market may be of more interest to the Japanese themselves than to some foreign investors, but its size means it is one overseas funds simply cannot ignore.

Looking at the new issues in more detail, the Bank of Japan breaks them down into interest-bearing long-term government bonds, interest-bearing medium-term government bonds, five-year discount government bonds and Treasury bills. Long-term bonds accounted for Y22 975 billion of 1994's issuance, or 41 per cent of the total. Interest-bearing medium-term bonds accounted for Y5750 billion or 10 per cent, five-year discount bonds for Y265 billion or less than a half per cent and Treasury bills for Y26 865 billion or 48 per cent. As for the amounts outstanding, long-term government bonds make up the vast majority—Y180 211 billion at the end of 1994 or almost 90 per cent of the total—reflecting the fact that Treasury bill issues and redemptions run at similar amounts each month.

Turning to the purpose for which 1994's total of Y55 855 billion in debt was issued, some 34 per cent was new financing and the remaining 66 per cent was refinancing. The total for new financing in turn broke down into Y17 476 billion of construction bonds and Y1518 billion of deficit financing bonds, issued from October 1994 at a rate of just over Y500 billion a month. In addition to these 'ordinary' government bonds, ranging from long-term issues to Treasury bills (confusing terminology, no doubt, for American investors, for whom the word 'bonds' means only debt issues with maturities of more than 10 years), Japan issues financing bills, split into Treasury financing bills, food financing bills and foreign-exchange fund financing bills. There are local government bonds too, as well as bonds issued by other bodies, such as public utilities, carrying a government guarantee. Issues of financing bills totalled Y174.6 trillion in 1994 and redemptions totalled Y173.6 trillion, raising the amount outstanding to Y24.8 trillion at the year-end from Y23.8 trillion at the end of 1993. The new issue volume consisted of Y45 407 billion (26 per cent) of Treasury financing bills, Y1013 billion (less than 1 per cent) of food financing bills and Y128 232 billion (73 per cent) of foreign-exchange fund financing bills.

Japan's Ministry of Finance puts issuance of local government bonds in 1994 at Y7643 billion and redemptions at Y2461 billion, raising the total outstanding at the end of 1994 to Y28 837 billion from Y23 655 billion at the end of 1993. As for government-guaranteed bonds, Japan's Bond Underwriters Association puts 1994 issuance at Y2747 billion and redemptions at Y1995 billion, increasing the amount outstanding to Y20 387 billion from Y19 635 billion.

To give an idea of the auction schedule, this is how it looked in the first six months of the 1995–6 fiscal year: 10-year JGBs were auctioned monthly in trillion dollar tranches on 25 April, 23 May, 27 June, 25 July, 22 August and 26 September; 20-year 'super-long' bonds were auctioned twice—Y400 billion on 6 June and Y300 billion on 8 August; two-year bonds were auctioned monthly in amounts from Y120 billion to Y170 billion on 27 April, 25 May, 29 June, 27 July, 24 August and 28 September (i.e. two days after the 10-year auction); four-year bonds were auctioned three times in Y500 billion or Y600 billion tranches on 10 May, 4 July and 29 August; and six-year bonds were auctioned three times in Y500 billion or Y600 billion amounts on 4 April, 30 May and 1 August.

The bid/cover ratio was respectable every time, ranging from a low of just under two to a high above six, and the tail—the difference between the highest accepted yield and the average yield—was typically two or three basis points. The frequency of the four-year auctions has been increased from bi-monthly to monthly and the size of the 10-year has been increased to Y1.2 trillion.

All JGBs are numbered, the number being used rather than the coupon and maturity used in other markets to identify issues, and bonds are quoted in the secondary market in terms of yield rather than price. Sweden is one of the only other major markets to use that convention. JGB coupons, which are fixed close to market yields at the time bonds are auctioned, are expressed in terms of an annual amount of interest paid per yen of nominal debt and are paid semi-annually on specified dates, with the accrued interest calculated on the basis of a 365-day year. Bonds are issued in both registered and bearer form and can in theory be called early at par, though this does not happen in practice.

Secondary trading is largely over-the-counter, conducted by securities companies and other financial institutions licensed to deal in public bonds. Some 500 institutions are licensed, far more than in most other world bond markets, but in practice Japan's 'big four' securities houses—Nomura, Nikko, Daiwa and Yamaichi—account for about 70 per cent of business. There are also several brokers' brokers, similar to US inter-dealer brokers. The government is a major buyer of bonds, with the Bank of Japan buying on behalf of the Ministry of Finance, which buys on its own behalf or for the Trust Fund Bureau. Small private trades also take place on the Tokyo and other Japanese stock exchanges. Bond loan and repo markets exist too. Taxation comes in the form of a 20 per cent withholding tax on JGB coupon payments, usually halved for foreign investors by double taxation treaties (and reduced to zero in special cases), and a transfer tax levied on the seller when a JGB is sold to a buyer located in Japan.

That then is how the Japanese government bond market looks, a large and important market. It is generally reckoned to be the world's second biggest after the United States and around three times the size of the German Bund market. It is therefore an important market for foreign as well as domestic investors if not, according to some analysts, a particularly attractive one. On the positive side, the government may well continue to support JGBs, and experience might suggest that its attempts to reflate the economy might not succeed. But on the negative side, increased supply and a weaker yen could harm JGBs badly.

BANK OF JAPAN (NIPPON GINKO)

As noted in an earlier chapter, Japan's central bank has little theoretical independence. In MMS International's ranking table it comes 17th out of 20 central banks, with an 'independence index' of just 20 per cent compared with 71 per cent for the top-placed Bundesbank and 51 per cent for the US Federal Reserve in fifth place. The table is based on a World Bank study conducted in 1993, which looked at the legal framework, the annual turnover of central bank governors and a questionnaire of monetary economists in each country. MMS notes, though, that while constitutionally the Bank of Japan has very little independence, in practice the Ministry of Finance delegates policy to it.

The Bank of Japan was founded in 1882, soon after the overthrow of the feudal system, as a joint-stock bank with a major shareholding by the government. Its initial task was to assist the government in retiring non-convertible bank notes. It started issuing bank notes itself in 1885 and these became convertible into silver the next year (rather than into gold as in many other countries, though the gold standard was finally adopted in Japan in 1897). It was also instructed to consolidate the country's banking system and promote industrialisation, was permitted to buy and sell government bonds, discount domestic and foreign bills and accept bankers' deposits. It was expected to smooth out seasonal fluctuations in interest rates and to avoid banking crises. Other services provided from its early years included clearing and settlement, oversight of financial institutions and monitoring of lending activities. A general supervisory role came later.

In 1942, much of this changed. The Bank's objectives became 'the regulation of the currency, the facilitation of credit and finance, and the maintenance and fostering of the credit system, pursuant to the national policy'. Management of the Bank passed to the Ministry of Finance and the government increased its shareholding to 55 per cent from 50 per cent.

As noted by MMS, the Ministry of Finance still has the ultimate power, given in 1942, to make important policy decisions. However, it is widely regarded as extremely unlikely that the government would resort to these provisions. It has never yet done so, and the Bank has therefore enjoyed very much more independence in practice than it has in theory. None the less, the government appoints both the Bank's governor, who serves for five years, and its directors, who serve for four. As at all the world's other major central banks, the governor can be reappointed at the end of the five-year term. The board consists of two government representatives, without voting rights, who represent the Economic Planning Agency and the Ministry of Finance, and four appointed members with knowledge of the business of the large city banks, regional banks, commerce and industry, and agriculture respectively.

The current Bank of Japan governor, Yasuo Matsushita, has a Ministry of Finance and commercial banking background. As president of Taiyo Kobe Bank in 1990, he oversaw its merger with Mitsui Bank to create Sakura Bank before taking over from Yasushi Mieno, a career central banker who became governor in 1989, at the Bank of Japan on 16 December 1994. Matsushita is the first governor since 1964 with a commercial bank background, but when his appointment was announced some commentators said his period at the Ministry of Finance's budget bureau might make him more willing to do the government's bidding than his predecessor and tip the scales towards monetary rather than fiscal action when faced with the choice. Time will tell.

DEBT RATING

Standard & Poor's Credit Analysis Service rates Japan's long-term local currency and foreign currency debt AAA and its short-term debt A-1+. These best-possible ratings were assigned in 1975 and 1981 respectively, and S&P said, in a note dated May 1995, that the outlook for these ratings was stable.

'The rating is based on Japan's highly advanced and diversified economy and its position as the world's largest net external creditor. The recent strengthening of the yen [it had only just begun to weaken when the report was published] will delay the long-awaited recovery from Japan's economic slowdown, now in its fourth consecutive year,' said the agency. As for the outlook: 'While the yen's appreciation will delay an economic recovery until next year, and ultimately reduce Japan's large current account surpluses, its strong net external creditor position will remain unchanged over the long term,' S&P added.

Moody's Investors Service rated Japan's sovereign foreign currency and domestic currency debt Aaa and its short-term debt P1, while European rating agency IBCA opted for an AAA sovereign rating too. In its note, Moody's described Japan as a country that is a linchpin in the world economic system, has a strong net creditor position with the rest of the world and a currency that plays a role as a reserve currency. It saw no threat to the ratings despite Japan's economic weakness and political upheaval but concluded that the appropriate extent of fiscal stimulus and deregulation of the economy were key issues.

THE ECONOMY

Japan is the world's largest net external creditor nation and has a highly advanced and well-diversified economy. But that economy is also firmly—some have said over—regulated, with strong non-tariff barriers against imports. Moreover, as hinted at in the comments above, the 1990s have been a terrible period for the Japanese economy. To the lay man or woman in the streets of America or Europe, Japan is still the powerhouse that has changed the world's economy so dramatically over the last few decades. But, in reality, growth of the country's real gross domestic product (GDP), year-on-year, dropped from around 6 per cent in early 1990 to below zero in mid-1992 and has been stuck close to zero ever since. GDP growth in 1995 was a real 0.9 per cent, up from a revised 0.5 per cent in 1994.

Inflation, that hated enemy in the West, has been almost completely wiped out of the system by this economic weakness with consumer price inflation down from over 4 per cent in 1991 to 0.7 per cent in 1994 and around zero in 1995, and wholesale price inflation actually below zero for all of that time, as wholesale prices were cut and cut again to try and stimulate demand for the wholesalers' products.

This economic malaise—far more than a simple recession—followed the bursting of what the Japanese call the 'bubble economy' of the late 1980s when credit was cheap, asset prices soared and profits jumped, created at least in part by American demands for strong economic growth to reduce Japan's trade surplus. It has been estimated that at its peak at the end of 1989 the Tokyo stock market was valued at 30 per cent more than the value of all America's listed companies. In 1990 Tokyo land prices were so high that the grounds of the Imperial Palace were calculated to be worth more than all the land in California.

As one vice-minister said soon after the bubble burst:

We became over confident, too bullish. We should learn not to become too pleased with ourselves. The Japanese are a very disciplined people, but they became intoxicated by the bubble and they somehow forgot their discipline.

Once the bubble had burst, asset prices slumped and the banks were left with enormous non-performing loans, particularly from

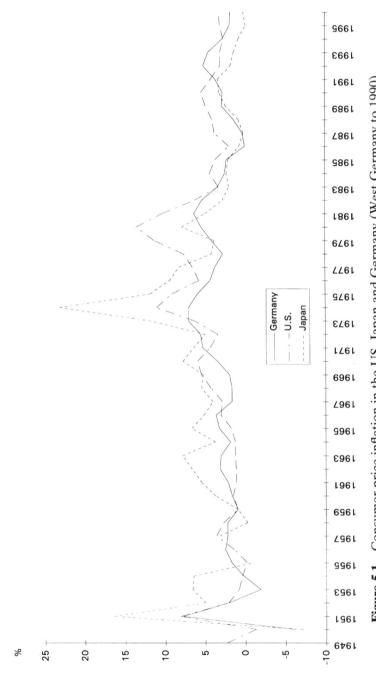

Figure 5.1 Consumer price inflation in the US, Japan and Germany (West Germany to 1990)
Source: 1949–1994 International Financial Statistics. 1995–1996, IMF World Economic Outlook, October 1995, projections

property lending in the late 1980s, when it was widely assumed that land prices would go on rising indefinitely. The authorities responded in all the usual ways, with package after package of stimulus measures, efforts to reduce the external value of the yen and cuts in interest rates, but all to no avail. The official discount rate, or ODR, was cut steadily from 6 per cent for much of 1990 and 1991 to a mere half of 1 per cent from 8 September 1995, a record low; yet in late 1995 and early 1996 many economists were still desperately gloomy about the economic outlook.

The economic stimulus package announced on 20 September may have marked a turning point. The package was worth Y14.22 trillion (though only some Y6.6 trillion of that was genuine new money), was designed to revive the ailing economy by boosting domestic demand and was the third to be announced in 1995. It is worth looking at in some detail. At the heart of the package was record public spending of Y12.81 trillion and it was designed, in the words of a Ministry of Finance official, to push up nominal GDP by more than two percentage points a year after implementation. At the time, the official forecast for nominal GDP growth in the 1995–6 fiscal year (April to March) was 3.6 per cent. Other observers were much more sceptical, both about GDP growth and the impact on GDP of the package.

The main points were:

- General public works spending totalling Y3.9 trillion, and an allocation for disaster reconstruction projects amounting to Y700 billion;
- The allocation of Y400 billion for science and technology, telecommunication projects and research facilities to help develop new industries and Y510 billion for education and welfare facilities;
- The spending of Y3.23 trillion to back up land-purchase projects by national and local governments and the private sector to promote the effective use of land;
- The earmarking of Y1.41 trillion for emergency reconstruction projects following the disastrous earthquake in January in Kobe;
- Local governments would be asked to increase public-works projects to a total of some Y1 trillion;
- Authorities would allocate Y1.11 trillion to help farmers trying to restructure after the Uruguay Round global trade liberalisation agreement;
- Loans from the Housing Loan Corporation, a public lending body, would be raised by Y520 billion to promote housing investment;
- The government's investment and loan programme would be used actively to digest national and local government bonds in the interests of a smooth implementation of the package's public works spending plans; and

- Japan would seek flexible and proper monetary policy steps, while watching domestic and overseas economic and currency conditions closely.

In addition, the government said it would take the following steps to overcome difficulties in the economy:

1. To promote effective use of land, the government would:
   - Allocate Y1.23 trillion to promote the purchase of land for future public use;
   - Allow a state-owned city development organisation to spend an additional Y500 billion on land purchase;
   - Ask local governments to increase their advance purchase of land for public use by Y1.5 trillion; and
   - Study land taxes based on current economic conditions and policies in present land law and seek a conclusion by the time it decides tax changes for the fiscal year beginning April 1996.
2. To promote the stock market, the government would:
   - Submit necessary bills to parliament during an extraordinary session starting in October for a temporary freeze on taxes levied on shareholders when companies buy back their own shares;
   - Abolish the interest rate limit on cash collateral for bond borrowing in transactions involving banks and securities houses;
   - Allow the Tokyo Stock Exchange to set up a futures market in medium-term government bonds by the end of March 1996;
   - Allow investors to trade shares in smaller lots from October; and
   - Allow the issue of commercial paper with maturities of less than two weeks as of October 1995. At the time, the maturity of commercial paper companies were allowed to issue was from two weeks to nine months.
3. To help small and medium-sized companies, a total of Y1.29 trillion in loans would be extended to help them cut their financial burdens, start new businesses and develop new technology.
4. Japan would set up a system within the Japan Development Bank to provide low-interest loans for the promotion of foreign direct investment in Japan.
5. The government would make efforts to complete an outline of measures to help resolve bad-debt problems at Japanese financial institutions by the end of September and finalise concrete measures by the end of the year.
6. The government would act to deregulate the economy by:
   - Implementing deregulation measures it had already announced as early as possible;
   - Reviewing price-setting methods for public rates such as electricity, gas, passenger transport and telecommunications; and
   - Considering cuts in international phone and mobile phone rates.

Launching this package, a senior Ministry of Finance official said: 'We've put aside a tight budgetary situation and done our best to include as many projects as needed to prop up the economy.' The ministry explained that the package would require state general budget spending of Y4.71 trillion and that Japan would issue national and local government bonds of some Y8 trillion to fund it. These would include construction bonds and deficit-financing bonds of some Y200 billion.

Masayoshi Takemura, who was finance minister at the time, said the decision to issue deficit-financing bonds reflected 'the government's strong stance to put the economy back on track for recovery' and said the government hoped to improve economic conditions by using all measures possible, including monetary and fiscal policy. He said he hoped the financial markets would give the package 'a positive assessment' and that the spending on land purchase would have a positive impact on the stagnant property market.

Separately, Trade Minister Ryutaro Hashimoto, who later became prime minister, said the package would send an appropriate signal both inside Japan and overseas and that it would be very good for the financial markets, coming at a time when the financial markets were already showing bright signs. At the time of writing it was impossible to tell whether the package and its many predecessors did indeed have the desired effects. It is perhaps worth noting, though, that the yen's persistent strength against the US dollar, regarded by many economists as the principal reason for Japan's economic woes, had already begun to reverse by the time the package was announced. From strong points just over 80 to the dollar and less than 60 to the German mark in April 1995, it had weakened to almost 100 to the dollar and 70 to the mark, as explained in more detail in the currency sector of this chapter.

Some economists were optimistic that a weaker yen would boost manufacturers' profits, revive the stock market and help the banks with their capital problems, all without creating an inflation problem. Many, though, remained pessimistic. The London Business School, for example, said in a report published a month before the package described above that the prospects for Japan were the weakest of any of the industrial economies and that 1995 growth was likely to reach only 1.4 per cent, held back by the strong yen and financial and banking problems. As mentioned earlier, 1995 growth was actually less than one per cent.

The Geneva-based United Nations Conference on Trade and Development (UNCTAD) said in a report released in September just before the package that the recession was likely to continue in Japan, with growth contracting to a mere 0.5 per cent. In stark contrast, UNCTAD noted that Asian countries generally were the most dynamic group in the world economy, with economic growth in the group as a whole likely to accelerate to 6 per cent in 1995 from 5.3 per cent in 1994. 'On the whole, Asian countries benefited from the further rise of the yen [early in 1995], which prompted Japanese industries to move labour-intensive manufacturing to other Asian countries,' the report said. China's economy, which had become an important locomotive in the region, would expand at a rate of 9.6 per cent in 1995 after three years of roughly 12 per cent annual growth, UNCTAD added.

THE CURRENCY

The extraordinary strength of the Japanese yen in the past few years may not be the only reason for Japan's economic woes, but it is certainly a key factor. Moreover, the soaring yen may have encouraged overseas investors to buy yen-denominated assets such as JGBs and Euroyen bonds. So the key question now is whether any sustained weakness in the yen would boost the Japanese economy and/or deter foreign investors from Japan's financial markets.

Hard though it may be now to believe, a US dollar bought almost 160 yen (see Chart 5.1) and a German mark bought almost 95 yen when the bubble economy was bursting in 1990. By April 1995, the dollar was buying only half as many yen and the mark was buying less than two-thirds as many. Against this background, the yen's weakness in late 1995 looks like 'nothing to write home about' even though the dollar had recovered some 23 per cent from its low by the autumn.

None the less, some economists were predicting continued yen weakness well into 1996, the trend helped by substantial Bank of Japan intervention in the foreign exchanges, measures to stimulate capital outflows, low Japanese interest rates, modest but well-timed Federal Reserve intervention in the currency markets and persistent attempts by officials in both countries to talk the yen down and the dollar up despite the risk that a weaker yen might boost the contentious Japanese trade surplus with the US still further.

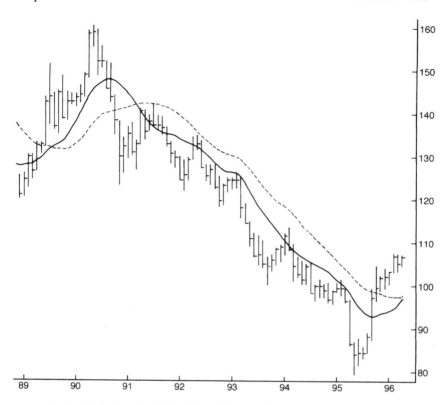

Chart 5.1 Dollar/Yen Monthly Bar Chart. Source: Reuters

Among the measures introduced by the Japanese to try and tame the yen was a set of steps unveiled in August to promote overseas investment and loans by Japanese institutions. The Ministry of Finance announced that Japan would, for example, scrap the limit on insurance companies' participation in yen-denominated syndicated loans and remove a 90-day 'lock-up' period during which Japanese investors had been barred from buying Euroyen bonds issued by non-residents.

'We believe these measures are very likely to become a good opportunity for investors to give more attention to investment overseas,' Finance Minister at the time Masayoshi Takemura told a news conference. Further measures were promised for the future, all part of a concerted attempt to weaken the yen by increasing capital outflows from Japan into foreign currency denominated assets. The response to the measures was cool among Japanese institutions but they were well received abroad, and the initiative was therefore more successful than many Japanese had expected, at least in reducing the value of the yen.

THE POLITICS

As in Italy, a turbulent, unstable, political scene seems such a permanent feature of life in Japan now that international investors have come to accept it and disregard it—an extraordinary state of affairs given that after two of the country's largest political parties merged in 1955 to form the Liberal Democratic Party (LDP) there followed a 38-year non-stop period of one-party rule. That party certainly brought prosperity to Japan but by the 1980s it had become extraordinarily corrupt, with public-sector contracts and business licences awarded in return for bribes, and an electoral system that allowed rural voters to keep the LDP in power in return for help for farmers.

In 1993, however, the LDP disintegrated and the government was finally thrown out and replaced: first, in August, by a coalition of reformers headed by Morihiro Hosakawa which forced through changes in electoral law; and then by a minority reformist government led by Tsutomu Hata. That in turn was replaced in August 1994 by a fragile new coalition led by the Social Democratic Party's Tomiichi Murayama. These coalitions included LDP members and seemed to have little coherent ideology but none the less made great strides towards cleaning up the dirty political mess left by their predecessors. In November 1994 no fewer than three reform bills became law, but by then the LDP was pulling itself together while its opponents were forming into a vast, complicated array of small new parties and splinter groups. The public became disillusioned and apathetic.

As 1995 began it seemed possible that Murayama would be forced out. However, Japan-watchers continued to advise overseas investors that a large political risk premium was not called for, if only because the country was still controlled by the people who had largely controlled it before—the powerful permanent bureaucrats. Against the odds perhaps, Murayama managed to stay in control even after Upper House elections in July resulted in a severe setback for his socialist party, which won only 16 of the 126 seats at stake and lost almost two-thirds of the seats it was defending. The Upper House, or House of Councillors, is much less powerful in Japan than the Lower House and the turnout among voters at the election was a record low 44 per cent.

Despite the setback, Murayama's coalition of socialists, liberal democrats, the small Sakigake Party led by Finance Minister Masayoshi Takemura and some independents held together, and Murayama immediately ruled out the idea of a snap general election as his supporters noted that Lower House elections did not have to be held until mid 1997. The big winner in the Upper House voting, incidentally, was the main opposition grouping called Shinshinto (the New Frontier Party). Formed in late 1994 and led by Toshiki Kaifu, it was facing its first electoral test, won 40 seats and emerged as the second-largest party behind the LDP. Shinshinto, a reformist grouping, said it favoured deregulation to slash red tape.

Prime Minister Murayama seemed intent as 1995 drew to a close to stay in power by pulling the economy out of recession. However, his cause was not helped in late September when *Euromoney* magazine voted his finance minister Takemura the 'Worst Finance Minister of the Year', and in January 1996 Murayama resigned suddenly, to be replaced by the LDP's Ryutaro Hashimoto. The new prime minister, leading the same coalition of conservatives, socialists and the Sakigake party, named socialist Wataru Kubo as his finance minister and deputy prime minister.

DERIVATIVES MARKETS

Japanese government bond futures are traded electronically on the Tokyo Stock Exchange (TSE) and the future trades to a lesser extent electronically on the London International Financial Futures & Options Exchange (LIFFE). The TSE also lists a 20-year government bond future and a five-year future was launched in February 1996. Euroyen three-month interest-rate futures are traded on the Tokyo International Financial Futures Exchange (TIFFE), which also lists a one-year Euroyen future. LIFFE plans to start trading a fungible three-month Euroyen future from April 1996.

The TSE's JGB future is based on a notional 10-year bond with a face value of Y100 and a coupon of six per cent. It trades from 09:00 to 11:00 and then from 12:30 to 15:30. Movements are in basis points (0.01) and there is a limit on price fluctuations of two yen either side of the previous day's close. Settlement must be made four working days after the contract date, while the delivery date is the 20th day of March, June, September or December. The final trading day is nine working days before the delivery date. Issues eligible for delivery are listed JGBs of seven to 11 years and commission is levied on new open interest, conversion, buyback and delivery. There is no securities transaction tax, but there is a TSE tax of 1/100 000 of the traded sum. The 'extra-long-term' future is based on a 20-year JGB and the details are essentially as above, though in this case the limit on price fluctuations is three yen either side of the previous day's close. Issues eligible for delivery are listed JGBs of 15 to 21 years.

TIFFE's three-month Euroyen future trades in lots of Y100 million. The contract represents 100 minus an interest rate in per cent on a 90/360-day basis. Movements are in basis points, with one tick equal to Y2500. There are no price fluctuation limits and there are March, June, September and December futures. Trading of a new contract starts during the first evening trading session after daytime trading on the existing contract's final day is over. The final trading date is two working days before the third Wednesday of the current contract month. If the third Wednesday is a bank holiday in New York, then the final trading day is only one working day before (where the working day must be a working day for both TIFFE and Japanese banks). Settlement must be by the next working day after the final trading day. Daytime trading takes place from 09:00 to 15:30 (or from 09:00 to 11:00 on the final trading day) though there is no matching from 12:00 to 13:30). Evening trading is from 16:00 to 18:00 on normal days only, with evening trades executed/carried forward to the next working day. TIFFE's one-year Euroyen futures are similar except that a tick equals Y10 000.

USEFUL ADDRESSES

Bank of Japan
CPO Box 203
Tokyo 100-91

Japan Institute for Securities
   Information & Public Relations
5–8 Nihombashi Kayabacho 1
Chuo-ku
Tokyo 103

Ministry of Finance
Kasumigaseki 3-1-1
Chiyoda-ku
Tokyo 100

6
United Kingdom

The UK has enjoyed the longest period of political stability of any country covered in this book, enabling the claim that it has never defaulted on its government bonds since the National Debt was created three centuries ago. This is formally true, a fact reflected in AAA credit ratings. However, after World War II the country relied largely on inflation to reduce the National Debt, from more than 200 per cent of GDP to around 40 per cent by the 1980s. This process has claimed its cost. Professional investors add a hefty inflation risk premium to bond yields, especially during bear markets. Few small investors in the UK buy government bonds: from 1945 up to the late 1980s, they were much better off buying shares and houses. UK government bonds may still be known as gilts on the grounds that they are gilt-edged securities, but there have been times when their yields have tracked those of double-to-single-A rated Italy more closely than those of AAA Germany.

The gilt market still enjoys the luxury of being located in the world's dominant financial centre. Old imperial connections also ensure a foothold for gilts in Asia, with easy access to Japanese money. Even so, the market does not win top marks for liquidity: its old age shows up in some creakingly quaint customs which irritate London's expatriate financial community. A decade after its first major post-war overhaul of the City of London, the Bank of England is undertaking further reforms of the gilt market, introducing an open gilt repo market and officially endorsed gilt stripping. Analysts say reforms of the Bank's idiosyncratic money-market operations are bound to follow.

However, the market would also like to see some reform of the Bank of England itself. The European Union's aspirations to monetary unity have generated intense debate about how much difference central bank independence makes to a country's inflation rate. Unfavourable comparisons between Germany and the UK have highlighted the extent to which the Bank of England, once a pioneer of techniques for controlling the money supply, has had to provide easy money for UK governments since it was nationalised after World War II. The politician currently in charge of the UK Treasury, Chancellor of the Exchequer Kenneth Clarke, has tried to reform the relationship. The governor now has a little discretion in the timing of the interest rate moves which Clarke decides. The Bank publishes a quarterly inflation report independent of any vetting by the Treasury; and the minutes of the monthly meeting between Clarke and Bank Governor Eddie George are published, albeit after a six-week lag. However, many analysts believe this is the worst of both worlds for the gilt market, since the new procedures merely publicise policy disputes without giving the Bank the clout to resolve matters in favour of monetary prudence.

What chance, then, of the politicians keeping inflation in check? In early 1996, after 17 years of power, political necessity was pushing Clarke's Conservative Party towards monetary and fiscal easing. But even with lower taxes and lower interest rates, it seemed likely to lose the election that it would have to call by May 1997, if not earlier. Opinion polls showed an overwhelming lead for the opposition Labour Party, which the gilt market had traditionally associated with profligate spending, punitive taxation and rampant inflation. This is not entirely fair: each party has inherited economic problems from the other and it was a Conservative government whose dash for growth in the early 1970s, coupled with the oil price shock, bequeathed the UK's record 24 per cent inflation rate to their Labour successors in 1975. But in any case, over the past decade the Labour Party has swung from the hard left to the soft centre of the political spectrum. A growing number of economists was prepared to give the benefit of the doubt to Labour's pledge to hold down inflation and the budget deficit.

Labour was also viewed as more likely to seek to lock the UK into low inflation by rejoining Europe's drive for Economic and Monetary Union (EMU). Labour would be able to distance itself from the acrimony which surrounded sterling's departure from

EMU's precursor, the European Exchange Rate Mechanism (ERM), in 1992. But UK voters share one prejudice with their German counterparts: they are equally reluctant to surrender their national currency. A split over European unity has all but paralysed the Conservative Party. The same division cuts across the Labour Party.

POLITICS

The 651-seat House of Commons, the lower house of parliament, is elected for a maximum five-year term. Members of the upper house, the House of Lords, either inherit their seats or are nominated to them, for life, by the government. The House of Lords can delay, but not prevent, any legislation from being enacted if the Commons approves it.

The British political system, which has famously evolved without the aid of a formal written constitution, has been widely blamed for the UK economy's tendency to lurch from boom to bust. The effect of the simple first-past-the-post electoral system has been to produce some decisive majorities and since World War II, power has alternated between Labour on the left and the Conservatives on the right. Apart from a brief period during the 1970s, the centrist party, now known after several identity changes as the Liberal Democrats, has had little opportunity to exploit the balance of power.

However, it took a lot more than just confrontational politics to stop and start the economy so abruptly and so often. For a start, Britain had to learn to live without the benefits of its empire, which it shed after the war; it was slow to appreciate the economic advantages offered by the European Union, which it joined in 1973. And it had to cope with an awkward imperial legacy, sterling's continued use as a reserve currency. The divergence between sterling's status and the post-war limitations of the UK economy ensured crisis and devaluation under the Bretton Woods system of fixed exchange rates.

The policy swings from left to right with each change of government were often more rhetorical than real. Until the mid-1970s, both parties used government spending to try to create jobs; both set ceilings on the nominal growth of wages, prices and bank loans to try to curb inflation. It was not Conservative Prime Minister Margaret Thatcher, but her Labour predecessor James Callaghan who announced in 1976,

> We used to think that you could . . . increase employment by cutting taxes and boosting government spending. I tell you, in all candour, that that option no longer exists, and that in so far as it ever did exist, it only worked by injecting bigger doses of inflation into the economy followed by higher levels of unemployment as the next step.

Thatcher's rule did not end boom–bust cycles: she presided over a 5 per cent surge in real GDP in 1988, followed by interest rate rises that helped to shrink the economy by 2 per cent in 1991, just after she had been ousted from the Conservative leadership. Her successor was John Major, who as Chancellor of the Exchequer had taken sterling into the ERM. He won election in his own right in 1992. However, his majority was slim, and it got slimmer as a combination of rebellion and mortality among Conservative back-benchers took its toll. His party lost some of its safest seats in by-elections. A Reuters survey conducted with the help of actuaries in late 1995 suggested a high probability that deaths in Conservative ranks might bring forward the general election that Major, facing almost certain defeat, could otherwise defer to May 1997.

Major's unpopularity dated back to the foreign-exchange market's assumption that the UK would not endure the high real interest rates which inflationary pressure in post-unification Germany was imposing on other ERM member countries. The market proved itself right. Major's government announced sterling's suspension from the ERM on the evening of 16 September 1992, a day when the market had sold the UK authorities several billion sterling at considerable profit. The government blamed the Bundesbank and spent the next three years struggling to discipline or placate the Eurosceptic wing of the Conservative Party which opposes any further UK integration with the European Union.

The leadership of the revamped Labour Party stops short of promising to rejoin the ERM, but it is far more enthusiastic about European Union than the current Conservative leadership dares to be. The Eurosceptics' high profile obscures the fact that the UK scores quite highly on most of the other economic criteria for membership of monetary union. Renewed efforts to meet all the

criteria—including making the Bank of England independent—
could only help the gilt market. But would the required austerity
keep voters happy? The opinion polls suggested that what they
really liked about Labour was its pledges to protect the UK's free-
to-all National Health Service and to halve a detested sales tax on
domestic heating fuel.

As Clarke admitted, UK voters were missing what he dubbed
the 'feel-good factor'. The gloom had a lot to do with job insecur-
ity, manifested throughout the European Union in double-digit
unemployment rates and exacerbated in the UK by labour-market
and welfare reforms undertaken in the 1980s. But some commentators believed the elusive feel-good factor was a close relative of
inflation. For more than four decades, British voters had invested
in houses, not gilts. They paid off their home loans through inflation. When a property price bubble burst in the late 1980s, the
unthinkable happened: house prices fell and went on falling,
through years when Clarke tried in vain to persuade the UK that it
was enjoying a textbook, export-led economic recovery. There was
some nostalgia for inflation among those voters who owed more in
home loans than their properties were now worth.

THE BANK OF ENGLAND

If there is a typical central bank, it is not the Bank of England. In
terms of its ability to chart the course of monetary policy, it lies at
the opposite end of the autonomy scale from the Bundesbank. Its
power has been wielded instead over the square mile that traditionally compromises the City of London. The Bank's reputed
preference for regulating by private influence, rather than by public reprimand and written rules, has served London well as a
financial centre. As sterling devalued, the City colonised the
Eurodollar instead, cornering the wholesale market not just in
foreign exchange but in the Eurodeposits and Eurobonds where
expatriate money is housed.

This market, at the forefront of innovation, co-existed
alongside a much more tradition-bound gilt market. Reforms to
both the domestic gilt and equities markets in 1986 generated a
cultural earthquake in the City. The Bank of England undertook
the gilt reforms largely as a defensive measure, in order to retain a

segregated market under its supervision for both debt management and monetary policy purposes. The changes included allowing foreign-based companies to join a new group of gilt-edged market makers (GEMMs). These primary dealers brought £600 million of capital to the gilt market and lost £200 million of it within two years as the competition drove 11 of the original 27 GEMMs to surrender their status. In early 1996 their number had recovered to 20, but most of the British-owned survivors of the initial turmoil had merged with or been taken over by foreign securities trading organisations.

Other central banks wrestle with official mandates to simultaneously curb inflation and ensure full employment: the Bank of England's brief is more closely bound up with that of the City of London. The Bank defines its objectives as maintaining the value of money; ensuring the soundness of the financial system; and promoting that system's efficiency and competitiveness 'so that the City of London can serve industry and commerce at home and maintain its place as the world's leading international financial centre'.[4]

The British sovereign is nominally responsible for appointing the Bank's governor, deputy governor and the other 16 members of its board, which is called the Court of Directors. In practice the prime minister and the Chancellor of the Exchequer choose at least the governor and the deputy-governor, who serve renewable five-year terms and cannot be sacked.[5] The directors serve renewable four-year terms; four of these posts expire each year to maintain a turnover. The Court meets weekly but the major issues, exchange rate and monetary policy, are decided elsewhere. The current governor, Eddie George, took office in July 1993 and is the first incumbent who graduated in economics. He is also unusual in having worked at the Bank for three decades before his final promotion: the job has more commonly gone to outsiders, recruited from the UK's long-established merchant banks.

The Bank carries heavier responsibilities for supervising the financial system than any other central bank. In July 1994, the Bank reorganised itself into two wings, one for analysing and implementing monetary policy, the other for all regulatory and supervisory work. The monetary stability wing is responsible for the quarterly inflation report and for the Bank's own market operations. However, the financial stability wing supervises market participants, including GEMMs and discount houses, and develops and oversees settlement systems. There are two executive directors in charge of each wing. The Bank's duties include intervening to defend sterling, but it is the Treasury, not the Bank, that owns the UK's foreign-exchange reserves.

CONTROL OF MONETARY POLICY

The Bank of England has some influence but no real control over the setting of interest rates in the UK. The decisions are taken by the finance minister, the Chancellor of the Exchequer. When the Bank of England was nationalised in 1946, parliament gave the Treasury the power to issue directions to the Bank. Although no such formal directive has ever been issued, 'the relationship is clearly understood to be one in which the Treasury takes the final decisions,' the Bank says.[4] Monetary policy is decided at monthly meetings between the Chancellor, backed up by a Treasury team, and the governor, backed up by a team including the Bank's deputy governor and chief economist.[5]

Since 1993 the Bank has had the right to choose the precise timing of an interest-rate move: current governor Eddie George told parliament at the time that the maximum leeway would be one month, but in practice he would probably implement the Chancellor's decision sooner. George pledged to use the Bank's quarterly inflation report to declare any difference of opinion on interest-rate policy. He went on to do so, pressing for a rate rise during much of 1995 before deciding the Chancellor had been justified in holding off. However, the UK government's own independent economic advisers are unhappy about the public disagreements which have already been aired in the inflation report and in the published minutes of the meetings between Clarke and George. George himself has indicated that he would like operational independence to pursue an inflation objective set by the government.

MONETARY POLICY TARGETS

When sterling left the ERM in 1992, the government set an explicit inflation target for the first time. The target range is 1–4 per cent, narrowing to less than 2.5 per cent by 1997 and beyond. The measure used is called the RPI-X, retail prices excluding interest payments on home loans. Home loan costs in the UK would otherwise complicate monetary policy calculations as much as they complicate monetary policy decisions: most UK home owners borrow at a variable rate which moves in tandem with short-term official rates.

From the end of World War II up to 1971, the UK authorities sought to control inflation largely by restricting the amount of credit on offer, including home loans. When the curbs were lifted, banks scrambled to expand their balance sheets and within two years the authorities felt obliged to impose a new constraint, dubbed 'the Corset', in 1973 to limit the growth of interest-bearing deposits. None of this did much to constrain inflation: it peaked at 24 per cent in 1975 and hit nearly 22 per cent during 1980, when the Corset was abolished in favour of monetarism. Thatcher's Conservative Party, which had won power in 1979, introduced a Medium-term Financial Strategy, to be updated annually at budget time, and set the first of several money supply targets. But these, too, proved a disappointment. The authorities decided monetary measurements were being distorted by their liberalisation of the financial system which included the lifting of exchange controls in 1979.

Next the authorities tried exchange-rate targets, at first informal, then, from October 1990, formalised through ERM membership. 'For the first 18 months, sterling's membership of the ERM was helpful in enabling base rates to be reduced from 15 percent to 10 percent as activity slowed and inflation fell [from 11 per cent to four per cent],' the Bank said.[3] Sterling was allowed a wide trading range of 6 per cent either side of its agreed central rate against each of the other currencies but crashed through its effective floor, at about 2.77 marks, on 16 September 1992.

The Bank says the UK authorities now use 'all available indicators' to try to chart the future course of inflation. The authorities still study measures of money supply growth, but the Bank says the 'monitoring ranges' which are now set for M0 and M4 are different from the 'targets' which were set when monetarism first became official UK policy in 1980. M0 is defined as notes and coins in circulation plus the settlement balances which banks hold with the Bank of England; M4 is cash plus private-sector deposits.

The Bank also constructs a Divisia index of money, a technique which aims to weigh the ease with which the various types of deposit included can be turned into cash.

IMPLEMENTING MONETARY POLICY

In order to implement monetary policy, central banks need to be able to keep a core group of commercial banks short of liquidity and so force them to borrow on central bank terms. One major clash between the UK authorities and the Bundesbank is over how directly this should be done. The Bundesbank has so far insisted that banks in Germany should hand over a proportion of their deposits as non-interest-bearing reserves. It views this minimum reserve requirement as essential to ensure it keeps a reasonably predictable degree of control over money market liquidity. The UK authorities reject this requirement; it offends the free-market purism proclaimed by the ruling Conservative Party. In this case there is probably little conflict between the Treasury and the Bank, which has traditionally preferred subtle pressure to direct intervention. Clearing banks keep balances at the Bank of England purely for daily settlement purposes. Explaining why it does not require minimum reserves, the Bank says that the technique amounts to a tax on the banking system and that it has enough leverage on the money market already through its sales of short-term paper: it says this attracts enough buyers to ensure that there is usually a daily liquidity shortage.

For some years the Bank also resisted the Bundesbank's technique of offering repurchase agreements involving long-term securities to the open market. The Bank of England preferred to restrict its own money-market dealings to a peculiarly British group of intermediaries, the **discount houses**, who sell short-dated bills to the Bank, either outright or under repurchase agreements, and channel the money to the wider market to relieve liquidity shortages. However, money-market dealers say larger commercial banks have found a profitable way to retaliate against the Bank's arms-length treatment of them. The bigger banks can brandish their capital clout by refusing to sell bills to the discount houses or by flooding the market with the paper. The result can be a sharp swing in overnight rates which the larger banks can exploit and which the Bank cannot readily control.

It was sterling's ejection from the ERM in 1992 that finally forced the Bank to add regular European-style **repos** to supplement its money-market operations—insisting all the while that these had no monetary policy significance. By buying up billions of sterling to try to stop the currency's plunge, the Bank had created a severe liquidity shortage. To get enough funds back into the market, it started repurchase agreements using longer-dated securities and open to all banks operating in the UK, for the first time relegating the discount houses to the same status as other market participants. This fortnightly facility was officially made permanent in January 1994. Since then the Bank has also overcome its reluctance to let participants in the wider gilt market strike repo deals among themselves. It has to sell a lot of gilts, and the lack of an open repo market was deterring some major foreign buyers.

Market analysts say the latest reforms will inevitably phase out the privileged role of the discount houses as conduits of central bank funds to the money market. As overall gilt repo turnover increases, they say, there will be a long overdue move to use an official repo rate to fine tune monetary policy. True, all markets complain now and then that their central bank is sending obscure or misleading signals. But UK economists say the Bank of England's current money-market methods have become so ossified that it has difficulty sending any clear or subtle messages to the wider market.

In 1995, the discount houses were still playing their traditional role, selling eligible paper to relieve daily liquidity shortages through the Bank's not-so-open **money-market operations**. These operations are meant both to fine tune monetary policy and to manipulate changes in the UK's main interest rate, the **base rate**, which is the benchmark that commercial banks set for calculating their lending and deposit rates. The impact of the Bank's operations on the base rate is indirect.

If the market is fairly orderly and the Bank has been able to choose its timing, it will probably signal any rate change—or underline its resistance to change—at around **09:45 to 10:00 London time**. This is when the Bank routinely announces its initial estimate of the daily liquidity shortage and may say it is inviting an early round of bill offers; if it does not, and there is a large shortage, the market may suspect that the Bank is withholding funds to punish attempts to push rates down too far or too fast. Normally, if there is a shortage of £1 billion or more, after a five or 10 minute wait the market gets a second part of the announcement. This says whether the Bank has bought bills from the discount houses, either outright or under a repurchase agreement, and gives the rates involved.

These operations normally involve **bank bills**, which are trade bills that have been guaranteed by one of a specified group of banks. Bank bills are grouped in four bands according to their remaining maturity. The Bank's **dealing rates**, expressed in 32nds of a percentage point, are closely related to, but not identical with, the base rate. In recent years the rate for outright buying of bills in the shortest-dated bands one and two has tended to be about a 1/8 point below the base rate, while the bill repo rate tends to be about a 3/32 point below the base rate. Until recently, when the Bank wanted to change monetary policy, it dropped a hint to the discount houses so they could change their bid rates. Its public announcement would not state explicitly that rates had moved: the wider market had to know what the previous day's rates were in order to work out whether the latest rates quoted were higher or lower. At the time of writing, the Bank was favouring more explicit announcements of rate changes. But it is always left up to the commercial banks to respond by changing their base rates by the same margin. If the market has been pressing for a rate change when the Bank is not prepared to budge, it can simply quote the same rates as the previous day's. The message is slightly stronger if the Bank announces a big shortage but offers little or no new liquidity.

The Bank routinely makes further **announcements at noon and at 14:00**, to say whether it has revised its forecast of the day's shortage and to detail any further activity. It can use these rounds of intervention to change rates. However, if the Bank has already dealt at the old rates in the early round, the market would not normally expect any rate changes in later rounds. In recent years liquidity surpluses have been rare; if there is one, the Bank will probably wait until 14:00 to sell T-bills to drain the extra cash.

The Bank may make one last public appearance at 14:45, to say whether it has provided **late assistance**. This is open to a slightly wider circle, including GEMMs, up to set limits. So far the late assistance round has never been used to change rates; often it is a fairly routine operation. However, it is used relatively frequently to punish the market for withholding bills from sale in anticipation of a rate cut. The interest rate for late assistance is not published, but the recipients will know whether or not it is penal and will pass the message on through the overnight rate.

These conventions have applied to many UK rate changes in recent years, but the Bank has other methods involving its **money-market lending rates**. The most explicit technique is to announce a minimum lending rate (MLR), which the Bank applies for a set period to all its lending to discount houses. Another method is to announce that the discount houses are invited to borrow at a set rate: this is now used mainly to combat market pressure for a rate change, in which case the rate cited will be the existing base rate.

The Bank's other major money-market operation is the auction every Friday of **Treasury bills**, discount securities whose sale is meant primarily to ensure a liquidity shortage rather than to finance the government. The three-month T-bill yield is currently not intended to convey any signals, a policy which took the market by surprise in July 1994. When the Bank accepted a three-month T-bill yield a 3/4 point higher than the previous week's, the bears assumed that was as near to an official rate rise as made no odds. They went on the rampage, driving down gilts and short sterling interest-rate futures. They were not greatly placated when the Bank announced that it had merely accepted a T-bill rate dictated by the market, with no wider implications. The débâcle has, if anything, increased the wariness with which the market watches the tender. Bids are due in by 12:30 London time each Friday and results are announced at 13:15, along with the size of the next week's tender. Settlement is any day the following week, at the buyer's discretion.

FUNDING, THE PSBR AND THE CGBR

Over the past two decades, the UK authorities and academic economists have agonised over what role, if any, gilt sales should play in monetary policy. During the early 1980s the Bank over funded, selling more gilts than were needed to fund the public-sector borrowing requirement (PSBR); the aim was to soak up some extra liquidity. The policy was switched to full funding, which was intended to have a neutral monetary impact, in 1985,

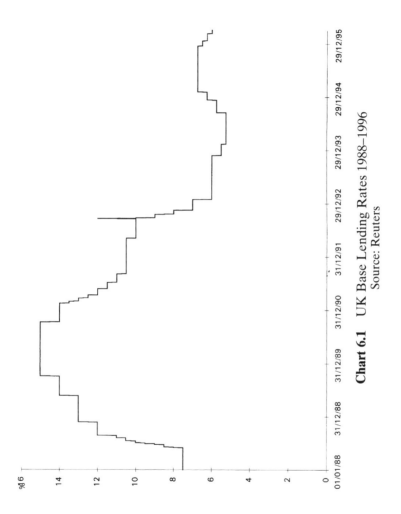

Chart 6.1 UK Base Lending Rates 1988–1996
Source: Reuters

on the grounds that gilt sales might otherwise 'crowd out' the corporate bond market. The new aim was to sell enough gilts, with at least three years to maturity, and enough National Savings products, aimed at small investors, to cover the PSBR, plus maturing debt, plus any net increase in the country's foreign-currency reserves. But the government continued to exclude gilt sales to banks and building societies (home loan institutions) from their funding calculations because such holdings were considered to fuel money supply growth by enabling banks to lend more to the private sector. This restriction was dropped in 1993. However, a monetarist taboo was maintained on counting instruments with less than three years to maturity, notably Treasury bills, towards funding the PSBR.

This will change in 1996. First, the government is relegating the PSBR calculation to the sidelines. The central financing measurement will become the CGBR, the central government borrowing requirement. Second, paper of any maturity will count towards funding the CGBR. The authorities say the changes merely reflect more accurately what already happens. The PSBR includes the debt of local authorities and public corporations, who have recently been making net repayments to the private sector. This means the CGBR is now bigger than the PSBR. The authorities have been making up the difference by issuing more short-term debt. They say the new framework 'will continue to provide the necessary discipline to ensure a prudent maturity structure for debt issuance . . . The government has no current plans to make significantly greater use than at present of short-term debt issuance.'

THE GILT MARKET

Like US Treasuries, gilts pay a semi-annual coupon and their cash and futures prices are calculated in 1/32 of a percentage point, rather than in 0.01 point as in most other markets. The gilt market also retains a few quirks in its terminology, such as calling bonds 'stocks', as opposed to 'shares' (equities). More importantly, foreign investors should note that what the gilt market calls 'long-dated' would be termed 'ultra-long' in most other markets. In the cash gilts market, **shorts** have less than seven years[1] to maturity,

longs have more than 15 years to go and those in between are called **mediums.** Up to now, gilts have not been issued with less than three years to maturity.

In the futures market, the LIFFE exchange compromises by allowing mediums with residual maturities of between 10 and 15 years to be delivered against its long gilt contract. Long gilt futures are therefore slightly out of line with Europe's other major bond futures contracts: bonds with seven to 10 years to maturity are deliverable against the MATIF exchange's French notionnel contract, while LIFFE's German Bund and Italian BTP contracts apply to bonds due in 8.5 to 10 years.

Supply and demand imbalances have also given gilts an idiosyncratic yield curve. Even when other markets' yield curves obey the textbook, rising consistently from left to right, the gilt curve tends to droop into the 20-year area. This is because short-dated gilts tend to match the liabilities of banks and building societies; longs match those of pension funds and insurance companies; but there is less domestic interest in mediums. The globalisation of bond markets has helped because 10 years is the international benchmark maturity popular with foreign investors. Even so, the gilt curve still tends to turn into a hump further out as fundamental demand meets relatively scarce supply. The Bank of England says that the difference between 10- and 20-year gilt yields averaged minus 25 basis points in the 15 years to 1995. This spread rose significantly into positive territory only when the 1993 bull market generated global demand for 10-year bonds.

The Bank suggests the hump becomes more pronounced in bear markets because money is also quicker to leave the benchmark 10-year area. Its main explanation for the hump is that it reflects the maturity of the UK's long-term savings industry. A related factor is that longer-dated bonds tend to have greater convexity than short-dated bonds which means that, compared with other bonds, their prices rise proportionately more in a rally than they fall in a selloff. This can offset the disadvantages associated with these bonds' long duration which means their prices fall as well as rise more sharply than those of short-dated bonds for any given change in yield. Since duration is primarily a measure of the timing of a bond's cash flows, pension fund managers usually need a fairly high proportion of long duration bonds to match their liabilities. Coupon payments reduce a bond's convexity and duration; stripping greatly enhances both properties. So the 'hump' might be smoothed out by the advent of stripped gilts, which should give pension fund managers a new choice of long-duration, high-convexity bonds to match their liabilities.

The Bank of England acts as agent and adviser to the Treasury in issuing gilts, but the Treasury is responsible for strategic decisions and for approving all debt issues. This used to involve the Bank in consulting Treasury ministers and officials on the fine details of funding, but since 1994 the Treasury has streamlined procedures by giving the Bank an annual remit.

REFORM—ROUND ONE

The Bank of England, anxious to maintain the invisible income generated by London as a financial centre and to prevent gilt trading from wandering offshore, has undertaken some major market reforms. The first round was in 1986 and coincided with the Big Bang reform of London's stock exchange. Until 1986, gilts were bought and sold wholesale on the floor of the London Stock Exchange by jobbers: brokers acted as intermediaries between the jobbers and investors, who paid them commission. The Bank scrapped the system on the grounds that it was illiquid—jobbers and brokers were undercapitalised with barely £100 million behind them—and that the commission structure penalised institutional customers.

Instead the Bank of England appointed primary dealers, who employ both market makers, to replace the jobbers, and salespeople, to advise investors. These dealers are called GEMMs, gilt-edged market makers. The GEMMs trade with each other anonymously using a screen-based service provided by inter-dealer brokers (IDB). A separate group of agency brokers mediate between investors and the GEMMs, although large investors also have direct access to the primary dealers. The GEMMs' perks, some of them lost in the second round of reform, included direct access to the Bank of England; the facility to switch gilts with the Bank; the facility to borrow gilts from Stock Exchange money brokers; access, along with the discount houses, to the Bank's daily late lending facility; and sole access to the IDB network. GEMMs must be separately capitalised from the rest of financial institutions which own them. The Bank also set up the Central Gilts Office, an early move to electronic book-entry handling of government bonds.

REFORM—ROUND TWO

Reform ran aground when the proceeds of privatisation combined with an economic boom to bring the UK government windfalls of revenue. The authorities stopped issuing gilts and started buying some back, at reverse auctions; the market dried up. The prompt return to budget deficits in the 1990s revealed the reforms had enhanced the gilt market's liquidity—but meanwhile other governments, notably France, had overtaken the UK in scrapping archaic practices and making both primary and secondary bond markets more user-friendly. Even Germany, whose bond market had emigrated to Luxembourg and London during the 1980s, had managed to repatriate a fair share of Bund trading to Frankfurt. In 1993, the Bank eased its grip on gilt settlement, allowing investors to use the international clearing operations Cedel and Euroclear as well as its own Central Gilts Office. The UK authorities also launched a major review of debt management.

This review proposed the moves to use the CGBR to calculate financing needs and the use of short- as well as long-term debt to meet them. In the process, the old argument about what debt management should contribute to monetary policy was shunted off into the sidings. Instead, the review made minimising the long-term cost of funding the prime objective, calculating that the UK would eventually save £25 million per year for every basis point that greater efficiency could shave off average yield levels. It approved efforts to give the markets much longer advance notice of gilt issuance plans; it toyed with a change in auction methods; and it sought to tidy up the Bank's older issuance methods. It also decided the authorities should hold more open and regular consultations with the market, proposing two sets of meetings, one with the GEMMs, the other with representatives of end-investors. These meetings will be annual and quarterly to coincide with issuance decisions.

The major reforms however, are the introduction of gilt-stripping and an open gilt repo market, which in turn necessitate a major overhaul of gilt taxation. GEMMs were not universally enthusiastic about the new repo regime, which undercuts their privileged ability to go short of gilts through their stock-lending facility. The reforms are certainly likely to generate a new shake-up in the City as the scrapping of curbs on stock-lending reduces or ends the need for some specialist services. However, analysts at some GEMMs reckoned the open repo could swiftly quadruple gilt turnover, providing plenty of new business for everyone. Daily turnover in cash gilts averaged £5.7 billion in 1994/95, while the weekly volume of stock lending averaged £13.2 billion.

DEBT ISSUANCE: STATISTICS AND METHODS

The nominal value of outstanding UK government debt totalled £297 billion at end-March 1995: £221 billion in gilts; £8 billion in Treasury bills; £16 billion in foreign-currency debt; and £52 billion in National Savings products. The market value of the gilts in market hands was slightly greater: £223.1 billion, against £218.5 billion in March 1994 and £168.1 billion in 1993 (see Table 6.1). Stock in market hands at end-March 1995 comprised: conventional shorts, 37 per cent; conventional mediums, 30 per cent; conventional longs, 15.3 per cent; index-linked, 14.9 per cent;

Table 6.1 Gilt Holdings, at Market Valuations (%)

	March 1993	March 1994	December 1995
Total UK	80.3	81.0	82.0
Public Sector	0.3	0.3	1.2
Banks	6.0	6.8	8.0
Building Societies	2.8	2.6	2.3
Insurance Sector	37.7	31.3	30.0
Pension Funds	18.2	12.7	12.3
Fund Managers	(no breakdown)	5.7	9.5
Other Financial	1.4	10.4	9.4
Other Companies	2.0	1.8	1.7
Individuals	11.9	9.3	7.7
Overseas	19.7	19.0	18.0
		Billion sterling	
Official Holdings	8.4	8.0	8.2
Total Market Value	168.1	218.5	220.7

Source: Bank of England, *Gilts and the Gilt Market, Review 1994/95*

floating-rate, 2.2 per cent; and undated 0.5 per cent. For 1995–6, the authorities aimed to make about 15 per cent of issuance index-linked, splitting the rest evenly between conventional shorts, mediums and longs. The longest-dated conventional gilt at end-March 1995 was due in 2017, but index-linked bonds went out to 2030.

The Treasury issues a Summer Economic Forecast at mid-year which gives a rough indication of gross borrowing needs for several years ahead, while the budget in November gives the first official estimate of the government's borrowing needs for the next financial year, which runs from April to March. In translating this into gilt issuance, allowance has to be made for National Savings and any other public-sector debt issuance; any change in net official reserves; gilt redemptions; and any over- or underfunding in previous years. Once the financial year starts, any deviation from the forecast borrowing requirement translates fairly directly into a change in gilt issuance.

Forecast June 1995, billion sterling

	1995–6	1996–7	1997–8	1998–9
PSBR[1]	23.6	16.1	5.0	—
Gilts maturing[2]	4.1	11.5	20	18

[1] The CGBR will be used instead in updates from April 1996.
[2] Does not include any estimates for gilts issued after March 1995.

In 1995, the UK authorities promised to try to make gilt issuance more predictable. In late March each year, they intend to publish an outline plan for the new financial year, giving an auction timetable; a forecast of total gilt issuance; and a sketch of how this is likely to break down between shorts, mediums, longs and index-linked gilts. At 15:30 London time on the last business day of each quarter, the Bank will announce the maturity ranges for the next quarter's auctions. Eight days before the auction, again at 15:30, it will give the final stock details, enabling when-issued trading to start. Bids have to be in by 10:00 on auction day and results should be out at 10:45, with settlement the following day.

The Bank has moved gradually since 1987 from tenders to auctions, where gilts are awarded at the individual bid price, with some paper reserved to be awarded at the average price to non-competitive bidders. In recent years, the auction size has been

£2–3 billion of gilts. To judge the auction a success, the market expects the tail, the difference between the average yield bid and the highest accepted yield, to be no more than one or two basis points: the average tail for 1994–5 was 1.46 basis points. The market also looks for a comfortable degree of oversubscription. Although gilts rarely attract the solid double cover which the French Treasury usually manages to drum up for its well-flagged bond auctions, the implication of an auction is that all stock must be sold. Hence the Bank's embarrassment, and the market's sharp selloff, in September 1995 when for the first time bids at auction slipped below full cover, to 99 per cent of the gilts on offer. The market rebounded when the next auction was covered 1.997 times. Cover averaged 1.58 times in 1994–5.

The authorities intend to stick with auctions for most conventional issuance but are considering experimenting with Dutch auctions, which the United States has been trying out since 1992. The disadvantage to the authorities is that every successful bidder is awarded paper at the highest accepted yield at Dutch auctions. But the method does offer an incentive to bid low yields because such bids will get the first shares of the paper on offer. Its main virtue is that it removes the disincentive to bid posed by conventional auctions where some 'successful' bidders have to pay higher prices than others. The theory is that Dutch auctions reduce risk, encourage participation and ultimately drive down the general level of yields bid to the greater benefit of the authorities.

The Bank of England used to issue gilts mainly through tenders or taps. Tenders differ from auctions in that the Bank sets a minimum price, bids are invited at or above that figure, the Bank calculates a strike price based on the bids and gilts are all awarded at that strike price. The Bank could decide to hold back some of the stock; undersubscription was relatively common.

Table 6.2 Official gilt sales

	1992–3	1993–4	1994–5
At auctions, per cent	37.1	64.1	71.0
Through taps, per cent	62.9	35.9	29.0
Total value, billion stg	33.4	50.9	27.6

Source: HM Treasury and Bank of England, *Debt Management Review, 1995*

Taps or tranchettes are gilts which the Bank holds back at tender or auction, or which the government issues directly to the Bank. When the Bank sees demand for these gilts, it makes them available to the GEMMs in amounts of a few hundred thousand sterling. The 1995 reforms embraced taps, including restricting their use. Index-linked gilts will still be sold largely by taps, but in future no more than 10 per cent of conventional gilts should be sold by this method. Tenders will be held if more than one GEMM bids for the tap stock.

TYPES OF GILT

The great majority of gilts are conventional fixed-rate bonds. Their dominant role should be reinforced by the advent of the gilt-strip market, which will require standardised bonds as its raw material and which will then customise them, saving the authorities the trouble of too many niche issues. Conventional gilts used to be scattered across a 30-year yield curve, but during the 1990s the UK has fallen into line with international demand for big benchmark issues at standard maturities. There were still 68 conventional gilt issues outstanding at end-March 1995, but 16 of them were issues of £5 billion or more.

The UK authorities have sometimes had to use considerable ingenuity to fund large budget deficits at times of high inflation. This is less of a problem in war time, and wars were largely responsible for the £3 billion which remains perpetually outstanding in eight undated gilt issues. But during the high-inflation 1970s in particular, the authorities felt obliged to innovate, even trying out a deep discount gilt at a time when the tax authorities had yet to plug the loopholes which such bonds exploited. Now the tax laws are being changed again to allow an official gilt-stripping market. If the Bank chooses, it will be able to issue zero-coupon bonds without facilitating tax evasion.

The Bank also pioneered variable-rate securities, tied to the T-bill rate, during the 1970s. The concept found its true home in the Euromarkets, but it is a convenient standby for governments during bear markets and a new floating-rate gilt was created in 1994. This issue has since been enlarged to meet market demand for a hedging vehicle, especially for repos.

The 1970s also gave birth to convertible gilts, which have more than one potential maturity date. Some convertibles give the government the option of early redemption over a period of several years. More commonly the option benefits the holder, who buys a short-dated gilt and can choose later on whether to convert it into longer-dated paper. The UK tried auctioning this type of gilt in 1994, but both the authorities and the market voiced frustration at the difficulty of reaching a standard valuation for the option embedded in the bond. Another 1970s' innovation which survived was partly paid gilts, where buyers pay only part of the price up front and the rest later, giving them the benefit of leverage. Such issues suit the Bank if it does not need the funds until the following financial year but wants to take advantage of a bull market.

However, the UK's best-developed niche market is in **index-linked bonds**. These were introduced in 1981 for pension funds but are now available to all investors. They are intended to encourage personal savings towards retirement and thus to ease the state's welfare burden. The redemption value and interest payments are updated in line with the Retail Price Index (RPI), albeit lagging the index by about eight months. Although nominal interest rates are low, around 2.5 per cent, the coupon payments will rise over time. However, most of the benefit—assuming, of course, that the UK does not encounter deflation during the life of the bonds—comes in the form of capital gains. This has been especially true for UK taxpayers, who have been taxed on their income but not on their capital gains from gilts. This regime is due to change ready for the new gilt-stripping market, but the authorities have pledged to protect the tax-free status of the inflation-proofing element of index-linked bonds.

These bonds are, naturally, most popular during inflation scares. They underperform when conventional gilts rally. They enable the authorities to pay low interest rates while increasing the capital value of the national debt without issuing new securities. Even so, many economists praise governments which issue index-linked bonds on the grounds that the authorities are renouncing their power to use inflation to erode their debt burdens. Some economists believed index-linked bonds would drive conventional bonds out of the market because once investors saw that inflation proofing was possible, everyone would want it. This has not happened yet. Index-linked bonds accounted for 15 per cent of the face value of market holdings of gilts in March 1995.[2] The sector remains illiquid, with most index-linked bonds held long-term to match the liabilities of a fairly small group of domestic institutions. The authorities are therefore seeking ways to generate more interest. They are keen to define a good hedging instrument, such as retail price index (RPI) futures, which would stimulate the market by attracting speculative interest. Another possibility would be to try index-linking gilts to average earnings.

At any rate, pension law changes in the UK should generate changes in gilt issuance, benefiting the whole market and the index-linked sector in particular. The legislation puts prudential pressure on pension funds to increase their gilt holdings at the expense of equities. It also requires future pension entitlements to rise by the lower of 5 per cent or the rate of increase in the RPI. The authorities are therefore considering issuing Limited Price Indexation (LPI) gilts to match this requirement. This is an area of the market where gilt stripping provides scope for innovation— although it also raises the risk of further fragmenting the liquidity of the index-linked sector.

TAX REFORM, GILT STRIPS AND THE REPO MARKET

The introduction of the open gilt repo market in January 1996, and of the gilt-strips market, due to start in early 1997, required an overhaul of gilt taxation which is set to take place in April 1996. This will, in general, end the practice of charging UK taxpayers income tax on gilt interest while exempting capital gains and losses from tax and tax relief. The new principle is that all returns on gilts will be taxed as income. Small retail investors will be exempt from the changes. The announcement of the reforms swiftly smoothed out tax-based anomalies on the yield curve such as the spreads of regular gilts over those designated FOTRA (free of tax to residents abroad). This is because most gilt holders should be able to receive interest gross from January 1996 in order to simplify repo transactions.

The repo allows all gilt-market participants to go short of paper if they want to, a privilege formerly restricted largely to GEMMs;

it also gives long-term bondholders a way to get extra income from their gilts. Repos can be used either to borrow money to finance a long position or to borrow securities to sell them short. The UK reform should level the playing field both for bond-lending and for access to money-market funds.

Stripping separates out a bond's principal and interest payments, so that a 10-year gilt, with its semi-annual coupons, would strip down into 21 payments. These could be viewed as 21 zero-coupon bonds; hence the need for the tax reforms. An official strip market has two big advantages: all the component payments remain the government's responsibility and therefore free of default risk; and arbitrageurs can maintain efficient pricing by recreating a recognised conventional gilt out of a bundle of strips. The authorities will have to adjust issuance to feed the market with suitable bonds, so that several different underlying gilts have completely interchangeable coupons.

For international investors, strips can offer a usefully bare-boned instrument to compare with other markets, easy to hedge against currency risk and free of the risk that coupon payments might have to be reinvested at lower yields. At the other extreme, strips can be individually tailored to produce a highly structured income stream. The Bank hopes the UK pensions industry will generate plenty of business for the strips market. Funds could buy principal strips timed to mature along with their liabilities; coupons could be linked to provide an annuity, giving a pensioner regular income but no lump sum; or a deferred payment bond could be created, paying no interest until retirement.

MEASURING SENTIMENT

London's futures and options exchange, LIFFE, chose gilts for the first government bond futures contract to be traded in Europe, in 1982. Options on the long gilts future were introduced in 1986 and now include serial options which expire in the nearest months, in between the traditional March, June, September and December expiries. The options market provides insight into underlying gilt market sentiment by offering, though the price mechanism, a way of measuring the degree and type of risk which participants expect. The implied volatility of the option on the long gilt future peaked at 14 per cent at the height of the 1994 bear market, against an average 7.8 per cent during the 1993–4 financial year. The rise was much sharper than that in German assets and in July 1994 implied volatility on options on long gilt futures was 6.5 points higher than that on Bund options. The spread fell back to 2.1 points in March 1995. Analysts attributed the high bear market spread largely to the way in which the UK's inflation history heightens uncertainty once investors go on the defensive. The same phenomenon can be seen in the cash market, in the 10-year yield spread of gilts over Bunds. That spread narrowed to a half-point at the height of the 1993 bull market, then shot out to nearly two points within six months as global greed turned to fear.

Analysts can use index-linked bonds to make more sophisticated attempts to quantify how much inflation the gilt market expects at different maturities. Studying the yield spread of conventional over index-linked bonds represents a considerable advance on other methods. But it remains an inexact science, because the spread cannot simply reflect inflation expectations. It may have been reduced, for instance, by the greater liquidity of conventional bonds. Then there is the difficulty of differentiating between the price premium which the market puts on protection against a generally expected level of inflation and the premium which it adds for protection against the risk that inflation will turn out to be even higher.

FOREIGN-CURRENCY DEBT

Eurosceptics or no, the UK pioneered the issue of Ecu Treasury bills in 1988. These are discount securities sold by monthly tender on a yield basis, unlike sterling T-bills which are quoted in terms of price. A 10-year Ecu bond was issued in 1991. In 1992, the UK started issuing three-year Ecu notes, sold in tranches by quarterly tender, with a new issue each January. Ecu issues top up the UK's foreign-exchange reserves and are not counted towards funding for the public-sector borrowing requirement.

Ecu is the only foreign currency debt in which the UK issues regularly. Ecu T-bill tenders are usually announced on the first

Tuesday of each month and held the following Tuesday, with bids in by 10:30, results at 13:00 and settlement two days later. Ecu T-note tenders are usually announced on the second Tuesday in July, October, January and April. Bids must be in by 10:30 the following Tuesday, with results at 13:00 and settlement a week later.

The UK has three issues outstanding in marks and dollars: a $4 billion floating-rate note due in September 1996, a $3 billion Eurobond due in December 2002 and a DM5.5 billion Eurobond due in October 1997.

THE ECONOMY

Annual UK retail price inflation slowed to 1.6 per cent in 1993, the lowest rate since 1960.[6] As the basic retail price index (RPI) climbed again, the authorities acted earlier than usual in tightening monetary policy, and base rates rose in three stages from 5.25 per cent in September 1994 to 6.75 per cent in February 1995. Meanwhile the government's current target inflation rate, the RPI-X, reached a low of 2.0 per cent in October 1994.

In September 1995, headline inflation was running at 3.9 per cent year-on-year and core inflation at 3.1 per cent. However, both rates had subsided below 3 per cent again by early 1996. Signs of slowing growth and weak inflationary pressures persuaded many economists that Chancellor Clarke had been justified in cutting rates in three stages back to 6 per cent. More troubling for the gilt market was the authorities' lack of success in curbing the budget deficit. The government raised its PSBR target for 1995–6 to £29 billion but many economists thought this was still too optimistic. As elsewhere in Europe, the budget was under pressure due to weaker-than-expected economic growth. GDP growth in fourth quarter 1995 was 1.5 per cent year-on-year and most economists thought Clarke's forecast of 3 per cent GDP growth in 1966 was optimistic. However, there were dissenting voices. Some economists saw the economic slowdown as temporary and said strong money supply growth could be storing up inflation for 1997.

In January 1996, Reuters published the results of a poll of 44 economists at banks, brokerages, universities and other institutions on their forecasts for the UK economy out to the end of 1997 (see Table 6.3). In general, they expected continued moderate economic growth and thought the government should be able to keep inflation below the ceiling of the 1–4 per cent target range, but they saw continued problems in restraining the budget deficit. The mean figures calculated from their forecasts for the PSBR were £29.9 billion for 1995–6, £23.9 billion for 1996–7, and £19.2 billion for 1997–8: all higher than revised official forecasts of £29 billion, £22.5 billion and £15 billion respectively. Mean forecasts for sterling/dollar were $1.4951 for end-1996 and $1.5156 for end-1997: sterling was trading at $1.5045 when the forecasts were published.

Table 6.3 Forecasts from Reuters Poll of 37 Economists for the UK Economy, January 1996

	Current	Q4 96	Q4 97	1996	1997
10-Year Gilt Yields (%)	7.4	7.64	7.94	—	—
UK Base Rates (%)	6.25	6.0	6.60	—	—
RPI-X (% y/y)	3.0	2.7	2.9	2.7	2.8
Producer Prices (% y/y)	4.3	3.2	3.6	3.5	3.4
GDP Growth (%) 1995 =	2.6	3.0	2.6	2.4	2.9
Current Account (£billion)					
Q3 95 =	–1.34	—	—	–5.3	–6.4
M0 Growth (%)	5.9	5.1	5.2	5.2	5.2
M4 Growth (%)	10.0	7.5	7.5	7.8	7.5
Unemployment (%)	8.0	7.7	7.4	7.8	7.4

Note: Current data are latest available when poll was carried out.

NOTES

1. Bank of England definition. Sometimes five years is used instead as the watershed between short- and medium-dated gilts.
2. Updated for inflation, the value was 17 per cent of market holdings.
3. Bank of England Fact Sheet, *Monetary Policy in the United Kingdom*, 1994.
4. Bank of England Fact Sheet, 1991, updated 1994.
5. *The Central Banks*, Marjorie Deane and Robert Pringle, Hamish Hamilton, London, 1994.
6. International Financial Statistics.

APPENDICES

Box 1—Credit ratings

Standard & Poor's rates Britain's domestic and foreign currency debt AAA with a stable outlook. S&P said:

> The ratings reflect the size, diversity and robustness of the UK economy, manageable inflation and public finances, as well as Britain's role as one of the world's most influential and stable democracies. The ratings are also supported by the government's commitment to tighter monetary and fiscal policies and by a substantially improved foreign trade performance . . . The opposition Labour Party has shifted towards the political centre and appears more electable now than for many years . . . The outlook reflects the expectation of continued austere macroeconomic policies, which result in a significant reduction in public sector borrowing.

Moody's also rates both the foreign and domestic currency debt of the UK as AAA. It says this is

> based on the country's stable political environment, the structural economic reforms undertaken during the past 15 years and London's position as a major world financial centre . . . The UK recovery picked up steam in 1994, with real growth doubling to four percent . . . Since then growth has been decelerating, reflecting a tightening of demand-management policies in response to concerns over rising inflation. A slight loosening of monetary policy might occur next year as the government attempts to improve its popularity ahead of elections . . . Looking towards the medium term, uncertainties include the prospects for a sustained European recovery and the fate of the planned monetary union. Questions also remain regarding the economic policy orientation of future governments.

Box 2—Futures and options on LIFFE

Long gilt future
Contract size £50 000
Notional 9% coupon
Residual maturity 10 to 15 years
Minimum price movement 1/32 point
Trading hours 08:00–16:15; APT 16:30–18:00

Short sterling
Cash settled, based on British Bankers'
Association Interest Settlement Rate for
three-month sterling deposits
Contract size £500 000
Minimum price movement 0.01 point
Trading hours 08:05–16:05; APT 16:22–17:57

Options are available on both the above futures contracts.
Short sterling options trade between 08:07–16:05, long gilt
options 08:02–16:15.
The minimum price movement on long gilt options is 1/64 point.

Delivery/expiry months are March/June/September/December.

Additional, serial options are available for long gilts, so that four expiry months, including the three nearest calendar months, are always available. APT is automated pit trading. Regular LIFFE trading is by open outcry.

7

France

OVERVIEW

Think of investing in French bonds and you probably think about the Maastricht criteria for European economic and monetary union (EMU), budgetary problems, political concerns, currency jitters—just about anything in fact except that the French government securities market, according to the country's Ministry of the Economy, is the second-most liquid in the world after the United States and therefore potentially very interesting to overseas investors. 'Since 1986, the French government has pursued a particularly attractive issuing policy from the point of view of the international investor,' says a foreword to a Ministry report on the market.

'This policy is based on a range of extremely simple products, highly liquid lines, and maximum regularity where market calls are concerned. This choice is the outcome of an extensive review of the situation in other countries, taking a deliberately long-term perspective,' it adds. Hyperbole perhaps, but between 1986 and 1993 it notes that foreign investment in French government securities rose from almost zero to 30 per cent of negotiable debt outstanding. It points to relatively low interest rates and the ability of the government to borrow much more money at a time of economic slowdown while increasing the average maturity of its debt.

It says the French Treasury was the first to issue long-term Ecu-denominated bonds in 1989 and the first to commit itself to a regular timetable of medium- and long-term Ecu debt auctions in 1994. It was the first in Europe to authorise the stripping of its securities, in French francs in 1991 and in Ecu in 1994. It looks after the secondary market, issues products appealing to specific groups of investors and is committed to providing information to intermediaries, investors and analysts to keep the market transparent.

It all sounds too good to be true, and some analysts say it is, because those concerns mentioned earlier—the economy, the currency and the politics—keep getting in the way. In 1995, when the Maastricht criteria were a dominant theme in the financial markets, it was noted that France was still some way from achieving the financial targets needed for it to adopt the single currency foreseen as part of EMU, and the financial markets remained sceptical about the new government's ability to put its economic house in order in time. The government was plumbing the depths in the opinion polls and the French franc was subject to periodic bursts of speculative selling.

Foreign investors in France certainly needed strong nerves, and in 1995 the total rate of return from an investment in French debt, at 17.01 per cent in French franc terms, was among the lowest in the major world government bond markets, according to data compiled by the US investment bank Salomon Brothers. In contrast, the return of 27.69 per cent in dollar terms was near the top. These topics will be discussed in detail later. First, though, the details of the market.

MARKET STRUCTURE

The Ministry's buzz words when describing the French market are simplicity, liquidity and transparency, and it notes the country's AAA long-term debt rating and the existence of a strong futures and options market, the MATIF. As far as simplicity is concerned, there are only three key instruments—OATs (*Obligations Assimilables du Trésor*), BTANs (*Bons du Trésor à Taux Fixe et à Intérêt Annuel*) and BTFs (*Bons du Trésor à Taux Fixe et à Intérêt précompté*). OATs are Treasury bonds with maturities up to 30 years that are used to raise long-term funds, BTANs are fixed-rate Treasury notes with maturities of between two and five years and BTFs are short-term Treasury bills with a maximum maturity of one year, issued at a discount.

Liquidity is enhanced by a policy of issuing fungible debt so that outstanding issues are regularly increased in size, by a policy of issuing debt regularly, by the establishment of a group of SVTs (*Spécialistes en Valeurs du Trésor*), which are primary dealers responsible for ensuring Treasury auctions are a success and making secondary markets, and by active intervention through the FSR (*Fonds de Soutien des Rentes*), the government debt management fund. Transparency is maintained by selling at auction via open competitive bidding, by publishing auction calendars at the beginning of each year, by issuing a monthly bulletin and by introducing new products.

French government debt auctions take place twice a month, with long-dated OATs auctioned on the first Thursday of each month and medium-term BTANs auctioned on the third Thursday. In addition, BTFs are auctioned each Monday, and every two months there is an issue of Ecu OATs or BTANs on the second Wednesday of the month. The securities and quantities to be sold are announced at least two working days in advance. The Treasury may also issue debt, though it rarely does, in the traditional syndicated form.

In the first half of 1995, these were the franc-denominated OATs and BTANs auctioned: ten-year OATs were auctioned each month, first a 7.5 per cent issue maturing in April 2005 and then, from April, a 7.75 per cent issue maturing in October 2005. One or two new 10-year OATs are created each year and act as the benchmark for the market. Thirty-year OATs were auctioned in January, February and June; in each case a 6 per cent issue maturing in October 2025. Two-year and five-year BTANs were auctioned most months, the most recent being a 7.25 per cent BTAN maturing in August 1997 and a 7.75 per cent BTAN maturing in April 2000. Other securities sold were an 8.5 per cent 13-year issue due October 2008, auctioned in February, March and May and an 8.5 per cent seven-year issue due October 2002, auctioned in June.

At the auctions, sealed bids may be handed in directly to the Bank of France, the central bank, though potential buyers may also use a computerised remote bidding system called Telsat. SVTs account for about 90 per cent of the securities sold. Highest bids are served first; lower bids are served in quantities decided by the Treasury.

Total government debt outstanding at the end of 1993 was FFr2458 billion, or 34.5 per cent of GDP, and negotiable securities represented 86.8 per cent of this, or FFr2132.8 billion. Of this, 63.3 per cent was long-term debt and the average maturity at the year-end was approximately 6.5 years. The volume of BTFs outstanding was FFr188.9 billion at the year-end. The Treasury issues one 13-week BTF each week and, alternately, a six-month BTF and a one-year BTF, though the initial maturities may be adjusted to attach them to existing lines.

THE SECONDARY MARKET

All bonds are tradeable on the Paris Bourse but, as elsewhere, the key secondary market is over-the-counter. French franc OATs are listed on screen and traded actively by the SVTs in discount-rate terms expressed as a percentage of par value. They tend to be traded in blocks of 50 million to 200 million francs and the bid/offer spread is generally between five and 15 centimes. All prices are quoted net of tax and costs.

BTANs and BTFs are only tradeable over-the-counter. The SVTs announce bid and offer prices, together with the volume available for trading on those bases. BTANs are traded on a yield basis and the rate of return is expressed as an annual percentage over 365 days (366 in a leap year). BTFs are traded on a money-market straight-line yield expressed as an annual percentage over 360 days.

OATs are cleared in France through the Paris Bourse's Sicovam clearing house. They may also be cleared and held in the Cedel and Euroclear clearing systems. The clearing conventions are three business days after the date of the trade domestically and seven calendar days after the date of the trade internationally. BTANs and BTFs are delivered and settled though the Saturne system run by the Bank of France. Lending, borrowing and repurchase of securities has grown rapidly. As far as supervision is concerned, the Ministry of the Economy has general authority over the financial markets while the newly independent Bank of France's role is to 'define and implement monetary policy' through the Monetary Policy Council. It is also responsible for supervising the money market.

Regulations governing financial institutions authorised to operate in France are laid down by the Comité de la Réglementation Bancaire, while the licensing of lending institutions and money brokers is in the hands of the Comité des Etablissements de Crédit. The Commission Bancaire ensures compliance by lending institutions with the relevant rules and laws, the Conseil des Bourses de Valeurs and the Société des Bourses Françaises supervise central operations in French bonds, the Conseil des Marchés à Terme and MATIF do the same in the futures market, and the Commission des Opérations de Bourse is the market watchdog. Investors in French government securities include the usual institutional investors, lending and financial institutions and industrial and commercial firms, but also UCITS funds including Sicavs, which are mutual funds/unit trusts, and fonds communs de placement, which are investment trusts. As for taxation, nonresidents are exempt from the flat rate withholding tax on OATs, BTANs and BTFs, and are not subject to any taxation in France for operations carried out on the MATIF, provided these operations are not attached to any institution liable for tax in France.

Is French debt worth buying? Well, as in so many other markets, that depends to a large extent on interest rate expectations. The key rates in France are the five-to-10 day repo rate (replaced sometimes by an emergency 24-hour rate) and the intervention rate, which generally act as the ceiling and the floor respectively for three-month money-market rates. Those money-market rates fell from above 13 per cent at one stage in late 1992 to below 6 per cent for much of 1994 but moved sharply higher in early 1995 before easing as the year progressed. By March 1996, the intervention rate had fallen to 3.8 per cent and the five-to-10 day repo rate to 5.5 per cent.

Economists quizzed by Reuters in late January had forecast that the intervention rate would fall for the first six months of 1996 but would rise slightly in the second half of the year and in 1997. The mean forecast was an intervention rate of 3.87 per cent at the end of the first quarter, very close to the actual level, a drop to 3.68 per cent at the end of the second quarter, but rises to 3.71 per cent at the end of the third quarter, 3.72 per cent at the end of the fourth and 4.38 per cent by the end of 1997.

As for the yield on the 10-year OAT, that was expected to rise in the second half of 1996 after holding steady in the first six months. The mean forecasts were 6.29 per cent at the end of the first quarter, compared with an actual level around half a point higher, 6.29 per cent at the end of the second quarter, 6.37 per cent at the end of the third, 6.56 per cent at the end of the fourth and 6.84 per cent at the end of 1997.

The 10-year OAT/Bund spread, the yield premium offered by OATs over German Bunds, was expected to remain close to 50 basis points throughout 1996. It was close to that level when the poll was conducted but the actual figure in March 1996 was nearer 25 basis points.

POLITICS

Putting a finger on why France is rarely at the top of international strategists' 'buy' lists is difficult, but politics must surely play a part. In 1995, the markets had to put up with an extraordinary amount of political uncertainty, both before and after the 23 April/7 May two-round election of Jacques Chirac as president, bringing to an end 14 years of socialist control of the Elysée. Following his election, the centre/right parties—the UDF (Union for French Democracy) and Chirac's own Gaullist RPR (Rally for the Republic)—had control of France at virtually every political level from the munici-pality and the region to the National Assembly and the presidency.

As essentially a conservative grouping, that might be expected to appeal to the financial markets. Instead analysts worried over the lack of an historical parallel for such all-embracing power and, in particular, about Jacques Chirac's election promise to wage war on unemployment. Moreover, he was soon very unpopular. He had come to power after a succession of 'sleaze' scandals which resulted in one former minister going to jail, another minister forced to resign and dozens more ministers, members of parliament, former members, prominent business people, other politicians, business people and their associates under investigation for corruption and in many cases charged and convicted. The ruling Socialists suffered badly, first losing control of the National Assembly in 1993—winning just 54 seats against the centre-right's 484—and then of the presidency in 1995. Unlike the presidential elections of 1981 and 1988, the centre-right won the presidency despite having two ser-ious candidates, with Chirac facing opposition from the then prime minister, Edouard Balladur. Chirac also won despite a reputation as a loser, having been beaten by the Socialist François Mitterrand in 1981 and 1988, and despite a patchy reputation as prime minister from 1974 to 1976 and from 1986 to 1988.

Then mayor of Paris, he beat the Socialist candidate Lionel Jospin, a candidate because former European Commission President Jacques Delors decided not to run, and once elected he chose Alain Juppé as his prime minister. Yet, as mentioned earlier, he had the briefest of honeymoons. An opinion poll in October 1995, just five months into his seven-year term of office, said that most voters expected the opposition Socialists to return to power in the 1998 National Assembly elections.

Analysts blamed the government's plans to raise taxes and mounting impatience about promised reforms to help the jobless, the homeless and the poor. Juppé narrowly escaped prosecution for awarding himself a city-owned flat with a cheap rent when he was deputy mayor of Paris in 1990 yet was still elected head of the RPR. The Paris prosecutor concluded Juppé had broken the law but let him off on condition he moved out—which he agreed to do.

Another poll a few days later showed public approval of Chirac continuing to fall and Juppé's standing at a record low, reflecting anger over an austerity budget, civil service pay restraint which sparked a one-day strike, concern at continuing high unemployment and opposition to the resumption of French nuclear tests in the south Pacific. Finance Minister Jean Arthuis faced problems of his own involving an allegedly illegal Swiss bank account kept by his Social and Democratic Centre party, and even Chirac faced questions at one stage over a flat he rented at cheap rates. All this cast a very long shadow over the economy and the attempts by Chirac, Juppé and Arthuis to fix it.

THE ECONOMY

Superficially, not a lot appears to need fixing. GDP growth in 1994 was 2.9 per cent year-on-year and in 1995 it was 2.4 per cent. Some economists forecast a rebound in 1997 after a weak 1996. Inflation was well under control. The problem was that the French themselves had made clear ahead of the election that they wanted action on unemployment and Chirac, some analysts said, had proved unable to square the circle of making job creation a priority—as promised in his election campaign—while at the same time cutting high French taxes and reducing government spending. His reward was the slump in popularity described above.

The government set itself the ambitious target of creating 700 000 new jobs in 18 months. However, it also promised to cut taxes and reduce the budget deficit from about 5 per cent of GDP in 1995 to 4 per cent of GDP in 1996 and 3 per cent in 1997 while failing to say where the spending cuts would come from, leading some analysts to write off its plans as not credible. The analysts also said the September 1995 budget offered little evidence the authorities were prepared to grasp the nettle with some analysts saying the measures announced were insufficient to meet the targets proposed. The budget aimed to cut the central government deficit to FFr290 billion in 1996 from FFr322 billion in 1995.

Some also said the franc could come under selling pressure at any time, targeted as a result of widespread scepticism about whether the government could achieve its budget deficit targets against a background of slowing growth. Specifically, there were fears of a loosening of monetary policy to try and reduce unemployment or alternatively to offset a tightening of fiscal policy to cut the deficit. The general government deficit to GDP ratio of 3 per cent or less is one of the key Maastricht criteria for the adoption of a single currency. Therefore, France's success in that area could actually determine whether or not there is a single currency in at least some European countries by 1999, as foreseen at Maastricht.

The government's economic difficulties were highlighted in October 1995 when five million public-sector workers staged their biggest strike in a decade in a 24-hour 'Black Tuesday' protest against the government's refusal to raise 1996 civil service pay beyond previously agreed levels. There were warnings of more strikes to come if the government attempted to rein back welfare and health care spending. The government had promised to cut the welfare deficit in half in 1996 and to zero in 1997 from FFr60 billion in 1995, though it had not at the time of the strike spelt out how that was to be done.

More details came shortly. Just a few weeks after the strike Chirac, in a television interview, appeared finally to come down on the side of belt-tightening rather than job creation or tax cuts, choosing mainstream financial orthodoxy rather than a uniquely French solution to the country's problems. He urged two years of budget austerity, stressing commitment to European integration, in an about-turn that some observers said had been forced on him by the financial markets and left the unions apoplectic. Chirac insisted that he had delayed rather than abandoned the war on unemployment but still appeared to have shelved the policies he had fought on during his election campaign. He scotched rumours he would abandon the '*franc fort*' policy and allow the franc to depreciate to boost economic growth, but he avoided a question on whether growth would be reduced by austerity measures. Analysts said that if growth slowed it would become harder still to meet the 3 per cent deficit/GDP target, and some again pointed to a lack of specific measures to reduce the deficit on the social security accounts financing health care, basic pensions and family allowances. None the less, international reaction was essentially positive.

At home, too, the future was looking brighter for Chirac by early 1996. Unemployment was still rising and had topped three million, with the jobless rate at 11.8 per cent in January based on International Labour Organisation (ILO) criteria. However, the government appeared to be inching towards a compromise on the issue of welfare reforms and the strikes of late 1995 had fizzled out in a stalemate. Polls showed Chirac's popularity with French voters rising sharply in March while Juppe's standing had edged upwards despite continued concern about rising unemployment and the government's proposed welfare reforms.

THE CURRENCY

The first thing that needs to be said about the French franc is that despite all the political and economic uncertainty described above, the franc has not historically been a weak currency. Just as the French bond market has been designed to attract investors, a long-standing '*franc fort*'—or strong franc—policy has shielded the currency from danger. The pun (*franc fort*/Frankfurt) is presumably intentional.

Chart 7.1 shows that between 1990 and 1995 the German mark climbed from a low below FFr3.36 to a high above FFr3.58, a drop for the franc of about 6.5 per cent. That is a very small decline, though, compared with the weaker European currencies such as the pound, the Italian lira and the Spanish peseta; at around FFr3.43 in early 1996, the franc was not far from the middle of its five-year range.

Moreover, Chart 7.2 shows the franc actually gained substantial ground against the US dollar since 1989, strengthening from more than FFr6.80 to the dollar to below FFr4.80 to the dollar at one stage. That strength reflects hard work by the French to defend their currency's link with the mark, if necessary by keeping interest rates high, despite the scourge of unemployment and the partial break-up of the European exchange rate mechanism (ERM) in 1993. France has appeared willing to let the German Bundesbank set the pace on rates, and its tight monetary policy has been seen as underlining its determination to save what remain of the links between Europe's currencies. It has also been blessed with healthy trade surpluses despite the *franc fort*.

None the less, maintaining the link with the mark has been no easy task at times. Take the autumn of 1995, for example, a politically turbulent period in France as described earlier. Strong

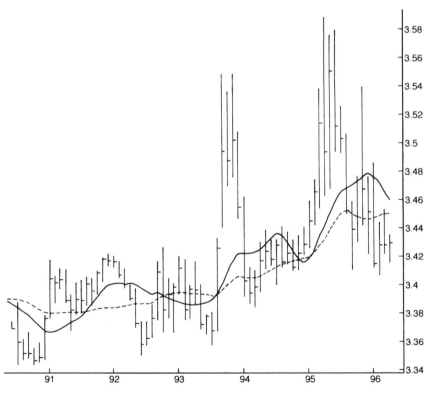

Chart 7.1   Mark/French Franc Monthly Bar Chart. Source: Reuters

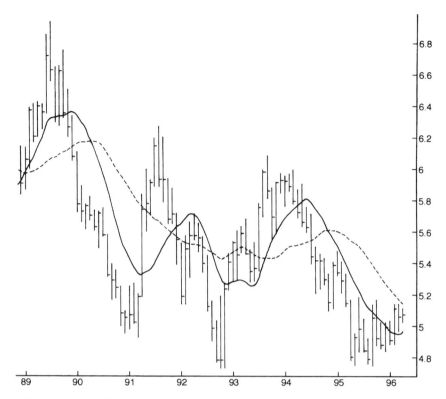

Chart 7.2 Dollar/French Franc Monthly Bar Chart. Source: Reuters

demand for the mark against all other currencies set warning bells ringing in France when the franc weakened at one stage above FFr3.47 to the mark. Bank of France intervention was widely suspected as the franc eased in response to the mark's strength and a wholly obvious admission by Alain Juppé that France was not ready for monetary union. Political scandal, the government's unpopularity and a weak dollar also tempted foreign exchange dealers to sell francs, a weak dollar being a factor because at times of dollar easiness dealers tend to buy marks and therefore push up the value of the mark against other European currencies.

Soon the Bank of France was acting decisively, closing its five-to-10-day emergency lending window, then 6.15 per cent, and opening an overnight 24-hour facility at the same rate to show its determination to defend its currency. These rates usually act as a ceiling on money-market rates. Dealers speculated that the central bank was defending an unofficial target of FFr3.50 to the mark by making it more expensive to borrow to short the franc and that it was determined not to allow the franc to weaken beyond that point. They noted it had taken similar (ultimately unsuccessful) action during the election campaign in March when the franc approached the same level amid general currency turbulence and as Jacques Chirac appeared to put jobs before fiscal conservatism.

That was on a Friday. Come Monday and the cost of overnight funds was raised by 1.10 percentage points to 7.25 per cent, helping the franc to strengthen; a week later it was cut back to 7 per cent, signalling an end to another mini French currency crisis. Analysts said the Bank of France had proved its readiness to support the currency with high interest rates, incurring little political opposition in the process, and had acted swiftly enough to reduce them again to avoid any economic damage.

Even so, a week later more franc selling emerged briefly—this time prompted by political upheaval in Italy—and underlining the currency's continued fragility. But Chirac said the independent Bank of France was right to make a reduction in public deficits the condition for lower interest rates and, in a television interview, added: 'There are no problems with the parity between the franc and the mark. That means there is no reason whatsoever to devalue the franc; no objective reason.' Bank of France Governor Jean-Claude Trichet followed the president's comments by noting that rates could come down if confidence returned, and analysts said the French were trying hard to force confidence back into the market. By and large, they succeeded, with the franc holding reasonably steady in late 1995 and early 1996.

THE BANK OF FRANCE (BANQUE DE FRANCE)

MMS International's table ranking the world's major central banks by their degree of independence, based on a World Bank study published in 1993, puts the Bank of France in 10th place out of 20 central banks, with an independence index of just 34 per cent. The study, though, was presumably undertaken before the Bank won its independence on 1 January 1994. The Independence Bill was presented to the public in May 1993 by the then

Minister of the Economy Edmond Alphandery. This is how it described the way the Bank now operates:

- The Bank of France defines and carries out monetary policy to maintain price stability within the framework of the government's general economic policy. The Bank may not ask for or accept instructions from the government or anyone else. (Alphandery said the reference to government policy was only to satisfy the French constitution and would be amended once the Maastricht Treaty came into force, outranking the constitution).
- Monetary policy is set by the Bank's Monetary Policy Council, comprising nine members: the governor, who chairs the council, and two deputies, appointed by the cabinet for renewable six-year terms. They can be sacked only for exceptional faults but must retire at the age of 65; six members appointed by the cabinet from a short-list of 18 independent figures drawn up by a college of representatives of six state institutions, including parliament and the judiciary. They have non-renewable irrevocable nine-year terms, with two replaced every three years. Of the first six, two, chosen by lot, will serve for only three years. Two more will serve for six.
- Members of the council must give up all activities that create conflicts of interest. They cannot hold elective office. They will also be given other, unspecified, official duties.
- The government controls exchange-rate policy and owns the foreign-exchange reserves. The Bank of France is free to use the reserves to pursue its monetary policy and the currency policy.
- The Monetary Policy Council must meet at least once a month (Alphandery said he would like it to meet once a fortnight) and the council can delegate powers to the governor temporarily.
- The Minister of the Economy or his proxy can sit in on council meetings and propose items for a decision but cannot vote.
- The governor must, as before, report once a year to the president of the Republic. Alphandery said he would like him to address parliament at least twice a year.
- The rest of the Bank's activities, aside from monetary policy, are run by the General Council. This consists of the nine members of the Monetary Policy Council plus a central bank employees' representative and a representative of the state, which remains the 100 per cent owner of the Bank of France.
- This state representative, the 'censor', is normally the director of the Treasury, part of the Ministry of the Economy. The censor has a veto over decisions taken by the General Council.
- The Bank of France continues to hold accounts for financial institutions and the Treasury but no longer lends to the Treasury. Only those commercial clients who had accounts before the reform can keep accounts at the central bank.
- The governor is no longer the de facto head of the Comité de la Réglementation Bancaire (CRB), which defines banking law. The Minister of the Economy, who remains president of the CRB, takes over de facto running of the CRB. The governor remains a member.

- The governor continues to head the Commission Bancaire, the banking supervisor, and the Comité des Etablissements de Crédit, which licenses banks. Bank officials run the Commission Bancaire.

Interestingly, the Bill effectively completed a full circle for the Bank of France when it was brought into law by Acts of 4 August and 31 December 1993. For when it was established by Napoleon in 1800, the emperor said: 'The government should hold it, but not too tightly.' In 1936, though, a new law increased the state's power over the Bank; and in 1945 it was nationalised to become fully subordinate to the government.

Interestingly too, the Bank of France gained its independence on the same day the process towards EMU entered its second preparatory stage on 1 January 1994. As Governor Jean-Claude Trichet said in his first annual report to the president and parliament as head of an independent central bank:

> France's monetary policy is based on stability, credibility and continuity. It is consistent with the process of European Economic and Monetary Union, which has been undertaken by the member states' governments and ratified by their parliaments. This process has just entered its second stage with the creation of the European Monetary Institute, which should help achieve greater co-ordination of monetary policies, ensure the smooth operation of the European Monetary System, remove the barriers to more widespread use of the Ecu in financial circles and, finally and perhaps most importantly, harmonise the statistical, analytical and monetary policy instruments so as to define the framework of the future European central bank's tasks.

Trichet concluded:

> The continued stance in favour of price stability and the stability of the franc *vis-à-vis* the other European currencies is also part of a more general move to improve the convergence of European economies, which is necessary for the completion of Economic and Monetary Union.

DEBT RATING

Moody's Investors Service Aaa rating of securities issued or guaranteed by the Republic of France and its short-term P1 rating 'recognises that France is and will remain a cornerstone of the Western economic and political system', the rating agency says in a report. Its competitors agree. Standard & Poor's Credit Analysis Service and the European agency IBCA both rate France's long-term debt AAA, and S&P's short-term rating is A1+, its equivalent of Moody's P1.

Moody's analysts write of France's 'large and diversified economy, extensive commercial relations and global political role', confirming its commitment to the system's stability. Despite the large borrowings that occurred from 1982 to 1984, Moody's says France's external debt remains small and its debt service burden light. None the less, the agency notes inevitably the growth of general government debt to more than 55 per cent of GDP in 1994.

Standard & Poor's, in a report dated March 1995, notes that it assigned its long-term rating in 1975 and its short-term rating in 1981 and that the outlook for both is stable. 'France's ratings principally reflect the country's position among the world's wealthiest, largest and most diversified economies.' 'France has taken a leading role in establishing the EU's market integration and fiscal discipline objectives'.

DERIVATIVES MARKETS

MATIF, the Marché à Terme International de France, was founded in 1986 and is now one of the world's largest futures and options markets. It is an open outcry market based in Paris and its key contracts are futures and options on a notional seven-to-10-year French government bond, the 'notionnel', and on three-month French interest rates or Pibor, the Paris interbank offered rate. There are also futures on a three-to-five-year medium-term French government security and on a long-term 15-year plus Treasury bond, Ecu bond futures and options, and other products outside the debt market, on the CAC 40 stock market index, for example.

The instrument underlying the notionnel future is, as stated above, a seven-to-10-year fictitious French government bond with a 10 per cent coupon, redeemable at maturity. The trading unit is FFr500 000 and price quotations are in per cent of nominal value to two decimal places. The tick size is two basis points (FFr100) and there are successive quarterly delivery months, March, June, September and December. The last trading day is the second business day preceding the third Wednesday of the delivery month (London basis) at 11:00 Paris time.

Delivery is based on the settlement price and bonds can be selected by the seller from an official list of seven-to-10-year eligible French government bonds redeemable at maturity. Open outcry hours are 09:00 to 16:30 Paris time, and the contracts can be traded outside those hours on the GLOBEX electronic system.

Pibor futures are based on three-month deposits, the trading unit is FFr5 million and price quotations are based on an index (100 minus three-month Pibor) quoted to two decimal places. Tick size is one basis point or FFr125 and there are successive quarterly delivery months. The last trading day is the second business day preceding the third Wednesday of the delivery month at 11:00 Paris time.

These contracts are cash settled, with the liquidation price equal to 100 minus a mean three-month Pibor, published on the last trading day and rounded off to two decimal places. Open outcry hours are 08:30 to 16:00 Paris time, with GLOBEX available for use outside those times.

MATIF's Ecu bond futures and options are the key contracts for these securities, while LIFFE, the London International Financial Futures & Options Exchange, is the principal exchange for Ecu interest-rate products.

USEFUL ADDRESSES

Direction du Trésor
Ministère de L'Economie
139 rue de Bercy
75572 Paris Cedex 12

Direction de la Communication
Banque de France
48 rue Croix-des-Petits-Champs
75001 Paris

MATIF SA
176 rue Montmartre
75002 Paris

Commission des Opérations de
  Bourse
Immeuble de Pont Mirabeau
39–43 quai André Citroën
75739 Paris Cedex 15

SBF – Bourse de Paris
39 rue Cambon
75001 Paris

Sicovam
5 rue du Centre Mont d'Est
93167 Noisy-le-Grand Cedex

Conseil des Marchés à Terme
18 boulevard Montmartre
75002 Paris

Comité de la Réglementation
  Bancaire
39 rue Croix-des-Petits-Champs
75001 Paris

Commission Bancaire
73 rue de Richelieu
75002 Paris

8
Italy

Italy was the government bond investor's favourite as the race for high yield took off in the second half of 1993. In many ways, it looked more like an outsider. Its foreign-currency credit ratings had just been downgraded again, to AA by Standard & Poor's and to a significantly less generous A1 by Moody's, putting Italian Eurobonds out of bounds for some institutional investors. The lira had been suspended from Europe's Exchange Rate Mechanism (ERM) in 1992. Yet the country was finally gripped by popular revolt against a political system blamed for systemic corruption—and Italy looked set to extend its rejection of the old regime to economics. Throughout the previous decade the Bank of Italy had been building its independence and seeking, with the Treasury, to modernise debt management. In 1992 trade unions had agreed to give up the *scala mobile*, a four-decade-old agreement to index wage increases to inflation. Now the quest for political reform held out the prospect of strong governments capable of transforming the national debt into equity through privatisation, of curbing public spending, of commanding compliance with tax laws—and of stabilising the supply of paper from the world's third-largest bond market. Confidence grew that Italy might even be able to persuade its European Union partners to let it join their planned Economic and Monetary Union (EMU). Salomon Brothers rated Italy the world's top performing major bond market, calculating lira investors gained 28.75 per cent during 1993.

But bonds and popular hopes tumbled through 1994 as electoral reform produced yet another coalition government, still plagued by corruption allegations and doomed to collapse in rather less than the post-World War II average of 11 months. By early 1995, the front-month Italian bond contract in LIFFE had tumbled 28 points from its all-time high of 119.15, reached in February 1994. Ten-year bonds were yielding nearly 14 per cent. That meant Italy was paying 6.6 percentage points more than the German government to raise funds, a massive increase over April 1994 when, at the height of the euphoria over the prospects for reform, Italy's yield spread over Bunds had shrunk to just 2.5 points.[7]

Investors in Italian equities can console themselves that the economy has been one of the most dynamic in Europe throughout the decades of political instability. Bond investors are bound to weigh Italy's chances of electing a government capable of surviving a full five-year term and confronting the spending pressures which inflated the public sector debt to GDP ratio to 125.4 per cent in 1994[1] from less than 60 per cent in 1980.

POLITICS

Part of Italy's debt burden and some of its political tensions can be traced to its relatively recent emergence as an independent nation. Unification in 1861 joined northern regions, endowed with embryonic industry and traditions of global trade and banking, with a south still largely feudal. State investment in industrial projects in the south has increased the national debt, failed to bridge the nation's economic divide and spawned northern demands for federalism. Italy's public sector is also in part a legacy of Fascist dictator Benito Mussolini, who founded public corporations including the state holding company IRI (Istituto per la Ricostruzione Industriale).

Mussolini backed Nazi Germany in World War II, which cut Italy apart again in 1943 when Allied soldiers occupied the south while Mussolini clung to power in the north, battling a largely Communist-inspired resistance movement. Many Italians endured civil strife and hunger. After the war, the backlash against Fascism inspired the creation in 1948 of an exceptionally pure form of proportional representation.

In practice this gave more than four decades of power-sharing to the Christian Democrat Party, which projected itself as a bulwark against the West's biggest Communist Party. While coalition partners swapped places, terrorism, corruption and organised crime took hold. In 1978, the extreme left Red Brigades murdered former Prime Minister Aldo Moro; in 1980 neo-Fascists bombed Bologna railway station, killing 84 people; and in 1981 extensive links were revealed between politicians and businessmen and a secret masonic lodge involved in financial and political scandals and right-wing terrorism. In 1989, a crackdown on the Mafia and its allies triggered violence including 200 killings in Naples.

The end of the Cold War had a profound impact on Italy, with the Christian Democrats rather than the Communists taking the brunt of the upheaval. As old political assumptions were called into question, Milan magistrates were emboldened to start unravelling a web of corruption which had entangled all political parties, but especially the Christian Democrats and one of their regular coalition allies, the Socialists. Italian researchers 'guesstimated' in 1993 that corruption—financed largely by inflating the value of the state contracts which the bribes were paid to win—could account for 10 to 15 per cent of Italy's budget deficits.[3] As the graft charges mounted, so did popular pressure for electoral reform. In a 1993 referendum, some 83 per cent of voters backed wholesale reform. As a result, a first-past-the-post system has been adopted for three-quarters of the 630 seats in the lower house of parliament, the Chamber of Deputies. Remaining seats in the lower house are awarded by proportional representation, but parties have to get at least 4 per cent of the vote to qualify for these. The 315 members of the upper house, the Senate, are elected on a regional basis in a single ballot which combines direct election and a proportional system.

The referendum result was translated into legislation under Italy's first non-political prime minister, former central bank governor Carlo Azeglio Ciampi. Meanwhile the old political parties underwent identity crises and a new party emerged, taking its name from the exhortation of the football terraces, Forza Italia. Its leader, media magnate and owner of AC Milan, Silvio Berlusconi, won the first polls held under the new voting system in March 1994. His honeymoon with the markets proved brief. Like all his postwar predecessors, Berlusconi proved dependent on reluctant coalition allies who brought down his government in December 1994.

Another former central banker, Berlusconi's Treasury Minister Lamberto Dini, took over in January 1995 to form Italy's 54th government since World War II. His limited but tough brief embraced a mini-budget; pension reform; and reform of the media, aimed at curbing Berlusconi's influence in television. Dini succeeded beyond the expectations of the financial markets in economic reform, but Berlusconi outmanoeuvred him on the television front. The media magnate rallied popular support against a referendum proposal to cut the number of stations he owned. At the same time, he sold a majority stake in Mediaset, the company which groups his television and advertising interests, in an ingenious deal which commentators said left him in effective control of his television channels.

However, Dini's unflappable style proved popular with Italians while the markets endorsed him by boosting the lira from its all-time low of 1275 per mark in March to around 1100 in September. Supported by leftists and centrists, Dini renewed efforts to guarantee parties equal access to the media and to get a reasonably austere 1996 budget through parliament. Dini said the lira might soon be ready to rejoin the ERM. Hopes revived that Italy might squeeze into an eventual monetary union via a loophole which would grant admission to big debtors who had demonstrated their determination to reform. Then the lira came tumbling down again. First, Germany expressed reluctance to bend the rules on EMU enough to admit Italy, at least initially. Next, Berlusconi challenged Dini in a parliamentary vote of confidence. Dini survived but largely thanks to a promise to resign as soon as the 1996 budget was approved. A general election was duly set for 21 April 1996. This time the political parties regrouped into two major coalitions: the Freedom Alliance under Berlusconi; and the centre-left Olive Tree bloc under economist Romano Prodi. Dini set up his own party, Italian Renewal, aligned with the Olive Tree. Opinion polls suggested the election might produce a new stalemate, with the vote evenly split between the two blocs.

Dini's most influential admirer was President Oscar Luigi Scalfaro. Only the president can dissolve parliament or nominate a prime minister, making Scalfaro a powerful figure in a country with Italy's history of coalition government. Scalfaro, who turned 77 in 1995, was elected to the post in May 1992 after a parliamentary career during which he was noted for his independence within the Christian Democrat party and his devotion to Roman Catholicism. With Italian politics still splintered into more than a dozen parties, he looks set to wield major influence throughout his seven-year term.

Any chance that the next election will produce a longer-lived government depends not just on the voting system but on which parties can find common ground. Here is a sketch of the most likely major players, starting from the left of the political spectrum.

Italy's communist party was never as dogmatic as others in Europe. It enjoyed regional power but, excluded from national government, was relatively untainted by scandal. It split at the end of the Cold War. The hardline, Marxist offshoot is called the **Communist Refoundation**. The biggest faction voted in 1991 to transform itself into the **Democratic Party of the Left (PDS)**, saying it is committed to a free market economy. It opposes proposals by Berlusconi for Italy to seek strong government through the direct election of a US-style president. Instead the PDS wants a French-style system with two rounds of voting, which would favour the left. It is the largest group on the Italian left, claiming a quarter of the vote in local elections in 1995.

The other old parties have fared much worse. The **Italian Socialists** are the remnants of the **Socialist Party** which was devastated by the corruption inquiries. The rump of the Christian Democrat Party relaunched itself in 1994 as the **Popular Party (PPI)**. Discredited by scandal and groping for a new political direction, neither could muster much popular support in 1995, but the PPI could get enough votes in a general election to tilt the balance of power. So too could a relatively new arrival, the **Northern League**, which emerged from a 1980s' backlash against state aid to the south. It toned down its federalist views to back Berlusconi but proved a volatile partner, eventually bringing down that coalition and splitting its own ranks in the process.

On the right, the major force is Berlusconi's **Forza Italia,** formed in 1994. It skipped the traditional process of setting up grassroots organisations and instead galvanised support through Berlusconi's television interests and the supporters' clubs of Berlusconi's AC Milan football team. Espousing free enterprise, its vote share swings between about 20 and 30 per cent.

Forza Italia's main ally has been the hard-right **National Alliance.** Gianfranco Fini created this party during 1994, using the organisation of the neo-Fascist **Italian Social Movement (MSI)** while seeking to divorce the new grouping from old images of stiff-armed salutes and old economic ideas like state corporatism.

The MSI formally dissolved itself in favour of the National Alliance in January 1995. Like the Communists, the MSI had been excluded from national power, and therefore from temptation, since World War II. This has helped the National Alliance gather up to 15 per cent of the vote during 1994 and 1995.

POLITICS, THE BUDGET AND THE DEBT BURDEN

It took a culture of widespread tax evasion, a generous social welfare system and a long tradition of subsidising heavy industry to transform Italy during the 1970s and 1980s into the world's third-biggest government bond market. It will take political commitment to tax reform, continuing inroads into welfare payments and some bending of the rules by Italy's European partners if the country is to realise its ambitions of becoming a founder member of European Economic and Monetary Union (EMU). Dynamic spurts of economic growth have not been enough to stop Italian debt ratios spiralling into realms where interest payments perpetuate themselves by creating secondary budget deficits and high-interest-rate risk premia. Economists reckon Italy needs to run primary budget surpluses of around 5 per cent of GDP over the next few years to stabilise the debt to GDP ratio effectively.

Italy's post-war decision to join the trading alliance which developed into the European Union played a major role in the country's rags-to-riches entry to the Group of Seven leading industrialised nations. The desire to stay in both clubs—the EU core and the G7—provides powerful motivation to at least try to cap the national debt. The uncovering of the nationwide corruption scandal in 1992 took place alongside the discovery of the urgency of the need for fiscal reform.[3] In June that year, Danish voters shattered European markets' faith in the inevitability of EMU by rejecting the Maastricht Treaty in a referendum. In July, Italy's government announced the liquidation of state-owned Efim, generating uncertainty about the fate of the creditors of the debt-encumbered company.[11] In August, Moody's downgraded Italy's foreign currency credit-rating by two notches, to Aa3 from Aa1. In September, the foreign exchange market hounded the lira out of the ERM.

It was a perilous time for the Italian bond market, with maturing debt refinanced largely thanks to the intervention at auctions of state-controlled banks.[3] However, the lira's suspension from the ERM galvanised the then government into economic action. It made unprecedented spending cuts and obtained an Ecu8 billion loan from the EU on tough terms to prove Italy still aspires to convergence with Europe's low-inflation economies. Since then, constitutional reform has vied with fiscal reform for political priority. But the two governments led by former Bank of Italy officials, Carlo Azeglio Ciampi and Lamberto Dini, have pursued major structural changes.

Under Dini, in 1995 Italy finally attained the elusive goal of staying within the annual public sector borrowing requirement target, revised down to L130 trillion. After 15 years of growth, the budget deficit to GDP ratio fell in 1995 to 7.4 per cent from 9.4 per cent in 1994. Dini was helped by a global bond market rally which reined in borrowing costs, but the structural curbs which he enforced through a 1995 mini-budget were also meant to reduce the overall budget deficit further in future years. He aimed to cut the 1996 budget deficit to L109 trillion. Presenting the set of rolling three-year financial targets which the Italian government announces in the middle of each year, in 1995 Dini claimed to have stabilised the debt to GDP ratio. His goal for 1998 was to rein in the debt to GDP ratio to 115 per cent and to reduce the budget deficit, which since 1992 has been composed exclusively of borrowing costs, to the 3 per cent of GDP advocated as the maximum permissible under EMU. However, economists questioned whether Dini's 1996 budget arithmetic would add up. They said economic growth and therefore tax receipts were likely to be lower than forecast and voiced scepticism about how much another crackdown on tax evaders would raise. Some also thought the government was optimistic in estimating that debt interest payments would total L189.4 trillion in 1996, just under the 1995 target. The Bank of Italy predicted there would have to be a L10 trillion mini-budget to meet the 1996 deficit target.

	1995	1996	1997	1998
Targeted deficit to GDP ratio	7.4	5.8	4.4	3.0

Dini also enforced reform to what he termed a 'pensions mechanism that for too many decades devoured resources and produced debts beyond any control'. The reform, intended to save a cumulative L100 trillion by 2004, switches Italy from an earnings-based to a contributions-based pensions system and makes it much harder for civil servants to retire early. However, the Bank of Italy[7] noted the savings amount to just 0.3 per cent of GDP per year and that no limit has been placed on the amount of benefit to be paid. The bank said that even when the reforms are fully phased in, the system will remain among the more generous in Europe, allowing Italians to retire relatively early on a relatively high proportion of their salaries. Economists complain the system retains a major structural flaw: the use of the contributions of those in work to pay the pensions of those who have retired. Italy's working population is projected to fall sharply over the next three decades and Dini's reforms, due to take full effect only in 2030, are probably not radical enough to ensure the long-term viability of the system. Much work remained, too, in enforcing compliance with tax laws. The Bank of Italy, estimating that evasion of Value-Added Tax (VAT) alone amounts to up to a third of what is due, said receipts were the lowest in Europe in relation to GDP.[7]

FUNDING THE DEBT

Managing the debt burden has spurred major reforms in the past 15 years, notably the 'divorce' of the Bank of Italy from the Treasury; the creation of a screen-based secondary market; and the speeding up of repayment of a withholding tax to inter-national investors. Along the way the authorities have worked doggedly to shift the debt out of the short-dated securities beloved of inflation-wary Italian households and into BTPs, the longer-dated, fixed-rate bonds convenient to foreign investors. In 1981, Italy met 66 per cent of its borrowing requirement with net issues of short-term BOTs and just under 8 per cent with BTPs. In 1993, aided by a bull market, it raised 4 per cent in BOTs and 77 per cent in BTPs, including a 30-year issue.[2]

The Italian authorities were unable to sell as high a proportion of BTPs into the 1994 bear market, issuing more seven-year floating-rate notes instead. This enabled them to continue in-creasing the debt's average maturity to three years at the end of 1994, from barely one year in 1982.[8] However, more than half of

Italy's outstanding public-sector securities are still linked to short-term rates. This makes for volatility in the scale of its interest payments, continually disrupting efforts to forecast the year's overall budget deficit. Even so, the debt management efforts bore some fruit in 1994 as interest payments eased to L174 trillion from L183 trillion in 1993.[7]

At the end of 1994, Italy's outstanding government debt according to the Maastricht Treaty definition totalled L2058 trillion (up from L1852 trillion in 1993). This included L134.8 trillion in Ecu and other foreign currencies.[7] Excluding Treasury bills (BOTs), 1995 redemptions were estimated at L194.58 trillion and 1996 redemptions at L194.43 trillion.

Italy embarked in the 1980s on a programme to privatise most of the massive state sector. Since 1993 any cash that accrues through selling off state enterprises is meant to go into a sinking fund, so that the Treasury can buy back bonds and cancel them. However, bond investors are not holding their breath. The benefits of privatisation have often lain mainly in ridding the state of burdens on the budget, and the Bank of Italy said there was L6 trillion in the fund at the end of 1994. The Bank started to buy back short-term paper at the end of 1995.

Italian budget deficits are financed almost entirely through the public issue of securities (see Table 9.1). Budgets have to be

Table 9.1   Stocks of Domestic Italian Government Securities

	L trillion		%	
	Dec 1993	Dec 1994	Dec 1993	Dec 1994
BOT	394	416	27.1	25.5
CCT	508	546	34.9	33.7
BTP	405	517	27.8	31.9
CTO	63	60	4.3	3.7
CTE	50	55	3.4	3.4
Other	36	29	2.4	1.8
Total	1455	1621	100	100

(Figures rounded. Excludes securities issued to finance the Treasury's new payments account and consolidate its old overdraft at the Bank of Italy.)

Source: *Banca d'Italia, Annual Report 1994*

approved by the end of each calendar year, when the Treasury publishes an annual calendar outlining its medium- and long-term bond issuance plans. It updates this with a quarterly announcement indicating the minimum size of each security it intends to issue. About a quarter of Italy's publicly placed debt remains in *Buoni Ordinari del Tesoro*, BOTs. These are discount securities, issued in three-, six- and 12-monthly maturities at fortnightly auctions.

Buoni del Tesoro Poliennali, BTPs, were spurned by domestic investors during the inflationary 1970s and 1980s before finding their market among foreign investors in the 1990s. Their attraction is that they are straight bonds paying a semi-annual coupon, although the market convention is to quote annual-equivalent yields. Demand for BTPs took off in 1991, spurred by the ending of capital controls, a government decision to start reforming withholding tax rules and above all the issue of a 10-year BTP benchmark.[3] By the end of the year, London's LIFFE exchange had established futures and options contracts on 10-year BTPs. Italy's own Mercato Italiano Futures was set up in 1992 and introduced a five-year BTP futures contract as well as its own 10-year futures. MIF now offers options on both these futures contracts. Successive BTP tranches, with maturities of three, five or 10 years, are auctioned fortnightly. Tranches of the 30-year BTP have become rare since the 1994 bear market made investors wary of very long-dated bonds, whose prices fall more drastically than those of shorter-dated bonds for a given rise in yield.

Certificati di Credito del Tesoro (CCTs) have played a crucial but controversial role in lengthening the average maturity of Italy's debt. These floating-rate notes were introduced in 1977 to wean households off shorter-dated paper by offering a degree of indexation to protect the holders against inflation. Until 1994, CCTs paid a spread over the average of yields at a series of BOT auctions. At one stage during the 1980s the market suspected that the Treasury had chosen this complex instrument, rather than a pure inflation index-linked bond, because it could hold down the yields at the appropriate BOT auctions through setting base prices, a practice it has since discontinued. The valuation of older CCTs is complicated by a time lag between when the coupon is set and when it is paid—up to 15 months for some which pay annually. Those CCTs do not behave like pure floating-rate notes:

the deferred coupon payments enhance the bond's value at times when yields fall and undermine the bond's price when yields rise. This does not matter to household investors intending to hold bonds to maturity, so CCTs continue to offer the Treasury a useful fallback when it has to issue into a bear market.[3] Since November 1987, CCTs have carried semi-annual coupons and since March 1991, they have been issued in seven-year maturities. During 1994 their link with soaring BOT yields attracted foreign investors and CCTs still accounted for a third of government securities on issue at the end of that year.[7] Since the start of 1995 they have been indexed to a single, six-month BOT auction, reducing the payment lag to six months.

There is also a secondary market in *Certificati del Tesoro con Opzione*, CTOs, although these have not been issued since 1992 and accounted for just 3.7 per cent of outstanding government securities at the end of 1994. They are similar to BTPs, but the holder has an option to sell the bonds back to the Treasury halfway through their nominal life. They have done little to assist the Treasury's debt management because investors effectively renew them, at above market yields, in bull markets, and demand redemption in bear markets.

In 1995 Italy began issuing two-year zero coupon notes, *Certificati del Tesoro a Zero Coupon* (CTZ), which have proved popular with retail investors. These securities will appear to reduce Italy's interest payments because they are issued at a discount which is added instead to the debt total.

ECU AND EUROBOND ISSUANCE

Certificati del Tesoro in Ecu, CTEs, offered the Treasury another means of lengthening Italy's average debt maturity. They were introduced in 1982, offering households some protection against inflation, as reflected in the lira's value against other currencies in the Ecu basket, as well as giving financial and other businesses a hedge against lira devaluation. Since June 1993, CTEs have had five-year maturities. They carry annual coupons at a fixed rate in Ecus and can be paid for in either lire or Ecu.

In 1995 Italy launched a five-year Ecu5 billion syndicated loan and a three-year Ecu floating-rate note in what syndicate managers said was part of a strategy to replace domestically issued Ecu paper on the Euromarkets. The strategy was cost-effective partly because of swap rates. However, Italy is still issuing new CTEs.

The Italian Treasury said it planned to raise $12 to $15 billion in foreign borrowing, including CTEs, in 1996. It said it issued a total $11.6 billion on the Euromarkets in 1995. Its aims in tapping the offshore market include issuing in low interest-rate currencies and swapping the currency exposure if necessary. It has also sought to extend maturities and to increase the liquidity of its issues to try to reduce its costs.

Despite the lowering of its credit rating, Italy had a spectacularly successful year on the Eurobond market in 1993, raising a net L22.2 trillion.[7] After a two-year absence, it made an innovative offer to swap illiquid dollar-denominated paper into two longer-dated issues. Take-up was modest, but it proved a useful way to test the water. Italy also won registration with the US Securities Exchange Commission (SEC). This cleared the way for Rome to issue one of the first global bonds, totalling $5.5 billion of paper in 10- and 30-year maturities.[6] It issued a net 16.1 trillion lire-worth in marks, dollars and yen in 1994.[7]

However, the government's foreign-currency denominated debt, including Ecu, still made up only 6.8 per cent of the total outstanding at the year-end. Italy's total net foreign debt has also remained modest, falling to 5.3 per cent of GDP at the end of 1995 from nearly 11 per cent at the end of 1992, according to Bank of Italy data. Standard and Poor's estimated the net external debt to exports ratio would be around 28 per cent in 1995 after 36 per cent in 1994.

TAX

Italian government bond yields are quoted gross of a withholding tax of 12.5 per cent, introduced on 1 September 1987. Italy took several years to activate a procedure for foreigners to claim reimbursement of this tax, and then it involved considerable form-filling and could take up to 10 months. It was not until 1994 that the authorities finalised arrangements to ensure prompt, computerised reimbursement to foreigners. The reform shifted the onus of handling the claims away from the government and onto investors' custodial banks in Italy. The Treasury says reimbursement should now take no more than 30 working days. Entitlement to reimbursement obviously depends on what form of tax accord Italy has with the investor's country of residence. The Treasury says it plans to have further reforms ready by the end of June 1996 which should prevent the tax being levied at all on most foreign investors.

PRIMARY MARKET

The Bank of Italy advises the Treasury on funding and organises the auctions at which government bonds are sold, usually in consecutive tranches to ensure that each issue is liquid. For BTPs, CCTs and CTEs, these are Dutch auctions. This means bonds are awarded to the highest bidders first, but all successful bidders pay the same price, known as the marginal price, which is that of the lowest accepted bid. Bond auctions are automated using the national interbank network. BOT auctions are US-style, with successful bidders paying the prices at which they bid. The Treasury does not set base prices but it does calculate an exclusion price, based on the average level of offers, to deter highly speculative bids. Ecu securities are settled three working days, and BTPs and CCTs two working days, after the auction.

SECONDARY AND FUTURES MARKET

Secondary market settlement is generally within three days. Bond denominations start at L5 million and Ecu5000 to accommodate small investors, who generally use the Milan stock exchange for trading. Professional trade is either over the counter in London or through the official market, the Mercato dei Titoli di Stato (MTS), known as the Telematico. The MTS was set up by the Treasury in 1988 and has greatly enhanced liquidity. This is a screen-based wholesale market with minimum lots of L5 billion or Ecu0.5 million. Average daily turnover in 1994 was L15.5 trillion and the average bid-offer spread was 29 basis points.[7] Since 1994, the authorities have operated a three-tier dealing system. At the apex are government bond specialists, market-makers who undertake to buy at least 3 per cent of bonds auctioned. In return they receive privileges, including the right to take up extra paper at the marginal price just after successful auctions. Then there are primary dealers, who have less onerous market-making responsibilities, and the ordinary dealers. The 16 specialists, trading more than 60 per cent of cash market volume, complained in 1995 that their status was not profitable and sought to abolish the role of the primary dealers. They reached a compromise with the authorities under which their secondary market trading obligations were reduced.

The MTS is open from 9:00 to 17:00 local time. The Italian authorities were able to use the same network to set up the futures and options exchange MIF in 1992 which makes arbitrage easy for approved dealers. Supervisory duties in the Italian bond market are shared by the Treasury, the Bank of Italy and Consob, the stock exchange commission.

PURCHASERS

Italy has been able to count on households to take up a much bigger proportion of its debt—about a third in the early 1990s—than is the norm in industrialised countries. Inflation rates peaking at 21.1 per cent[5] in 1980 ensured these purchases focused on short-term BOTs and floating-rate CCTs. Families bought government securities partly because they distrusted the stock exchange and because institutional investment opportunities such as mutual funds were slow to develop. Besides, the yields attracted less tax than bank deposits and real interest rates were high, averaging about 6 per cent between 1983 and 1993[4] as the Bank of Italy sought to establish its anti-inflation credentials. At the end of the 1980s, government securities constituted a third of families' financial assets. One side-effect is that an official interest rate rise in Italy can boost income in many households, at least at first, partly offsetting the more usual impact of monetary tightening in choking off demand.[3]

This strong domestic demand base is likely to be eroded over the years. Italy's household savings ratio, although still the highest among the Group of Seven nations, had slipped to 15 per cent in

1994 from just over 20 per cent 10 years earlier.[1] Besides, alternative forms of investment are developing, especially as state pension reforms take effect and Italians join private pension funds. Since capital controls were lifted at the start of the 1990s, Italian families have also been moving some of their savings into foreign securities, either directly or through investment funds. At the end of 1994, their foreign portfolios accounted for 4.6 per cent of their financial assets.

Banks lead the field of other major domestic investors, although some commentators have suggested that the privatisation of state-controlled institutions will make it harder for the issuing authorities to rally support for their debt auctions at times of market turbulence. The banks, too, are likely to seek to increase their exposure to foreign investment.[3] None the less, the debt burden is shouldered primarily at home. Foreign holdings of lira-denominated Italian government debt were around 13 per cent at end-1994.[7]

THE ECONOMY

Italy's 1992 ejection from the ERM was not all bad news for its economy. The lira's plunge generated an export boom, which turned around the current account to a surplus of 1.5 per cent of GDP in 1994. International Monetary Fund projections showed that over the rest of the decade, Italy is the only G7 member apart from Japan likely to record large current-account surpluses.[7] Economists expected 1995 would show a current account surplus of about 2 per cent of GDP and GDP growth of around 3 per cent.

The downside of the lira devaluation was an upsurge in inflation. The central bank brought it down to a 25-year low of 3.6 per cent in July 1994, but a year later, aided by rises in indirect taxes, it had surged to nearly 6 per cent. Trade unions representing government employees, who had accepted pay settlements on the basis of over-optimistic inflation forecasts, demanded the government should make up the difference and Dini set aside L6 trillion in the 1996 budget to placate them. Economists were sceptical of government forecasts that inflation would average 3.5 per cent in 1996, saying 5 per cent was more likely. They also doubted the

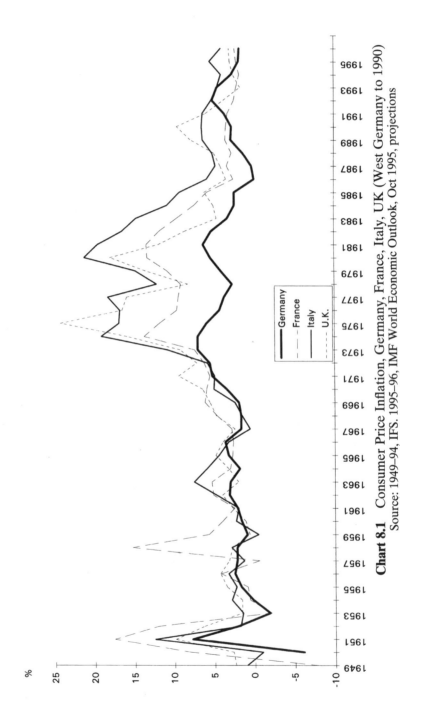

Chart 8.1 Consumer Price Inflation, Germany, France, Italy, UK (West Germany to 1990)
Source: 1949–94, IFS. 1995–96, IMF World Economic Outlook, Oct 1995, projections

official 1996 growth forecast of 3 per cent, expecting GDP to grow by about 2.5 per cent.

Italy's most market-moving economic indicator is usually the preliminary data on consumer prices in nine major cities, released towards the end of the month to which it refers. Final figures take another two weeks. The other major market-mover is the monthly public-sector borrowing requirement number.

The economic reform drive, due partly to European Union pressure to phase out subsidies for heavy industry, has accentuated the north/south divide in Italy. In mid-1995, the unemployment rate in the south, where the state has traditionally been the main employer, was running at 21 per cent against 8 per cent in the north.[7]

THE BANK OF ITALY[6,9]

The Banca d'Italia, founded in 1893, is now both legally and in practice among the world's most independent central banks, although it sometimes has to fight hard to repel political interference in its affairs. The governor, currently Antonio Fazio, is only the sixth incumbent since World War II and is appointed indefinitely by the independent 16-member Supreme Council. The Bank has a free hand in both monetary and exchange-rate policy. It is not state-owned: its shareholders are banks and insurance companies. They choose the 12 directors who sit on the Supreme Council, making the selections on a regional basis. The directors must not have active political roles and serve for renewable terms of three years. The Treasury can send a representative to the council's monthly meetings who can speak but not vote.[6,9]

However, the prime minister, treasury minister and president must ratify the choice of governor and nominations for the three posts immediately below in the Bank hierarchy, those of the director-general and two deputy directors-general. Traditionally all four posts are filled by promotions within the Bank. The current director-general, Vincenzo Desario, is an insider whose appointment was pushed through by the bank in 1994 only after a five-month standoff with Lamberto Dini, who was then treasury minister in the Berlusconi government. Dini, who had himself joined the bank in 1979 from the International Monetary Fund, argued that it was time to hire another outsider. The squabble followed hard on the heels of the Bank's decision in August 1994 to switch monetary policy from easing to tightening. The government was given no warning of the discount-rate rise, and financial markets were convinced that the government's motive was to find an outside candidate who might prove more malleable. Governor Fazio won that round with the help of much stronger legal protection for the Bank than existed in 1979, when one of his predecessors, Paolo Baffi, was forced to resign under government pressure.

The Bank finally managed to get its independence enshrined in law in the early 1990s, with the help of the Maastricht Treaty which makes central bank autonomy a condition for eventual entry to monetary union. In practice, independence evolved rather than being conferred. The government co-ordinated the merger which created the Bank of Italy in 1893 in response to a banking crisis. For four decades it remained a private institution, although the government had to approve the appointment of its governor. From the start it acted as the official depository for state funds, advised the state and arranged loans of last resort in banking crises; and in 1910, the Treasury took over the power to set its discount rate. Mussolini was largely responsible both for consolidating the Bank of Italy's status as a central bank and for depriving it of any control over the money supply. He gave the Bank sole rights to issue bank notes and supervise other banks in 1926.[9] At the same time, he sought to solve Italy's post-World War I debt problem by unilaterally lengthening the maturity of outstanding securities. The state's credibility was shattered and the central bank had to print money to fund it.[3] This practice was formalised in 1936, under legislation which set no formal limit to how much government debt the Bank could hold. The same law incorporated the Bank under public law and limited its ownership to other public companies.[9]

After the war, the Bank's liberty in law was curtailed further, with authority over monetary policy formally vested in the government in 1947. However, in practice the succession of unstable coalition governments enabled the Bank of Italy to rebuild its independence and turn itself into one of the country's most respected institutions. This process accelerated during the 1980s under the leadership of Ciampi. He initiated the 'divorce' of the

Bank from the Treasury with a 1981 agreement that the Bank need no longer buy unsold Treasury bills at auction, the essential first step towards autonomy in monetary policy. The final divorce settlement took a lot longer. It was not until 1994 that the Treasury's overdraft with the Bank was effectively written off and replaced with a cash account which complies with the standards of central bank independence set out in the Maastricht Treaty.[10] In July 1995, the Treasury's account was a healthy L80 trillion in credit.

The settlement enabled the Bank of Italy to start relaxing reserve requirements, which had been among the toughest in Europe, forcing commercial banks to deposit reserves of more than a fifth of their short-term liabilities with the central bank. The ratio was reduced to 15 per cent in May 1994.

The Bank's formal monetary policy target measure is M2 money supply, aiming for annual growth of 5 per cent. In fact M2 grew by 3.1 per cent in 1994, when the Bank started tightening monetary policy, and by 7.9 per cent in 1993, when the Bank was easing. In practice the desire to get the lira back into Europe's Exchange Rate Mechanism has kept the Bank's monetary policy heavily dependent on that of the Bundesbank. Any easing tends to follow German rate cuts and any German rate rise is likely to force disproportionate tightening by the Bank of Italy. The Bank won credibility during the 1980s through its readiness to tighten policy sharply to counter inflation and defend the lira. It has held real short-term interest rates high: generally above 5 per cent for the past 10 years. Ciampi and Fazio have pursued this policy despite the economic conflict created by Italy's debt burden, which ensures that any short-term rate rise pushes up borrowing costs and therefore the budget deficit. The central bank's determination to establish its credibility has therefore added urgency to the efforts to shift Italy's debt into longer-dated, fixed-rate bonds.

It has come in for some criticism since it allowed the discount rate, which usually forms the floor for money-market rates, to bottom out in May 1994 at 7 per cent, barely three points above the consumer price inflation rate. Some economists believe it then tightened too slowly. By May 1995, the discount rate was 9 per cent and the fixed-rate advances rate, intended to act as a ceiling, was 10.5 per cent. Both these rates and the repo rate can signal monetary policy changes. The discount rate can be used for rediscounting BOTs and other eligible securities but is now more commonly used for commercial bank borrowing using agreed credit lines with the central bank called ordinary advances (*anticipazioni ordinaire*).

Repos are held at least weekly, in lire and often in foreign currencies, usually dollars or marks. The market reads little, if any, monetary policy significance into the foreign currency repos. Lira repo rates, too, tend to reflect short-term market conditions rather than medium-term monetary policy. At the middle of each month, for instance, banks have to reconcile their reserve requirements and this can have quite an impact on the repo rate. The repo takes the form of a competitive auction, with the Bank announcing in advance the amount of funding it will make available. Occasionally, however, the Bank sends a strong signal that it does not want money-market rates to ease further by refusing to cover the amount it initially offered, rejecting bids below a certain rate.

The fixed-term advances rate (*anticipazioni a scadenza fissa*), also known as the Lombard rate, generally comes into play when the central bank wants to tighten. It then offers fixed-term advances instead of a repo and at higher rates. The Lombard rate is meant to form a ceiling for the money market. However, the Bank can ration the supply of fixed-term advances to domestic banks, while foreign operators are not eligible at all. This means that sometimes excess demand for emergency funds can push the repo rate above the fixed-term advances rate. Dealers say that sometimes the central bank also intervenes in the bond market to hold down long-term rates.

The Bank of Italy has broad authority over the Italian payments system and oversaw the modernisation of the inter-bank network in 1989. It also has supervisory duties for securities firms as well as banks. It has a huge branch structure, with about 100 offices, to help it carry out this role, as well as reporting on local economic conditions. This did not enable it to prevent fraud destroying Italy's Banco Ambrosiano, whose president Roberto Calvi was known as 'God's banker' because of his links with the Vatican. Calvi was found hanged under London's Blackfriars Bridge in 1982, and the Bank of Italy had to rescue depositors. Convictions for the fraud were secured 10 years later. Appeal hearings began in late 1995.

CONCLUSION

Could another Italian government ever decide to follow the lead of Mussolini and unilaterally reschedule the state's debt? Financial analysts say no. Any form of default would be political suicide while such a high proportion of debt is held domestically and by small investors. Although Mussolini's effective confiscation of Italians' savings in 1926 has not burned itself into the folk memory as deeply as hyperinflation did in Germany, it caused widespread hardship and his term debt 'consolidation' remains a dirty word in Italy.[3] Bank of Italy governors have insisted repeatedly that budgetary discipline is the only way to reduce Italy's debt burden; and soon after taking office, the current governor Antonio Fazio dismissed any talk of alternative methods as 'iniquitous'. With the Bank held in high popular esteem, his words matter.

But what of the risk to foreign creditors of an enforced default? When Standard & Poor's gave Italy's lira-denominated debt an AAA rating in 1995, they were buying some strong arguments as to why Italy's debt burden is quite different from those of Latin America. Only a small share of Italy's debt is denominated in foreign currencies or held by foreigners. This is no problem while the lira exchange rate remains competitive, keeping exports buoyant and the current account in surplus. It is not an insupportable burden even if an Italian government insists on getting the lira locked back into the European Exchange Rate Mechanism (ERM) at too high a valuation. Although the domestic investor base may be eroding with lower savings rates and the lifting of capital controls, Italians are not going to switch their collective portfolios into Bunds or Swiss francs overnight.

Why, then, does Italy have to pay such high yields to fund its debt? Belgium, with a higher debt to GDP ratio, pays far less of a premium over Bunds. The reason is inflation. Italian households have ensured that Italy cannot use inflation to get rid of its debt, by their refusal over the years to buy fixed-rate paper. Too much of Italy's debt is floating rate for inflation to hold much attraction to the authorities as a way of eroding the real cost of redemption. But the memory of double-digit price escalation keeps real interest rates so high that borrowing costs alone sustain the debt burden.

Hence the enthusiasm of the authorities to re-enter the ERM, preferably in time to have served the two-year qualifying period set for eventual membership in 1999 of Economic and Monetary Union (EMU). The widening of the fluctuation band permitted within the ERM to 15 per cent in 1993 might appear to have made readmission easier. But the lira has proved itself capable of devaluing by 15 per cent in a matter of months. In early 1996, Italy looked unlikely to be welcomed back with open arms, and any readmission would have to be at a rate well over L1000 per mark, compared with L770–765 when the currency was forced out.

If it gets as far as re-entry to the ERM, would Italy ever be allowed into an eventual EMU? Like monetary union itself, this depends far more on the will of continental Europe's politicians than on economics. It is obvious that Italy's debt to GDP ratio, double the 60 per cent laid down as the maximum normally permissible, will bar it from admission to EMU—unless it is granted a special dispensation on the grounds of evident penitence. But such an exemption would almost certainly require strict adherence to other criteria such as a much lower inflation rate than Italy was running in 1995. Otherwise, Italians might ask themselves whether they wanted to belong to an anti-inflationary club which would have their country as a member.

Yet it might prove unwise, as well as uncharitable, to be too cynical about Italy's ability to sort out its finances. After all, the country has run primary budget surpluses since 1992, despite the political turmoil. Two of its most popular recent prime ministers have been former central bankers, intent on austerity. There has been an overwhelming popular rejection of a political system geared towards the doling out of influence rather than the pursuit of policy goals. As long as Italians are willing to buy the bulk of their government's securities, and as long as some form of economic convergence remains a European goal, adventurous investors are likely to enjoy spectacular rewards—albeit at considerable risk—in Italy's government bond market.

NOTES

1. OECD *Economic Outlook, 58*, December 1995. Debt to GDP ratio calculated using Maastricht Treaty definition.
2. *A Guide to the Government Bond Market*, The Treasury Board July 1994, Rome. © Direzione Generale del Tesoro.

3. *I Titoli di Stato*, Tiziana Barghini, Milan (1993). Le Guide de Il Sole 24 Ore. Il sole 24 Ore Società Editoriale Media Economici.
4. UBS Global Research.
5. International Financial Statistics, IMF publications.
6. *The Central Banks*, Marjorie Deane and Robert Pringle.
7. Banca d'Italia 1994 *Annual Report*, presented 31 May 1995.
8. Figures from the Italian Treasury and Bank of Italy. The 1994 maturity figure excludes ultra-long-dated bonds issued in 1993 and 1994 as a final settlement in the separation of the two institutions.
9. *The Future of Central Banking: the tercentenary symposium of the Bank of England*, Forrest Capie, Charles Goodhart, Stanley Fischer and Norbert Schnadt.
10. In December 1993 the Treasury issued L30 trillion of bonds to finance its new account with the central bank. It has to tell parliament if the monthly balance on this account falls below L15 trillion or if the monthly balance falls below L30 trillion for three months in a row. In November 1994 it issued a further L76 trillion of securities to consolidate its old overdraft. Sources: Treasury and Bank of Italy.
11. Italy later made arrangements to reimburse EFIM's creditors.

APPENDICES

Box 1—Credit Ratings

Moody's awards Italy the lowest sovereign rating of any country with a reasonably mature bond market. Long-term debt denominated in lira, as well as foreign currency debt, gets a mere A1. Moody's says:

> The ratings take into account the advanced income level of the country, the robust nature of the private sector, as well as the overall flexibility of the economy in dealing with economic challenges . . . The ratings also take into account the very high level of public sector debt. High debt levels make the economy particularly susceptible to changes in investor confidence . . . Uncertainty regarding the ability of Italian governments to tackle the country's fiscal problems has caused upward pressure on interest rates, as well as sharp downward pressure on the exchange rate. Political uncertainty has a high economic cost.

Standard & Poor's is markedly more sanguine, awarding an AA for long-term foreign-currency debt, albeit with a negative outlook, and a full AAA with a stable outlook for the government's lira debt. It says:

> Italy's very strong creditworthiness reflects the wealthy and diversified economy and considerable external flexibility . . . The local currency ratings reflect a stronger capacity to service lira-denominated debt than foreign currency debt, due to the government's taxation powers and control of the domestic financial system, and are supported by Italy's record of moderate inflation, responsible financial management by its autonomous central bank, a consistently high savings rate, and broad domestic and foreign ownership of the republic's debt. The negative outlook on Italy's foreign currency debt reflects the increasing risk that Italy's weak political leadership will fail to address the country's growing, serious fiscal and political problems . . . The prospect of continued policy and political uncertainty threatens to undermine the market confidence necessary to sustain Italy's robust domestic and external economic performance.

Box 2—Futures and options

Futures contracts on LIFFE and MIF

BTP: Nominal contract value L200 million L250 million
  Notional coupon   12 per cent
  Residual maturities   8 to 10.5 years
  Min. issue size   L4 trillion L3 trillion
  Delivery   March, June, September,
          December
          10th of the month (or next
          working day in Italy)
  Last trading day   12:30 Italian time, four Italian
          working days before the
          delivery day.
  Trading hours   08:00–16:10; APT* 16:21–17:58
          09:00–17:00; 17:10–19:00
  Monthly volume*   1.09 million 0.24 million

Medium-term BTP: MIF only; details as for MIF BTP future
 except:
  Residual maturities   3.5 to 5 years
  Monthly volume*   9987

Three-month Eurolira: LIFFE only; contract value one billion lire
        Quotation 100 minus interest rate
        Trading hours 07:55–16:10;
         APT 16:23–17:58
        Monthly volume 0.42 million

American-style options: expiry months March, June, September,
 December
BTP: Trading hours   08:02–16:10 09:00–17:00
  Monthly volume*   91 066 16 288

Eurolira: LIFFE only; Trading hours 07:57–16:10; *Monthly
 volume 15 655

Minimum price moves for all futures and options 0.01
*Monthly volumes for September 1995, compiled by Reuters
 Daytime LIFFE trading is by open outcry.
**APT is Automated Pit Trading.

9

Canada

The bond market was generous to Canada in the 1980s. It was the decade of unraisable taxes and incurable welfare spending in most developed countries, and Canadian governments were not alone in letting the public debt to GDP ratio ratchet up: their companions included the leaders of the United States, Japan, Italy and Sweden. Canada's liquid bond market helped attract funding for its government deficits. Its government bonds offer a convenient high-yielding alternative for US investors, mirroring many of the features of US Treasuries. Canada was a low-risk alternative in the 1980s, too. It plays a leading role in international affairs as a member of the Group of Seven nations, it is rich in natural resources and its post-war prosperity seemed to underpin its political stability. The market tended to overlook Canada's separatist tensions after the predominantly French-speaking province of Quebec rejected independence in a 1980 referendum. Investors helped Canada's net debt interest payments to balloon to 5.2 per cent of GDP in 1991 from 1.9 per cent in 1980. Its gross debt to GDP ratio rose during the decade to 80.4 per cent from 44.3 per cent and was over 95 per cent by 1994.[1]

But by the early 1990s, investors were starting to pass some harsh judgements on the big government debtors. The United States and Japan were protected by the size of their economies and by their reserve currency status. But Canada's population of just under 30 million was relying increasingly heavily on foreigners to finance a high standard of living, via twin budget and current account deficits. Canada's household savings ratio, the second highest among the G7 nations in 1982 at just over 18 per cent, was falling steadily: it hit 7.9 per cent in 1994.[1] Canada's federal system has empowered its provinces to tap the Euromarkets, extensively in some cases, pushing the net public external debt to exports' ratio above 100 per cent by 1991.[2] With its economy heavily dependent on US direct investment, the outflow of dividends and interest payments now leaves Canada with the biggest current account deficit in relation to GDP among the G7.[1] And Quebecois nationalism will not go away. In 1980, Quebec voters rejected independence by a margin of nearly 20 per cent. In October 1995, they rejected separatism again, but this time the margin was just 1 per cent. Canada remained intact thanks to 52 000 votes.

The referendum threw unwelcome light onto the debt burden which an independent Quebec and a truncated Canada would have to carve up between them. By 1995, even Canadian voters had begun to agree that austerity was the best policy. Federal and, in some cases, provincial governments were winning mandates to curb spending and sell off state-owned utilities. But the process added to the challenge of defining a national identity in the face of Quebec's separatist demands. For many Canadians, their generous welfare system—notably free, universal health care—symbolises the cultural distinction between their country and the United States. Spending cuts threaten Canada's tradition of capitalism tempered with compassion. Besides, welfare helped to bind together the federal and provincial governments in the task of providing nationwide services: any erosion of common health care standards, for instance, could also erode federal loyalties.

By the end of 1995, foreign investors could be forgiven for doubting the depth of federal loyalties in the world's second-largest country. The rapid increase in the scale of the country's debt burden must claim primary responsibility for the lowering of Canada's credit ratings and the raising of its real yields in recent years. But the constitutional deadlock over the relationship between Quebec, the federal government and the other provinces has not helped. Years of inter-provincial squabbling have roused an awareness that Canada's roots as a nation are shallower than those of the rest of the G7.

VIVE LE QUEBEC LIBRE?

The differences between English- and French-speaking Canadians start with the date when colonisation began. For the English, it was 1497; for the French, 1534. But it was the French who built the first major settlements at Montreal and Quebec City. British incursions were sporadic until Anglo-French colonial rivalry intensified in the mid-18th century. Britain seized Quebec, aiming to secure Canada's fur and fish trade and to safeguard its American colonies to the south. Just two decades later, America declared independence. Quebec was invaded again, this time by British loyalist refugees. Economic depression sparked popular revolts in English- as well as French-speaking areas in 1837, but in Quebec, a second defeat by British troops left particularly bitter memories. However, fears of conquest by the United States helped to persuade Quebec's politicians to join New Brunswick, Nova Scotia and the core of Ontario in forming the Confederation of Canada, a self-governing British dominion, in 1867. It took another 80 years to complete the federation of Canada: Newfoundland remained aloof until 1949. Railways helped to unite the rest of the country under European rule, encouraging settlement and creating a nation-sized debt burden. The expansion revealed a wealth of natural resources. Industrialisation had begun by the time of confederation, with many of the early factories sited in Quebec. But two sources of tension have persisted: Canada's relationship with the United States; and Quebec's relationship with the rest of Canada.

Canada's major internal squabbles over its relationship with the United States are more than a century old. The central issue, arguably resolved by the union of Canada, Mexico and the United States in the North American Free Trade Area (NAFTA) in 1994, is Canada's economic dependence. NAFTA seems to have consolidated Canada's status as a 'branch-plant' economy, heavily dependent on US direct investment. The secondary issue, which surfaces whenever the western provinces are particularly fed up with Quebec, is Canada's political independence. Some westerners threaten to line up behind Puerto Ricans in the queue for US citizenship if Quebec chops the heart out of Canada.

The cultural differences between the Quebecois and the later colonists were accentuated by the French-speakers' tendency to stay at home, leaving the British to win the Canadian west. There is a religious divide, too: Quebec is mostly Catholic, the rest of Canada mainly Protestant. Since 1867, Anglo-French tensions have flared over issues ranging from educational choices over religion and language to attempts to conscript young Quebecois to fight alongside British troops in two world wars. Separatism finally grabbed international attention in Canada's centenary year, through an unlikely alliance between the radical youth culture of the 1960s and France's right-wing president General Charles de Gaulle. Invited to Montreal by a nationalist provincial government in 1967, de Gaulle rocked English-speaking Canada by proclaiming to the crowds, '*Vive le Quebec libre*'!

Canada reacted by electing a dynamic, bilingual federalist, Pierre Trudeau, as its prime minister. Quebec, too, elected his Liberal Party to provincial power. In 1969, Trudeau made Canada officially bilingual as part of his strategy to hold the nation together. But Montreal youths were talking revolution and in 1970 a Front de Liberation du Quebec kidnapped a British diplomat and a provincial minister. When young radicals at mass rallies chanted their adulation for the kidnappers, Trudeau called it an insurrection, suspended civil liberties and sent in the army. The diplomat was rescued, the minister found murdered. Opinion polls at the time showed overwhelming support throughout Canada, including Quebec, for Trudeau's unprecedented crackdown.

Longer-term, support grew for a new Parti Quebecois. It won provincial power in 1976, ordered businesses to display their names in French only, and called a referendum in 1980 on what it called 'sovereignty-association', under which Quebec would become politically independent while retaining close economic ties with the rest of Canada. Trudeau promised constitutional reform in return for a 'No' vote and was rewarded with a turnout of 88 per cent and a 59.5 per cent rejection of the separatist proposal. But Canadian prime ministers had been thwarted for decades in their efforts to get all of the country's 10 provinces to agree an updated constitution. Trudeau was no exception. He did get nine provinces to accept a compromise, the 1982 Constitution Act. The British parliament approved it, ending an anachronism under which it had been responsible for Canadian constitutional change. Quebec refused to sign.

For three years from 1987, Progressive Conservative Prime Minister Brian Mulroney tried again. His Meech Lake accord would have met Quebec's demand for power to preserve and promote its 'distinct society'. Mulroney got initial agreement from all 10 provincial premiers. Then public protest broke out. Many Canadians feared the accord, which offered more powers to all the provinces, would weaken the federal government so much that it would lead to the country's disintegration. The constitutional wrangles also infuriated Canada's indigenous people, especially the Indians in Quebec, who protested that their rights were being trampled. Manitoba and Newfoundland refused to ratify the Meech Lake accord and it died in 1990.

The accord's opponents took a grim satisfaction in watching Quebec call in Canadian troops a few weeks later to quell protests by Mohawk Indians claiming land rights. But since then other provinces, too, have been on the receiving end of growing militancy among Canada's half-million Indians, as cuts in native affairs budgets have sharpened resentment at the constitutional impasse over their claims to autonomy.

Mulroney did not give up on Quebec. In 1992 he offered the Charlottetown accord, which would have guaranteed the province a quarter of the seats in Canada's House of Commons (lower house of parliament), reformed the Senate (upper house) and recognised aboriginal rights to self-government. This package was rejected in a national referendum by 54 to 46 per cent. In 1993, Mulroney stood down and one of the most devastating defeats in electoral history left his party with just two seats in parliament. That election also gave Canada a separatist party as its official parliamentary opposition: the Bloc Quebecois, led by Lucien Bouchard, one of Mulroney's former ministers and a charismatic orator. In 1994, the Parti Quebecois under Jacques Parizeau won provincial power and called the 1995 referendum on independence. Voters, 82 per cent of them claiming French as their first language, were asked, 'Do you agree that Quebec should become sovereign, after having made a formal offer to Canada for a new economic and political partnership?'

The implications of sovereignty

In contrast with his predecessor Pierre Trudeau, Canada's Liberal Prime Minister Jean Chretien at first refused to promise any constitutional rewards to Quebec in return for a 'No' vote. Instead he called sovereignty a one-way ticket out of Canada. Most Canadians believed him, but the campaign revealed a gulf in expectations between them and Quebec's voters. Polls showed that most people in Quebec believed that an independent Quebec could continue to share the Canadian dollar and would reach some form of agreement on sharing out the federal debt burden. Canadians outside Quebec thought all this was highly unlikely. They opposed Quebec's separation and were split on whether a sovereign Quebec should be allowed to forge a new economic partnership with their provinces. But as separatist support surged and Canadian complacency eroded in the last weeks of the referendum campaign, the government began to talk again of constitutional concessions.

For Canada, Quebec's departure would be a geographical disaster. Ontario and the other provinces to the west would be severed from the eastern Maritime provinces, which would also be separated from each other if Quebec held onto its St Lawrence estuary coastline. Separatism, or annexation by the United States, might be a more attractive option for the western provinces than domination by Ontario in a truncated Canada. Cree Indians and Inuits would demand that the boundaries of an independent Quebec should be redrawn to exclude their traditional hunting grounds to the north. This would not be much use as a geographical link for the rest of Canada, whose population is concentrated in the south, along the US border. But the indigenous people's land claims would disrupt the activities of the heavily indebted Hydro-Quebec electricity company, which the Indians say is devastating their environment.

Quebec's economy is quite big enough for statehood—its gross domestic product was estimated during the run-up to the referendum at C$165 billion, comparable to that of Denmark. But its debt burden at independence would be crippling. Some studies suggested Quebec should take on about 23 per cent, or C$133 billion, of Canada's net direct federal debt, reflecting its share of the population and of the economy. The Conseil du Patronat, Quebec's largest employer group, said in that case the independent province would have been liable for debt totalling C$280 billion at 31 March 1996. The separatists' calculations, giving Quebec a 17 per cent share of federal liabilities, would still have debited the new state with C$156 billion, high enough to raise a serious risk of default. Inevitably, the two sides disputed the scale of the province's existing debt burden, but Moody's projected Quebec's net direct and guaranteed debt for 1996 at C\$83.4 billion, excluding wholly provincially owned Hydro-Quebec, whose long-term debt in 1994 was C\$37.7 billion.[10] Foreign investor confidence is critical for servicing costs. The Patronat said that in 1993, about 40 per cent of Quebec's debt and more than half of Hydro's was held by foreign investors.

An independent Quebec would depend for its survival on uninterrupted trade with Canada and the United States. The separatists sought assurances from the United States that an independent Quebec could remain part of NAFTA: they received none. However, mutual economic dependence would probably force the rest of Canada to be conciliatory towards Quebec if separation ever happened.

The implications for market sentiment

Analysts outside Quebec suggested before the 1995 referendum that a 10-point margin of victory for the 'No' lobby would be enough to settle the market's nerves for at least 10 years. Opinion pollsters and political and financial analysts in Montreal cautioned all along that this was over-optimistic. In the event, 93 per cent of voters turned out for the referendum and of these, 49.44 per cent voted for divorce negotiations. Separatists promptly began preparing for a third referendum. Their chances of victory next time are enhanced by the likelihood that some of those who voted 'No' in 1995 will decide to move out of the province.

Meanwhile, the rest of Canada will have to try yet again to persuade Quebec to sign a common constitution. Quite apart from the federalist urge to do something in response to the referendum vote, Canada is obliged to review its 1982 constitution in 1997. This will ensure that the Quebec issue crops up often enough to have a major impact on bond market sentiment. And if the cliffhanger vote of 1995 scares Anglo-Canadians into recognising Quebec's claims to be a 'distinct society', Indians and Inuits will have ample grounds for pressing their claims to land and self-rule. There could be years of hard bargaining ahead, during which the Canadian bond market will be vulnerable to periodic surges of support for separatism and to continual uncertainty over whether Quebec will ever sign the country's constitution.

POLITICS AND PROVINCIAL DEBT

The British monarch is Canada's head of state and is represented by a governor-general, appointed on the advice of the Canadian prime minister. In practice the House of Commons (lower house of parliament) is sovereign. Its 295 members are elected on a first-past-the-post basis for a maximum five-year term. The Senate, the upper house, has up to 112 members who are appointed by federal governments for life. The Senate has limited powers.

Canada's 10 provinces have their own premiers, chosen by elected, single-chamber legislative assemblies which also serve five-year terms. The provinces share with the federal government the cost of national schemes for health, welfare and tertiary education. They have considerable powers to raise taxes and loans on their own accounts. Ontario, the most populous, is the biggest non-sovereign borrower in international capital markets.[3] An equalisation programme transfers funds via the federal budget to Canada's poorer provinces, notably Quebec.

Since 1867, federal power has alternated between Liberals and Conservatives, who renamed themselves Progressive Conservatives during World War II. But these parties have often been rendered irrelevant in provincial elections. A left-wing grouping, founded in 1932 during the Great Depression and renamed the New Democratic Party in 1961, has won power at different times in most of the provinces, although never at federal level. Quebec has always had its own French-speakers' party. West of Ontario, a peculiarly Canadian form of radical populism was born during the Depression years. Called Social Credit, it mixed opposition to both socialism and the banking system with ideas such as giving consumers more purchasing power and spending on major public works. It evolved towards a more orthodox populist conservatism, now represented nationally by the Reform Party which swept British Columbia, Alberta, Saskatchewan and Manitoba in the 1993 federal election.

The Reform Party is the most radical cost-cutter among the parties now vying to halt the country's debt spiral. It opposes any special status for Quebec and, with only two fewer seats in the national parliament than the Bloc Quebecois, proclaims itself the true federal opposition. For opposite reasons, the Reform Party and the Quebec separatists ensured the defeat of the 1992 plan for constitutional change.

The Reform Party approves of Alberta's Progressive Conservative government which, elected in 1993, has eliminated the provincial deficit—albeit with the aid of oil and gas revenues. Alberta has broken with the principles of Canada's national health insurance scheme to offer faster treatment for patients prepared to pay. Ontario's Conservative government, elected in 1995, plans to privatise Ontario Hydro, a huge power utility which has amassed debts of C$32 billion, and has promised to eliminate the budget deficit by the year 2000. Ontario accounts for about 40 per cent of Canada's GDP. Conservatives were also re-elected in Manitoba in 1995, with a mandate to balance the budget and to cut provincial ministers' salaries if they slipped into deficit.

The Liberals won New Brunswick in 1995 and the other three Atlantic provinces, Nova Scotia, Newfoundland and Prince Edward Island in 1993. They have balanced budgets or narrowed deficits in all these states. The New Democrat Party, which formed a powerful lobby for the creation of Canada's federal welfare programmes, has lost a lot of ground in the cost-cutting 1990s, winning just nine seats in the 1993 federal election. However, it was re-elected in Saskatchewan in 1995 and is due to seek another term in British Columbia by May 1996. It, too, has cut deficits significantly, antagonising some of its trade-union supporters in the process.

In late 1995, Moody's Investors Services estimated provincial budget deficits in 1995–6 would total about C$13 billion, some C$2.5 billion less than the previous year and well below the record C$25.6 billion of 1992–3. But, Moody's added, 'the progress has been uneven with the improvement being much more moderate in the two largest provinces, Quebec and Ontario'.

CANADA'S BUDGET

The federal government estimates its net debt for the end of the fiscal year 1995–6 at C$579 billion. The government estimates this will rise to C$603 billion in 1996–7 and C$620 billion in 1997–8, about 74 per cent of GDP. The OECD estimates gross debt to GDP at 97.3 per cent in 1995 and 1996.[1]

With debt servicing costs accounting for over a third of federal government revenue, the Liberal government has been forced to start selling state enterprises, notably a C$1.7 billion stake in Petro-Canada. This cuts its ownership of the company, which was founded to protect the country's oil industry from US domination, to 20 per cent. The equally emotive sale of the historic Canadian National railway company in November 1995 raised C$2 billion. Other potential candidates for what the government preferred to call 'commercialisation', rather than privatisation, included the airports, the St Lawrence Seaway, a stake in the Hibernia oil field off the east coast and Atomic Energy of Canada.

Canada's fiscal year runs from 1 April. By the time the 1996–7 budget was announced, it looked as if structural spending cuts initiated in the previous budget had been effective in curbing the deficit to C$32.7 billion, or 4.2 per cent of GDP, in 1995-6, from 5.1 per cent in 1994–5. The goal for 1996–7 was 3 per cent, which would be the lowest ratio for more than 20 years, and 2 per cent in 1997–8 (see Table 8.1). The ultimate aim was to balance the budget but the government declined to set itself a deadline for that. The 1995 cuts will mean the loss of about 45 000 jobs, 14 per cent of federal employment. The 1995–6 budget left untouched the equalisation programme, which benefits lower-income provinces and which has been renewed to the year 2000. However, the government announced plans to lump other transfers to the provinces, for health, welfare and tertiary education, into a single block grant in 1996–7 and to cut the total. It also cut subsidies to business and agriculture. Economists and ratings agencies approved of the gradual deficit reduction but said there was no room for government complacency, pointing out that the absolute debt level was still rising, albeit much more slowly than in the early 1990s.

Table 8.1   Fiscal Outlook from 1996–7 budget (C$ billion)

	1995–6	1996–7	1997–8
Revenue	130.6	135.0	141.0
Total spending	160.8	156.8	155.0
of which Public-Debt Charges	47.0	47.8	49.0
Deficit	32.7	24.3	17.0
Financing Requirement	20.0	13.7	6.0
Deficit as percentage of GDP	4.2	3.0	2.0

ECONOMY

In 1991 the government and the Bank of Canada agreed to bring inflation to the midpoint of a target band of 1–3 per cent by the end of 1995. This target band has since been extended to the end of 1998, using an underlying measure of consumer prices excluding food, energy and the effects of indirect tax changes. It hit the target early, by 1992. Underlying inflation in 1994 was 1.8 per cent but it nudged as high as 2.7 per cent year-on-year during 1995. The Bank said in early 1996 that it expected core inflation to move back to the midpoint of the target range in coming months. Noting improved productivity and low wage growth, it thought Canada would share the benefits of moderate growth and low inflation in the United States during 1996.

Headline inflation in Canada has been more volatile since the government gave up a vain battle to tax cigarettes more heavily than the United States in 1994. This cut headline inflation to just 0.1 per cent that year, then flung the total consumer price index back above 2 per cent in early 1995 as the tobacco tax effect fell out.

The economy grew rapidly in 1994, helped by a boom in exports generated largely by the sharp fall in the external value of the Canadian dollar during the 1990s. Membership of NAFTA helped, accelerating economic deregulation, as did strong growth in the United States, which accounts for more than 80 per cent of Canada's merchandise exports. The trade boom helped to narrow Canada's current account deficit to C$13.1 billion in 1995, the lowest in 10 years. However, domestic growth slowed in 1995, partly because the Bank of Canada had to tighten sharply in

Table 8.2 Canadian Government Forecasts, 1996–7 Budget, per cent

	1995	1996	1997
Real GDP growth	2.2	1.8	2.6
10-year government bond yield (average)	8.2	7.7	8.2
91-day Treasury bill rate (average)	7.0	5.8	6.6

Note: All figures estimated except 1995 average interest rates. Estimated interest rates are higher than private sector forecasts, adding 'prudence factors' of 0.5 point in 1996 and 0.8 point in 1997. The government says this is partly to allow for the risk of revived separatist debate, especially in 1997.

January and February to defend the Canadian dollar when Mexico's crisis revived foreign concerns about Canada's debt and political uncertainties. The IMF calculated that the Canadian dollar depreciated by 25 per cent between 1990 and early 1995 in real terms.[6]

THE BANK OF CANADA

The Bank of Canada was set up to bolster the country's independence from the United States rather than out of any purely economic necessity. The country had experienced little of the financial turbulence which spurred the creation of the US Federal Reserve system: the Canadian banking culture was far more conservative. The banks ran their own clearing system and the government discounted securities for them when necessary, untroubled by any ideas about controlling the money supply. What shocked the government into calling for a central bank was the discovery, prompted by Britain's suspension of the gold standard in 1931, that Canada's transactions with London had to be made via New York. The new bank, which began its operations in 1935, was modelled to a large extent on the Bank of England, which encouraged its creation.

The Bank of Canada Act, approved by parliament amid the Depression, required the new institution

> to regulate credit and currency in the best interests of the economic life of the nation, to control and protect the external value of the national monetary unit and to mitigate by its influence fluctuations in the general level of production, trade, prices and employment, so far as may be possible within the scope of monetary action, and generally to promote the economic and financial welfare of the dominion.

The Bank was located in Ottawa rather than upsetting one of the two rival financial centres, Montreal and Toronto, and was set up under private ownership, but a change of government led to its nationalisation by 1938. Its governor is appointed by the government for a seven-year term. The current governor, Gordon Thiessen, was appointed in 1994.

World War II helped to elevate Canada to the status of a major player on the international economic scene. A war-time boom in employment and manufacturing developed its economy and it was able to lend heavily to Britain and other Allied countries to help in post-war reconstruction. Its officials mediated between the United States and Britain in the Bretton Woods agreement and in the setting-up of the International Monetary Fund and the World Bank; and Canada lobbied for the trade liberalisation which led to the first General Agreement on Tariffs and Trade in 1948.

The Bank of Canada Act had left it far from clear how independent the Bank was meant to be. In any case, for the first 20 years of its existence the central bank had few weapons for enforcing monetary policy because there was no domestic money market. It took dogged effort to wean Canadian banks off their dependence on the New York money market. After a sustained campaign of reforms by the Bank of Canada, a Canadian money market finally sputtered into life in 1954. With the conditions finally in place for the Bank to pursue a more active monetary policy, a new bank governor, James Coyne, sought to keep a tight rein on the money supply. From 1957 Coyne found himself at odds with a high-spending Conservative government. Their conflict became public when C\$6.4 billion in war bonds matured and Coyne urged a higher coupon for the refunding than the government was willing to pay. Coyne quit in 1961.

The issue of the Bank of Canada's independence was not resolved until 1967, when the Act was revised to enable the finance minister to give the governor a detailed written directive, covering a specified period, in the event of any disagreement over monetary policy. However, monetary economists regard the publicity involved in such a procedure as a deterrent to government intervention[4] and the provision has never been used. In practice Canada's inflation record has been relatively good: far better than that of Australia or the UK and only a little worse than that of the United States.[5]

WHAT MOTIVATES MONETARY POLICY MOVES

The exchange rate plays a leading role in Canadian monetary policy, thanks to the country's twin dependence on world demand for commodities and on US demand for manufactured goods. The money market often pushes the crucial overnight rate up or down in direct reaction to a rise or fall in the external value of the Canadian dollar. The Bank of Canada constructs a Monetary Conditions Index (MCI) which gives a shorthand measure of the combined impact of short-term interest rates and the exchange rate. This helps the Bank to decide whether it needs to adjust monetary policy in order to pursue its 1–3 per cent target range for inflation.

The MCI uses the 90-day commercial paper rate and the trade-weighted exchange rate against the Group of 10 leading industrialised countries. It gives a higher weighting to the interest rate, judging a one-point change in interest rates to have much the same impact on the economy as a three-point change in the exchange rate. The nominal level of the MCI does not matter: the index is just a way of tracking the trend in monetary conditions. The Bank says it

> does not try to maintain a precise MCI level by adjusting interest rates in response to every exchange rate wiggle . . . In addition, there are occasions when Bank actions cannot be devoted to achieving the desired MCI because of the need to cope temporarily with disorderly markets.[8]

The Bank also studies the output gap, which tries to measure the difference between actual and potential economic growth. The idea is that as the actual growth rate rises close to the potential rate, supply bottlenecks start to drive prices up. However, measuring potential output is an inexact science. The Bank says its approach, focusing on factors including labour supply, unemployment, real wages and productivity, tries to incorporate more information than most conventional methods. But it acknowledges there is still a wide potential margin of error in its calculations.

It monitors several other indicators to try to gauge inflationary pressures. It has to watch demand trends in the United States closely. It follows the expectations which are influencing Canadian prices and wages through the Conference Board of Canada's Quarterly Survey of Forecasters; and it follows financial markets' inflation expectations by comparing the 30-year yields on the government's conventional and index-linked real return bonds.[9] It also watches two money supply measures: M2-plus for forecasting inflation one or two quarters ahead and real M1 for forecasting output growth.

HOW MONETARY POLICY IS IMPLEMENTED

The Bank of Canada wields its influence over the money market mainly via the overnight call loan rate. When turbulence hit bond markets in 1994, the Bank sought to increase the effectiveness of its monetary policy by announcing target ranges, usually about a half-point wide, for the overnight rate. This range has fluctuated sharply, reflecting Canada's economic exposure. The Bank cut the overnight rate target range three times in mid-1994, only to have to start tightening again in November. It changed the range no less than 14 times in 1995, raising it five times during January and February to a peak of 7.75–8.25 per cent, mainly to try to calm markets unnerved by the Mexican currency crisis. However, by early 1996 the range had eased to 5–5.5 per cent, with the help of US rate cuts. The Canadian dollar tends to become very vulnerable if short-term spreads with the United States dip into negative territory.

The Bank has two mechanisms it can use to encourage or deter market pressure to raise or lower the overnight rate. It can control the supply of money to 12 major credit institutions for their final daily settlements, forcing them to borrow or encouraging them to lend overnight; and it can reinforce or temper the message by using overnight repos. Sometimes it also intervenes to influence the result of the weekly three-month T-bill tender, through outright sales or purchases in the cash T-bill market. But it prefers to rely mainly on its control of settlement balances, viewing this mechanism as leaving most scope to market forces.

The overnight rate affects other rates because money-market dealers usually finance their inventories using overnight funds. The Bank Rate, the overdraft rate which the central bank rate charges the 12 direct clearing institutions, used to be linked to the weekly three-month T-bill tender rate, but since February 1996 it has been pegged to the top of the overnight rate target range. The T-bill is likely to remain an important trigger and guide for Bank action. If short-term rates are falling faster than the Bank wants, it may push the overnight rate above the three-month rate to deter speculative purchases of T-bills using one-day funds. If short-term rates are rising against the Bank's wishes, it will add liquidity to bring the overnight rate below the three-month T-bill rate.

The Bank does most of its fine-tuning through the drawdown/ redeposit mechanism. This gives the Bank a retroactive power to withdraw or redeposit funds from the accounts which the federal government holds with the 12 direct clearing institutions. The Bank can withdraw funds from this inner circle, reducing the cash available for overnight loans, when it wants to push the overnight rate up, and it can give the clearers extra funds to lend when it wants the overnight rate to ease.

The system works, despite the fact that Canada has now abolished reserve requirements as an unnecessary tax on banks, because the direct clearers still keep accounts with the central bank for settlement purposes. They will try to keep that amount to a minimum because the Bank pays them no interest on their balances. Every night, it assesses the clearers' expectations to see if the pool of settlement funds which they will share the following day will be the right size to keep the overnight rate within the target range. On the following morning the Bank will shift funds between the government's accounts with itself and with the clearers—but with effect from the previous night. This keeps the direct clearers guessing overnight as to whether they have enough money to meet the next day's settlement needs and provides the Bank with the power to surprise that enables it to keep the overnight rate on track.

The Bank of Canada is unusual in that the drawdown/redeposit mechanism is the only tool it uses to add or drain liquidity. It intervenes on the open market purely in order to demonstrate the interest rate it thinks appropriate: it neutralises the liquidity effects of these operations. In fact, a lot of the funds that it shifts through the drawdown/redeposit mechanism have no monetary policy purpose except to offset open market and other official transactions. This makes the daily drawdown/redeposit figures hard to interpret.

There are more clues in the foreign-currency swap deals detailed in the Bank's balance sheet, published every Wednesday. If the Bank wants to add liquidity, it will buy foreign-currency assets from the government's Exchange Fund Account, with a commitment to sell the assets back at a future date; meanwhile it credits the government's account with the purchase money, which it then redeposits with the clearers. If the Bank wants to drain liquidity, it withdraws these deposits and reverses the swaps. If the balance sheet shows higher net foreign currency sales commitments, the Bank has been easing, while a smaller net figure suggests it has been tightening.

Although reserve requirements have been scrapped, the direct clearing institutions have to keep their settlement accounts on average at zero or in credit. They can get overdrafts from the Bank, at the Bank Rate, but these funds are not counted in calculating their average settlement balances. The averaging period is the four or five weeks up to the third Wednesday of each month. The clearers are charged the equivalent of a one-day loan at the Bank Rate on any negative overall balance. A bigger deterrent to going overdrawn too often is the risk of rumours of liquidity problems.

If the overnight rate looks like straying from the target range, then the Bank can use overnight reverse repos or repos to nudge the rate back on track. It uses the reverse repos, SRAs (Sale and Repurchase Agreements), to set the floor; sometimes just the offer of these sends a strong enough message to halt a fall in market rates. It offers SPRAs (Special Purchase and Resale Agreements) to set a ceiling for rates. These repos are known as 'specials' to distinguish them from PRAs, the regular repos which the Bank offers to finance the inventories of the jobbers. A senior bank official[7] has cautioned against reading too much into open market operations in isolation, saying, 'Open market operations are used to complement and often to moderate the impact of the drawdown/deposit mechanism.'

THE T-BILL MARKET

The T-bill rate has had a crucial but indirect signalling role in Canadian monetary policy, thanks partly to its former link with the Bank Rate. Sometimes when the market has driven rates too fast, the Bank has bought or sold T-bills, outright and publicly, through the jobbers. The jobbers are market-makers, committed to making firm two-way quotes in Treasury bills.

Canadian T-bill issuance multiplied during the 1980s as the federal government relied on them increasingly for funding. If the government exceeds the limit for new financing set by parliament in the annual Borrowing Authority Act, it has to fall back on T-bills of six-month terms or shorter. As the volume of T-bills has grown, the proportion held by banks has fallen, while foreign interest has grown sharply, to 13 per cent in the early 1990s. Canadian individuals and small businesses also greatly increased their holdings during the 1980s, although some of these investments were diverted into money-market mutual funds during the early 1990s, when payments from these funds lagged declining short-term interest rates.

Canada has an active when-issued market, where forward contracts in the following week's T-bills start trading as soon as the details of the next auction are announced.

The Bank of Canada auctions three-, six- and 12-month T-bills every Tuesday, with settlement on Thursdays. The one-year bills are issued in two successive tranches to ensure liquidity, with the first tranche dated 364 days and the second 357 days so that the bills become interchangeable. Banks, investment dealers and the central bank all submit competitive bids on a yield basis, electronically, by 12:30 Toronto time on Tuesdays. The Finance Ministry has the right to reject bids. At 14:00, the Bank announces the results and the amounts to be sold next week. The auctions are US-style: the bidders pay what they bid; those who bid the lowest yields get the first shares of the allotment; and those who bid the highest accepted yield—the cut-off yield—often get only a proportion of the bills they sought. The Bank also holds ad hoc tenders to meet government cash needs, issuing bills with an irregular term whose maturity date will match that of a regular issue. It buys bills at auction itself, usually aiming to make neutral bids and to acquire the paper it needs for open market operations. If it wants to adjust the maturity profile of its portfolio, it will usually do so through switches, buying and selling offsetting amounts of T-bills of different maturities. These operations have no monetary policy implications. However, sometimes the Bank will use the auction to try to slow a rise in market interest rates, by bidding at below-average yields.

Three-month T-bill rates fell to 20-year lows of less than 4 per cent in January 1994, with a spread of less than one point over the

United States. But rates soared to more than 8 per cent a year later, with the spread widening to more than two points. After the Quebec referendum, rates eased to around 5.25 per cent by March 1996.

GOVERNMENT SECURITIES

At the start of 1995, Canadian government securities outstanding totalled C$435.2 billion (see Table 8.3). More than a third of these were Treasury bills. Bond maturities extend to 30 years. The Bank of Canada put bond redemptions due in calendar 1995 at C$14.1 billion and at C$28.9 billion for 1996.

The total had risen to C$463.39 billion by the end of January 1996, the Finance Department said. US Pay instruments are US-dollar denominated and used to replenish foreign exchange reserves to defend the Canadian dollar. Foreign-currency-denominated debt also includes two US dollar global bonds issued in 1995, a $1.5 billion five-year issue in May and another $1.5 billion in July.

The government has issued some Canadian dollar bonds which it had the right to redeem early, but only one small issue is still in existence. It has purchase funds for some other bonds to enable it to buy back some of these issues on the open market. Canada also issues real return bonds, which are linked to the consumer price index. Interest is calculated on the principal sum adjusted for inflation to date, and a lump sum to compensate for inflation throughout the bond's life is paid along with the nominal principal

Table 8.3 Government Securities Outstanding at 1 January 1995 (C$ billion)

Treasury Bills	159.55
Marketable bonds	226.19
US Pay—Canada Bills	5.65
US Pay—Notes, Bonds	7.89
(Non-marketable bonds)	
Canada Savings Bonds	32.42
Issued to Official Pension Fund	3.49
Total	435.19

at maturity. Apart from these index-linked bonds, Canadian government bonds pay fixed-rate coupons semi-annually. The Bank of Canada uses swaps where necessary to enable the government to receive fixed-rate interest and pay floating rates at a spread below the three-month Canadian Bankers' Acceptance rate. The Bank publishes details of these swaps, whose notional value totalled C$7.08 billion at 1 January 1995.

THE PRIMARY BOND MARKET

Canada has issued all its marketable bonds by auction since 1992. It publishes quarterly calendars giving auction and settlement dates, amounts maturing and the maturity of each issue. It gives other details, including the size of the issue, a week before the auction. It focuses issuance on benchmark two-, five-, 10- and 30-year bonds.

The Bank of Canada administers the primary market on behalf of the Department of Finance. The primary distributors, a syndicate of investment dealers and banks, are eligible to bid at bill and bond auctions and to trade with the central bank. The dominant group among them are the jobbers, who are obliged to provide firm two-way quotes for both bonds and bills; to ensure between them that auctions are covered; and to give the bank feedback on market conditions. The jobbers play a central role in monetary policy operations. They have dedicated phone lines to the central bank and access to its repos. Jobbing companies which are investment dealers can finance their inventories through regular repos; bank jobbers cannot, on the grounds that they already have overdraft facilities with the central bank. All jobbers can take part in 'special' repos which the central bank initiates, often in order to give a monetary policy signal. Investment dealer jobbers have to belong to the Investment Dealers Association of Canada. Bank jobbers are supervised by the Office of the Superintendent of Financial Institutions.

THE SECONDARY BOND MARKET

Canada was among the first countries to drop capital controls when the Bretton Woods exchange rate system collapsed in 1973, and its government bonds are unusually liquid for a relatively high-yielding market. However, it has proved harder to build up liquidity in exchange-traded bond derivatives, and bond options are mostly traded over-the-counter. Foreigners hold nearly 30 per cent of Canadian government debt. The 10-year spread over US surged above 200 basis points at the height of the 1994 bear market from a low of a half-point in 1992.

OUTLOOK

Quebec's 1995 referendum has ensured that investing in Canadian bonds is no longer a simple play on how a commodity-based economy performs through the economic cycle. This is not to suggest that economic factors will now play a secondary role in influencing market sentiment. In fact, any resurgence of the risk that Canada's debt burden may have to be reallocated at some point tends to intensify the bond market's scrutiny of the country's track record on inflation, the current account deficit and provincial and federal budget deficits. However, the Quebec factor will greatly enhance the rewards of investors skilful—and lucky—enough to go long of Canada when federalist morale is low and to take profits as it peaks.

NOTES

1. *OECD Economic Outlook*, 58, December 1995.
2. Standard & Poor's Corporation.
3. Economist Intelligence Unit.
4. Stanley Fischer, 'Modern Central Banking', in *The Future of Central Banking: the Tercentenary Symposium of the Bank of England.* Cambridge University Press, Cambridge.
5. Rated in *The Central Banks*, Marjorie Deane and Robert Pringle, Hamish Hamilton, London, 1994. Twenty-year inflation rates annualised to a constant rate, 1971 to 1991. Canada's rate was 7.1 per cent, compared with 3.8 per cent for Germany (1st), 6.3 per cent for the United States (17th), 9.1 per cent for Australia (46th), 9.9 per cent for the United Kingdom (55th) and 39.9 per cent for Mexico (101st).
6. International Monetary Fund, *World Economic Outlook*, October 1995.

7. 'The implementation of monetary policy in Canada', Bruce Montador, Chief of the Securities Department, Bank of Canada, in *Canadian Public Policy*, Vol. XXI:1, 1995.
8. *Bank of Canada Monetary Policy Report*, May 1995.
9. See Chapter 6 for more details on index-linked bonds.
10. *Sovereigns, Supranationals Credit Opinions*, Moody's Investors Service Global Credit Research, September 1995.

APPENDICES

Box 1—Ratings

Standard & Poor's rates Canada's domestic debt AAA with a stable outlook and its foreign currency debt AA-plus with a negative outlook. After the Quebec referendum, S&P President Leo O'Neill said the ratings depend on progress in cutting deficits. He added, 'Especially with the referendum's narrow margin, how the discussion [over Quebec's concerns] is conducted is almost as important as its outcome. Canada's cost of access to international capital markets is at stake.' S&P's last formal review of Canada, in March 1995, said the ratings reflect

> Canada's diversified, export-oriented economy and wealth of resource endowments . . . weak but improving fiscal performance; moderately high net external debt position; and stable political system, despite the uncertainties associated with . . . Quebec . . . The higher local currency rating reflects the government's flexibility in taxing, its influence over monetary matters and its commitment to low inflation . . . The negative outlook on the foreign currency debt reflects the possibility of a downgrade, should the slow pace of deficit reduction fail to ease the government's debt and interest burdens over the next few years.

Moody's downgraded Canada in April 1995 to Aa2 for foreign currency and Aa1 for domestic currency debt, citing 'the sizeable portion of the fiscal debt financed by foreigners, as well as the relatively short maturity structure of the debt', as factors. In a statement after the referendum, Moody's said

> lingering constitutional uncertainties have negative implications for Canada's medium-term ratings outlook . . . The narrowness of the [federalist] victory, as well as the difficulties involved in resolving the constitutional issues facing the country, all lead towards a heightened concern regarding the federal government's ability to deal with the referendum's challenges contemporaneously with the strains inherent in any medium-term fiscal stabilisation program . . . Failure to successfully address these constitutional issues may lead to another referendum in the not-so-distant future, the results of which would be difficult to predict. In a highly-indebted country such as Canada, such heightened levels of uncertainty may create a more difficult economic and financial environment.

Box 2—Futures and options

Futures Contracts Montreal Exchange

One-month Canadian Bankers	Contract size C$3 million, minimum price move C$25
Acceptances (BAR)	Contract months: nearest six
Three-month Canadian	Contract size C$1 million, minimum price move C$25
Bankers' Acceptances (BAX)	Contract months: March/June/ September/December
10-Year Canadian	Contract size: C$100 000, minimum price move C$10
Government Bonds (CGB)	Contract months: March/June/ September/December
Five-Year Canadian	Contract size C$100 000, minimum price move C$10
Government Bonds (CGF)	Contract months: March/June/ September/December
	American-style options on:
10-year CGB Futures (OGB)	Contract size C$100 000, minimum price move C$10 Contract months: March/June/ September/December
BAX Futures (OGB)	Contract size C$1 million, minimum price move C$25 Contract months: nearest four BAX contracts

Trading hours: 08:20–15:00 local time

The Chicago Board of Trade offers similar futures and options contracts on 10-year Canadian government bonds, trading at the same hours (07:20–14:00 local time).

10
Australia

Australia is traditionally a higher-yielding competitor to Canada among government bond markets, since both are commodity-based economies. Canada's lower yields have mainly reflected the considerable liquidity of its market, modelled closely along the lines of the neighbouring United States. Canadian yields also used to reflect higher foreign-currency credit ratings than Australia's, as well as the fact that Australia has the poorer inflation record of the two. Furthermore, Canada's economy diversified much earlier and that factor, combined with its higher diplomatic and geopolitical profile, enabled it to squeeze into the Group of Seven leading industrialised nations.

However, by 1995 rapid growth in Canadian government borrowing had changed the picture. In a major reversal, Moody's downgraded Canada's domestic currency debt to Aa1 while keeping Australia on AAA. S&P rates both countries AAA for domestic debt. Meanwhile the two countries' foreign-currency credit ratings had been moving closer and the shift in relative investor confidence helped their 10-year domestic yields to converge in the bull market of 1993. In 1994, the Australian economy took off, reviving inflation fears, and the spread moved once more into Canada's favour. However, the difference was around one point in 1995 compared with 3.5 points in the late 1980s.

The ratings revisions mainly reflect the role of federal and provincial governments in raising Canada's external debt burden to a scale similar to that which has long weighed on Australia. Australian public-sector spending has been comparatively restrained but private investment has been particularly dependent on

Table 10.1   Canadian and Australian Debt Burden Compared

	Canada		Australia	
	1995ᴾ	1994ᵉ	1995ᵉ	1994
Net external debt/exports	141.8	149.2	157.0	158.1
Net external public debt/exports	106.9	100.3	78.4	86.4

p = projected, e = estimate, exports of goods and services, plus net transfers

Source: Standard & Poor's Ratings Group

imported capital (see Table 10.1). High current-account deficits, fuelled by overseas interest payments, are now a major problem for both economies.

There are political similarities, too. Both countries are former British dominions, grappling with the twin challenges of integrating more recent waves of immigrants from other cultures and redressing the grievances of aboriginal inhabitants. But by the end of 1995, Australia looked a lot more stable than Canada. Despite a surge in Australian inflation, the nominal 10-year spread narrowed to around 75 basis points in late October as Canadian bondholders began to fear that French-speaking separatists might win a referendum in Quebec province.

After the separatists lost the vote, the Australian market felt bearish as the nominal spread over Canada shot back out above 110 basis points. However, the Quebec separatists' margin of defeat had been just one percentage point and they were vowing to try again. A closer look revealed that, in real terms, Australian bonds were doing surprisingly well. Consumer prices were rising 5.1 per cent year-on-year in Australia, against just 2.3 per cent in Canada. On a current basis, Australian real yields were nearly two points below Canada's, suggesting that Australia retained the political advantage.

POLITICS

Australia was the last great landmass to be colonised by Europeans, in the late 18th century. British settlement of the island, much of it desert and semi-desert, was haphazard, with limited communications between the six states: New South Wales, Queensland, Victoria, South Australia, Tasmania and Western Australia. When the states united as the Commonwealth of Australia in 1901, they conceded only limited federal powers. Each of the states, regardless of population, sends 12 representatives to the Senate,[2] which can reject legislation passed by the nationally elected lower house of the **Commonwealth parliament**. All the states have their own parliaments and have tapped the Euro-markets in their own right. Elections for the 148-seat House of Representatives must be held at least every three years. Senate elections are also held every three years. Senators have a six-year term, half retiring at each election. Voting is compulsory in Australia. A general election took place in March 1996. There is a complicated preferential electoral system.

For much of the 20th century, Australian governments resisted any form of identification with **Asia**, clinging instead to trade ties with Britain. But World War II dislocated these loyalties. Britain made heavy calls on Australian troops, leaving Australia itself acutely vulnerable to Japanese advances and engendering a national phobia that the sparsely populated country could be invaded without knowing it. It was the United States that came to Australia's rescue and as the Cold War set in, Australia joined the US crusade against communism in Asia. Under the slogan 'populate or perish', immigration policies were relaxed to admit first East European, then Asian refugees. The population remains tiny in relation to Australia's size, about 18 million.

Australia's enhanced awareness of its Asian hinterland, which includes some of the world's fastest-growing economies, could prove crucial to its ability to restrain the current-account deficit. Australia already counts Japan as its main export market, but that trade is commodity-dominated and chronically vulnerable to the global economic cycle. The government now seeks to sell a far greater range of goods and services to Asia. But that could require some persuasive diplomacy in order to lower trade barriers with countries whose human rights records Australia has criticised in the past.

Meanwhile the British sovereign remains the country's head of state and the monarch's representative has the power to dissolve parliament. This power was used in 1975 to sack radical Labor Prime Minister Gough Whitlam after a hostile Senate held up the budget. There was no immediate popular backlash: in fact, Labor's opponents won a crushing victory in the ensuing election. But as the UK forged new trade ties in Europe at the expense of Australasian farmers, the seeds of **republicanism** spread. Former Labor prime minister, Paul Keating, defeated in the 1996 election, sought a referendum on making the country a republic as part of a campaign to galvanise Australians of British descent into recognising their Asian neighbours.

Keating's **Labor Party** is a far more pragmatic organisation than Whitlam's was. It had been in power since 1983, initially under the leadership of former trade union leader Bob Hawke. It was under Labor, not the more right-wing Coalition of the Liberal and National parties, that Australia floated its currency, reformed its bond market, cut both government spending and corporate tax and dismantled its protectionist tariff barriers. Hawke was deposed by Keating, his finance minister, amid some acrimony in 1991.

Since Keating had defended his austerity policies by telling Australians that recession was doing them good, most commentators were taken by surprise when he won election in his own right in March 1991. That victory was attributed largely to the unpopularity of a central campaign policy of the Liberal and National party **Coalition** for a general goods and services tax. Many economists believe the potential benefits of such a tax in curbing consumption, and thus easing the current-account deficit, would outweigh its inflationary impact. But neither political party was willing to risk advocating it in the 1996 election campaign. Instead the victorious Coalition, under Liberal Party leader John Howard, planned tax concessions to encourage domestic savings. The Coalition also promised radical industrial relations reforms, which trade unions threatened to resist. In foreign policy, too, there was a major shift of emphasis: the Coalition asserted that it would not let traditional ties with the United States and Europe unravel.

THE ECONOMY

Australia's central economic problem is that the cost of servicing its overseas loans outweighs any trade surplus, keeping its current balance in the red. The fact that primary and manufactured commodities make up more than 80 per cent of exports further complicates the picture, especially for bond investors. The external value of the Australian dollar is highly leveraged to commodity prices, so it will tend to strengthen, offsetting domestic inflationary pressure, during an economic boom. But global bull bond markets require slow growth or recession in the United States and Japan, Australia's major export markets. This weakens the Australian dollar, raising the inflation risk for bond investors. Nor does the trade balance necessarily swing into surplus during a recovery because when Australian business expands, it imports machinery. The net income deficit, too, tends to grow in a recovery. Floating-rate interest payments are likely to rise and, as foreign capital flows into commodity-related equities, more dividend payments flow back out of Australia.

The International Monetary Fund calculated that by mid-1995, the Australian dollar's real effective exchange rate had depreciated by about 20 per cent from its 1990 value—although the Canadian dollar had done worse, depreciating by about 25 per cent. The IMF linked such currency weakness partly to historical inflation but also to high current-account deficits, noting markets had become more aware of such external imbalances after the crisis in Mexico in early 1995. It urged fiscal consolidation in Australia to encourage domestic savings as well as to constrain inflation, saying the authorities had yet to prove the credibility of their inflation policies. See Table 10.2 for further IMF forecasts.

The Economist magazine took up the Mexican theme pointedly in November 1995. In a leading article headlined 'Guess who's looking rather like Mexico', the British weekly described Australia's dependence on foreign capital. Acknowledging that it would be scare mongering to talk of 'an Antipodean Mexico', it recalled that Keating himself had once warned Australia that without a proper economic policy, it could end up as a banana republic. 'It still could,' concluded *The Economist*. Most market

Table 10.2 IMF Statistics and Forecasts for Australian Economy (%)

	1994	1995	1996
Current Account/GDP	−4.8	−5.7	−5.3
Real GDP Growth	5.4	3.8	3.6
Consumer Price Inflation	1.9	4.5	3.4

Source: *World Economic Outlook*, October 1995

analysts said the article was unfair, but it prompted some overseas selling of the Australian dollar.

In its budget[3] for the fiscal year to 30 June 1996, Keating's Labor government forecast a **current account deficit** of A$27 billion, or 5.5 per cent of GDP, saying that although import demand would ease and export growth accelerate, income payments overseas would rise. The deficit came in at just over A$27 billion in 1994–5, although the monthly deficit in May 1995 was a record A$3.1 billion. This was due partly to a drought which slashed farm exports. The officially advocated long-term solutions to the current-account deficit are to encourage domestic savings— Australian household savings rates are among the lowest in the OECD—and value-added exports.

Australia issues quarterly official figures on its **foreign debt**. Data to December 1995 put gross external debt at A$232 billion and net external debt at A$185 billion. The net external debt to GDP ratio hovered just below 40 per cent during 1995. Australia emerged from a severe recession to record real **GDP growth** of 5.4 per cent in calendar 1994, raising fears of overheating. However, sharp rises in official interest rates in late 1994 helped to moderate growth and the OECD's outlook for 1966 was benign. 'A soft landing is projected for Australia, with growth slowing . . . to 3.5 per cent in 1995, then remaining at 3 per cent or so over the next two years . . . With the slowing in domestic demand growth, rising terms of trade and the breaking of the drought, a sharp fall in the current account deficit is projected, from 6 per cent of GDP in the first half of 1995 to 3.5 per cent by 1997,' it said.[4] Although its external **debt** to export ratio is high, Australia's public debt to GDP ratio is more respectable, at an estimated 38 per cent in 1995.[4]

Australia's **unemployment** rate has generally been higher than the OECD average, especially during the early 1990s when it peaked at more than 11 per cent. By 1995 the rate had fallen to around 8 per cent, but it stalled there.

INFLATION AND INTEREST RATES

Australia's inflation rate surged into double figures after the 1973 oil price shock and remained above that of its major trading partners through most of the 1980s. As governments around the world tamed inflation in the early 1990s, Australia succeeded better than most. Its consumer prices rose just 1 per cent in 1992[4] and official interest rates came down from a 1989 peak of nearly 18 per cent to a low of 4.75 per cent. The central bank duly stamped on the monetary brakes as economic growth soared in 1994, raising the official cash rate to 7.5 per cent between August and December. But inflationary pressures went on building during 1995, due largely to a weak Australian dollar, increases in indirect taxes from July and wage rises.

The Reserve Bank of Australia (RBA) has an informal target of limiting **underlying inflation** to an average 2–3 per cent. However, it says this is not so much a fixed range as 'indicative of where we would like to see the average rate over a run of years.'[1] Consequently, the Bank did not move to raise rates during the latter half of 1995 when underlying inflation was rising at an annual 3.2 per cent, the highest since 1991, with headline inflation at 5.1 per cent. The Bank said it expected underlying inflation to move back below 3 per cent during the latter half of 1996. Some economists[5] agreed but others thought a new growth spurt might force the Bank to tighten in late 1996.

Underlying inflation is calculated by the Treasury. It removes the influence of past increases in home-loan rates but not the impact of tax rises from the headline rate, the **consumer price index (CPI)** published quarterly by the Australian Bureau of Statistics. The underlying rate also excludes consumer debt charges, some public-sector charges and volatile items such as energy and some fresh food prices.

The RBA seeks to tighten monetary policy, by raising its target for the overnight **cash rate**, before inflation actually rises. It says the economic indicators which may help to determine monetary policy changes include data on capacity utilisation, the labour market, wages and price expectations. It also looks at money-supply data but abandoned its attempt to use M3 money supply as a policy anchor in 1985 on the grounds that financial deregulation and market innovation continually upset linkages between money and income.

Since 1983, Labor governments had negotiated national frameworks for wage deals with the trade unions, with an increasing emphasis on enterprise bargaining. Under the latest accord,

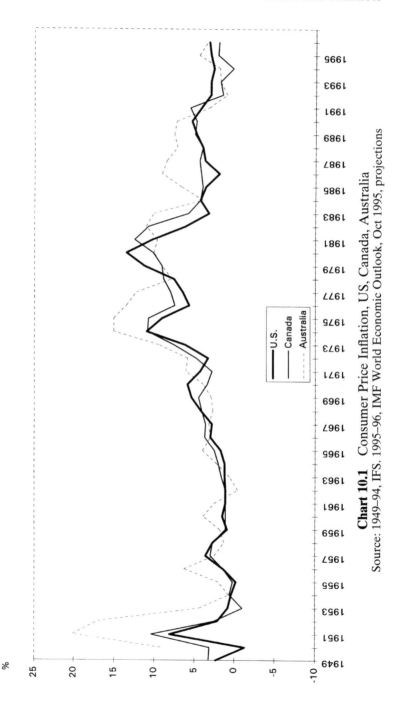

Chart 10.1 Consumer Price Inflation, US, Canada, Australia
Source: 1949–94, IFS. 1995–96, IMF World Economic Outlook, Oct 1995, projections

unions agreed to set pay demands to keep underlying inflation within the RBA target range, while the RBA said it could tolerate higher wage growth providing productivity rose too. During 1995 **earnings growth**, measured by average weekly ordinary time earnings (AWOTE) pushed against the RBA's 5 per cent tolerance ceiling. The new Coalition government planned to let wage restraint accords lapse.

Inflationary pressures did not stop a few economists suspecting there might still be a rate cut just before the general election in 1996. There was not: RBA governor Bernie Fraser has long denied such linkages. 'Some commentators persist in their mistaken beliefs that the Reserve Bank is not independent . . . It has not, as some commentators like to imagine, been pressured to adjust (or not adjust) interest rates for political motives,' he said in late 1994.[1]

BUDGET

Although Australia ran budget surpluses in the late 1980s, recession drove up spending and sapped revenue during the early 1990s. Keating's government took analysts by surprise and left them sceptical by announcing the 1995–6 budget would be in surplus by A\$718 million, after a 1994–5 deficit of A\$12.2 billion, or 2.7 per cent of GDP. The surplus hinged on economic growth of 3.75 per cent in 1995–6, and on the sale of government stakes in Commonwealth Bank and Qantas Airways. Without the asset sales, the 1995–6 budget would have been in deficit by A\$4.5 billion.

The scepticism proved justified. The Qantas stake was sold in July 1995 for A\$1.45 billion, rather less than expected. The Senate, where the Coalition had a majority, blocked a series of Keating's revenue-raising and cost-cutting measures. When the Coalition took office in March 1996, it announced the 1995–6 budget outcome was likely to be a A\$280 million deficit. The new Treasurer, or finance minister, Peter Costello, also rejected the previous government's projections of budget surpluses over the following three years, saying that in fact it would take major spending cuts just to restore the budget to balance by 1997–8. He promised to do so without raising taxes, planning instead to cut spending by a total A\$8 billion over the two fiscal years 1996–8. He scheduled his 1996–7 budget announcement for August.

Meanwhile both the Australian dollar and bonds remained vulnerable to any upset over the sale of Commonwealth Bank, which the new Coalition government said would proceed as soon as market circumstances permitted.

RESERVE BANK OF AUSTRALIA (RBA)

Australia's capital markets have been transformed in the past 15 years.[6] Until 1986, the government was able to borrow directly from RBA by selling the bank Treasury bills at a 1 per cent discount rate. The government needed central bank funding because it was offering securities to the public at pre-set interest rates. Since the market could not decide the yield, it decided the amount instead, which was often less than the government needed. The market also decided the volume of the RBA's foreign-exchange intervention because the exchange rate was quasi-fixed and the RBA had to defend it. All this left the RBA with no real control over the flow of cash to and from the market. Reform began in 1979, when tenders were introduced for Treasury notes, giving the market greater say over interest rates and the authorities more control over volume. Bond tenders began in 1982, and the Australian dollar was floated in 1983. However, it was not until 1986 that the government formally abandoned its claims on central bank credit. It now has an overdraft facility at the RBA but on penal terms. The RBA acts as agent and adviser to the Treasury on debt management, and the central bank buys Commonwealth Government Securities (CGS) purely for use in market-smoothing and monetary policy operations.

The RBA's main instrument of monetary policy is the overnight cash rate. Since 1990, RBA policy on rate changes has been to make a public announcement, usually at 09:30 Sydney time, stating that it wants the cash rate to rise or fall and explaining why. Its board meets on the first Tuesday of each month, but any decision to change rates is usually implemented some time later. The RBA carries out daily open market operations, involving repos or outright sales or purchases of federal government securities. It also offers to buy back Treasury notes with less than 90 days left to maturity, but this discount rate carries a penalty margin and is rarely used.[7]

Australia's 1959 Reserve Bank Act sets the central bank the multiple task of pursuing policies that 'will best contribute to:

(a) the stability of the currency of Australia;
(b) the maintenance of full employment in Australia; and
(c) the economic prosperity and welfare of the people of Australia'.

The current governor, Bernie Fraser, interprets this as giving the bank an 'obligation to the broader community to do what it can to sustain economic activity and employment'. He defends his mandate against those who compare the RBA unfavourably with, for instance, the Reserve Bank of neighbouring New Zealand (RBNZ). New Zealand has become an increasingly serious rival for the attention of foreign bond investors since the RBNZ was given complete operational independence in 1989 to pursue the sole goal of price stability. Australia's Fraser said his mandate 'suits the complexity and uncertainty of the real world better than simple, single goals'.[9] He added, 'It is regrettable that central banks with an attachment to more than one objective are often treated with suspicion.' Denying that the RBA believes permanent jobs can be bought with ever-higher inflation, he said, 'Our aim is to pursue price stability while doing what we can to smooth the business cycle.'[1]

Fraser also defended the degree of independence granted to the RBA. Its governor and board members are appointed by the government, the bank must consult the government before making monetary policy decisions and the government can overrule the bank's recommendations. However, no such confrontation has ever taken place and if it ever does, the government is obliged to table its objections before both houses of parliament. Fraser said what matters more than this legal framework is the RBA's use of market reforms to enhance its practical independence in setting monetary policy.

Australian economists generally agree the RBA operates independently, but say overseas investors are sceptical. Such doubts been fed in recent years by the Coalition, whose leaders repeatedly accused Fraser of being too close to Labor's Keating. Fraser defended Labor government policies against Coalition attack, saying he saw nothing wrong in supporting policies which he considered appropriate for the economy.

Despite the rhetoric, Coalition sources told Reuters in 1995 that they were unlikely to propose changes to the current Reserve Bank Act if they won the 1996 election because they considered the bank has acted reasonably independently in recent years. However, Fraser's seven-year term as governor expires in September 1996 and new Prime Minister John Howard said he believed that Fraser did not intend to seek reappointment.

BOND SUPPLY

The federal government planned to raise A$8.5 billion from the bond market in 1995–6, after more than A$21 billion in 1994–5. Its planned 1995–6 budget surplus is not due to accumulate until late in the fiscal year, so the funding schedule included an extra A$2–A$3 billion of bonds to plug the gap. This was meant to leave the Treasury with spare cash at the end of the year, reducing 1996–7 funding needs.[8] Gross funding needs will clearly depend heavily on Costello's spending plans. However, gross funding must also cover redemptions, estimated to rise from about A$6 billion in 1995–6, to A$8 billion in 1996–7, just under A$11 billion in 1997–8 and roughly A$13 billion in 1998–9; and pension commitments of about A$1 billion a year for public trading enterprises.

The Treasury aims to keep about three-quarters of its domestic debt in fixed-rate bonds and Treasury Indexed Bonds, known as

Table 10.3 Actual and Planned issuance by security type (A$ billion)

	Treasury bonds	Indexed bonds	TABs	Debt total* (%)	Debt/GDP (%)
On issue end-June 1995	81.03	3.23	3.70	95	21
Gross issuance 95/96	5.0–6.0	0.75	2.0–3.0	100	21

* Estimated totals, for fiscal year-ends, include Treasury notes and debt repayable in foreign currencies. But exclude borrowings undertaken on behalf of the states and Northern Territory under an arrangement which ended in 1990.

Source: Data including Treasury estimates supplied by the RBA.

TIBs, with the rest in floating-rate notes and Treasury Adjustable Rate Bonds, known as TABs. Treasury Fixed Coupon Bonds pay semi-annually. Their stock has fluctuated widely, falling to A$31 billion in June 1991 after three years of budget surpluses but soaring in the following four years. The authorities have boosted liquidity by consolidating the paper into benchmarks. There were 20 of these 'hot stocks' in August 1995, with maturities out to October 2007 and issue sizes ranging from just under A$2 billion to nearly A$6 billion. Foreign holdings of Treasury bonds were estimated at about A$28 billion at end-March 1995.

Australia is one of four major bond markets[10] which offers inflation-indexed issues. TIBs have a niche role, appealing mainly to institutions such as pension funds. In Australia the market for these bonds remains small and they are longer dated than conventional bonds, limiting the scope for comparisons with conventional bonds which offer a useful guide to inflation expectations in bigger markets such as the United Kingdom. Australia has issued indexed bonds since 1985. Issuance plans are approximate because of the need to tailor supply to demand for specific maturities.

Australia introduced TABs, floating-rate notes with maturities of three and five years, after yields shot up during 1994 and significant amounts of fixed-rate bonds had to be issued at a discount. The coupons on TABs are linked to the Australian Bank Bill Index. The notes proved popular and the aim was eventually to sell them by tender, but in late 1995 issues were still being handled by an underwriting syndicate group. Apart from offering investors an efficient hedging instrument, TABs are meant to lengthen the maturity profile of the Treasury's floating-rate debt and enable the Treasury eventually to halve the amount of short-term Treasury Notes on issue from a peak of around A$20 billion during 1994–5.[8]

The RBA said a further A$3.1 billion of paper repayable in foreign currency was on issue at the end of calendar 1994. The Australian government used to raise some of its funds on the Eurobond market, but its long-term foreign currency ratings have been downgraded since 1986 and the last such issue was in 1987. The Treasury now uses the swaps market to make extensive changes to both the currency and interest-rate balance of its debt portfolio. Its aim is to keep about 15 per cent of the total portfolio in foreign currencies, with nearly all of this in US dollars and 70 per cent of it in floating-rate paper. Australia can exploit the differential between its foreign-currency rating and its AAA local-currency rating by issuing on the domestic market and swapping the principal into foreign currencies. However, the amount of money the country saves this way depends on the swap market, and the Treasury does not rule out returning to direct issuance offshore at some stage.

PRIMARY MARKET

Tenders for bonds and short-term notes are held using the RBA's electronic Information and Transfer System, known as RITS, and are US-style, with successful bidders paying the prices they bid and higher bidders standing to get more paper. The market watches the weighted-average yield.

There is no set timetable for fixed-coupon bond issues, but as of August 1995 the Treasury planned to hold tenders for them roughly every four to six weeks during 1995–6 and to weight issuance towards the first half of the year. Details of these tenders will usually be announced at noon on Mondays with results at 14:00 Sydney time on Tuesdays and settlement on Thursdays. For indexed bonds, the announcement is on a Wednesday, results on Thursday and settlement by the following Monday. TABs were initially issued through a syndicate of underwriters, but the authorities intended to bring the securities into the usual tender process. Tenders for Treasury notes are usually announced at 16:00 every Tuesday, with results at 14:00 on Wednesdays and settlement on Thursdays.

SECONDARY MARKET

Liquidity in the secondary federal government bond market has soared since tenders were introduced, with turnover in Treasury bonds rising to around A$5 billion a day in 1994–5 from about A$100 million in 1982–3. Trades are usually arranged by telephone and then registered via the electronic RITS system. The market's maturity has also been hastened by the early development of interest-rate futures and options contracts on the Sydney Futures Exchange (SFE), which introduced its 90-day bank bill contract in 1979, 10-year bond futures in 1984 and three-year bond futures in 1988. Liquidity in both cash and futures is concentrated at these maturities. Australia has traditionally attracted Japanese investors in search of high yield at low risk, so the market tends to rally on moves by the Japanese authorities to encourage overseas investment.

SEMIS

There is also an active market in 'semis', the semi-government bonds issued domestically by Australia's six states. However, 'semis' carry no formal guarantee from the Commonwealth government, and the states' credit ratings can vary along with their economic performance and debt management.

OUTLOOK

No domestic bond market can escape the impact of global bond market sentiment in a deregulating world. But Australia is particularly exposed. Its domestic-currency yields inevitably reflect its overall dependence on foreign confidence, plus the risk that persistent current-account deficits might erode the external worth of Australian-dollar debt. 'Australia needs, over time, to lessen its dependence on foreign savings and reduce its vulnerability to destabilising changes in market sentiment towards it,' Central Bank Governor Bernie Fraser has said.[1] There is also little doubt that, despite the capital-market reforms introduced during the 1980s and growing Japanese investor interest, Australian government bonds remain illiquid compared with Canada's.

However, the political uncertainty generated in late 1995 by the imminent Australian general election was more than offset by the fundamental doubts about Canada generated by the Quebec referendum. The Australian bond market is likely to continue to depend heavily on political sentiment towards Canada. For much of the next year or so, the Australian–Canadian yield spread looks set to be driven by the Canadian government's success or failure in reducing the debt burden and placating the Quebecois. On the Australian side of the equation, any narrowing in the spread will depend on the authorities' ability to restrain inflation, the electorate's ability to accept tight fiscal policies, and the country's ability to diversify the export base to service foreign-currency debt.

NOTES

1. 'The art of monetary policy', *Reserve Bank of Australia Bulletin*, October 1994.
2. The local governing bodies of the Australian Capital Territory and the Northern Territory have more limited powers. These two territories each send two representatives to the Senate.
3. Announced in May 1995.
4. OECD *Economic Outlook*, 58, December 1995.
5. Reuters surveys.
6. 'The separation of debt management and monetary policy', *Reserve Bank of Australia Bulletin*, November 1993.
7. *The Reuter Guide to Official Interest Rates.*
8. Details of debt outstanding and types of bonds available were supplied by the RBA. Details of funding plans, debt management strategy and new tender arrangements are taken from papers presented to the Australian Financial Markets Association by Tony Hinton, first assistant secretary, investment and debt division, Commonwealth Treasury, on 16 March and 21 August 1995.
9. 'Central bank independence: what does it mean?', *Reserve Bank of Australia Bulletin*, December 1994.
10. The others are the United Kingdom, Sweden and Canada. The idea has also been tried in Brazil, Finland, Israel and France.

APPENDICES

Box 1—Credit ratings

Standard and Poor's rates the Commonwealth of Australia's domestic currency debt as AAA but downgraded its long-term foreign-currency debt to AA in 1989. Its outlook is now stable (Canada: domestic currency AAA, foreign currency AA-plus with negative outlook). S&P says:

> The Commonwealth of Australia's ratings balance its diverse and increasingly competitive industrial and natural resources-based economy with a still-high net external debt burden . . . The local currency rating reflects a stronger capacity to pay Australian dollar than foreign currency debt due to manageable inflation and public finances, as well as the Commonwealth's taxation powers and control of the domestic financial system . . . However, Australia's credit standing also hinges on firm adherence by the Commonwealth to conservative financial policies . . . Despite historically low . . . inflation and a tighter monetary stance, the credibility of the Reserve Bank's inflation target is not yet firmly established.

Moody's rates Australia's foreign-currency debt Aa2 and its domestic debt Aaa (Canada: domestic currency Aa1, foreign currency Aa2). Moody's says:

> The principal medium-term challenge facing Australia is to reduce its reliance on foreign savings. In order to maintain the country's present level of investment activity, Australia relies quite heavily upon foreign financing. This is not automatically a negative, except that after a certain point, the burden of repayment has the potential to decrease a country's medium-term growth rate . . . The government's policy response [to the current account deficit] has been to propose moving the Commonwealth budget to surplus in 1995/96—thus increasing domestic savings through decreasing government dissavings. This appears to be an appropriate policy response. The question is whether this will be enough to reverse the current account adequately. From today's vantage point, it appears that further measures will probably be needed if the current account deficit is to be reduced significantly in the medium term.

Box 2—Futures and options, Sydney Exchange

Contract months for interest rate futures and options: March,
June, September, December

Trading hours: Floor 08:30–12:30   14:00–16:30
SYCOM (computerised) 16:40–06:00

Options are American-style, i.e. they can be exercised on
any business day up to and including the day of expiry; exercise prices at intervals of 0.25 per cent annual yield.

The SFE also offers European-style overnight options on
bond futures. These contracts, traded during SYCOM hours,
expire at the end of each SYCOM session. Holders of in-the-
money options receive a futures position at the strike price.
Nine strike prices are available, with others added at the
exchange's discretion, on the nearest delivery month.

Futures and options on 90-Day Bank Accepted Bills of exchange

Contract unit: A$1 million; total volume (futures and options)
1994: 10.3 million

Futures delivery: bank accepted bills or bank negotiable
certificates of deposit

Futures quotation: 100 minus annual percentage yield to two
decimal places

Futures settlement: second Friday of delivery month; options
expire one week earlier

Futures and options on 10-year and 3-year Commonwealth
Treasury Bonds

Contract unit: Face value A$100 000, 12 per cent coupon; cash
settlement

Total volume (futures and options) 1994: 7.6 million 10-year;
10.2 million 3-year

Futures quotation: 100 minus yield per cent per annum in
multiples of 0.005 per cent for 10-year bonds, 0.01 per cent for
three-year bonds

Futures settlement: middle of delivery month; options expire one
day earlier

11
Summary and conclusions

At the end of the day, the global investor who is given reasonable freedom to take decisions and is planning to allocate funds has an extraordinary number of decisions to make: bonds or equities, Germany or the United States, hedged or unhedged, the short end or the long end and many, many more.

The decision between asset classes—bonds or equities, property or commodities, fine art or cash, say—will depend on a host of factors including the economic cycle. The decision on where to allocate funds geographically will be a similarly tough one. Some investors must compare their performances with various benchmarks, will be relatively conservative and must think in terms of overweighting or underweighting; others will have a much freer hand to 'make a bet' wherever they see fit. Some will have restrictions placed on them in terms of the credit rating of the assets they are allowed to invest in or the proportion of funds that must be kept at home or in equities. Some will regard the currency as an integral part of the attractions of a market, others will look at currencies as a separate asset class, others will see currency risk as a problem to be dealt with. Having made a choice of, say, German Bunds, there is still the decision to make about where on the curve to invest—the duration required and finally the exact instrument.

In this book we have tried quite simply to look at some of the world's biggest government bond markets and give our impressions of the plus and minus points of each. This book is not yet another textbook, detailing bond analytics; nor is it one more handbook enabling the professional investor to understand the intricacies and complexities of each market covered. Instead, what we have tried to do is give the investor some ideas, plus details of where to go for more. Above all, the opinions expressed are not ours or Reuters but have been picked up from talking to and reading the thoughts of many of the financial world's top analysts, economists and strategists.

Some regard the economics as crucial, others the technical picture, others the psychology of markets. We have tried in this book to satisfy each group, for an investment decision must take into account many factors from the degree of risk the fund manager is prepared to take—given that higher risk can mean higher profits but also higher losses—to the level of liquidity in each market.

Germany, at the time of writing, was still seen as the core European bond market: relatively low risk and safe although some domestic investors were concerned about the impact of eventual monetary union. Italy, Spain and Sweden were seen as the high risk European markets, offering considerably more in terms of yield but perhaps potentially less in terms of the total rate of return.

Obviously there are key factors to consider in each market:

- The politics are crucial because political uncertainty can wipe points off a market in just a few hours.
- The standing of the central bank is important. Can it be trusted to do the right thing if political pressure is put on it to do the wrong?
- The market structure is important because buying bonds at auction can be cheaper than buying them in the secondary market.
- The secondary market itself is important because fund managers need to know that they can buy and sell quickly, easily and cheaply.
- Debt ratings are important for some funds may be barred from buying assets with too low a rating. A decision by Moody's or Standard & Poor's to cut a rating—or even signal a possible downgrading—can cause enormous uncertainty and lead to instant losses.
- The economy may not be as important as some economists think but news of, say, a US employment report well out of line with expectations can send shudders through markets that can last for days.
- The technical, or chart, position is crucial, if only because traders worldwide look at charts and listen to what technical analysts have to say. For some, combining economics with technicals is a good way to look at a market—offering ideas both on direction and on entry and exit points.
- Behavioural psychology is massively important too; how else do you explain how markets can shoot up or down, overshoot, move back? It

has to be the way the financial markets are a crowd and, as psychologists will tell you, crowds behave in specific ways.

- The currency is crucial whether the investor manages debt risk separately from currency risk or decides on a geographical location for his or her funds after looking at both the debt market itself and the currency.
- We have looked only at central government debt in this book but there are plenty of alternatives—municipal, agency and corporate bonds, and sovereign Eurobonds to name just a few.
- The investor might want to look at some of the markets we have not included: Ireland rather than the United Kingdom, Portugal rather than Spain, the Netherlands rather than Germany for example.
- The professional investor might also want to consider some of the emerging markets in Latin America, Eastern Europe or Asia; true, most early emerging market investment is in the form of equity or venture capital, but there are plenty of debt instruments available in countries like Russia or Mexico.
- The derivatives markets have never been more important than they are now. An investment in bond futures might be a good, liquid alternative to an investment in the cash market.

All these are factors to be thought about. It is possible, moreover, to be more sophisticated than ever before by using options strategies, box trades or a host of other devices.

Inevitably a book that describes the markets country by country will give less attention to the spreads between markets, yet that is where an increasing amount of business takes place. The markets are full of phrases like the TED spread (between Treasuries and Eurodollars) or the Siesta spread (between Spain and Italy). How will the markets compare in 1996? If bond markets do best in a recession, because a recession tends to lead to lower interest rates and subdued inflation, then Japan could be a candidate unless the government succeeds in stimulating the economy and the yen remains weak, enabling GDP to climb rapidly from the depressed leve's of 1994 and 1995. The United States could be a candidate, too, if growth continues to slow in 1996 as it did in 1995. In contrast, the United Kingdom and Italy could be among the least attractive markets, if both economies continue to grow at a reasonable clip in 1996 as they did in 1995.

But what of inflation? Again, Japan could be the best bet, with inflation as near to zero as makes no difference; and Italy could be among the worst bets, with inflation around twice the G7 average both in 1995 and 1996. Yet, oddly enough, there was little enthusiasm for Japan in the international bond markets in late 1995, and plenty of strategists were tipping Italy—if the political scene would only calm down. Perhaps part of the answer lies in interest rates: high enough in Italy to make that market attractive; low enough in Japan to make it unattractive—perhaps.

One thing seems certain: global capital will still flow around the world, imposing discipline on individual governments of a kind they have never had to face before. Another certainty is that the performance of the dollar will be crucial. If it continues to gain ground, much US money will stay at home, while plenty of overseas money will head across the Atlantic, and more importantly the Pacific, for America.

In many ways 1996 could mark a turning point. There could be a new president in the White House. Japan's economy could finally emerge from recession. It could become clearer whether there is to be a single currency in parts of Western Europe and, if so, in which countries and when. The reformed UK gilts market could succeed in attracting new investors, Italy's fraught political situation could stabilise. Interest rates could fall further in many key economies.

These fundamentals certainly help the well-informed international investor or trader make the right decisions. In the words of the International Monetary Fund, in its *World Economic Outlook* published in October 1995:

> It seems clear that fundamentals do influence market sentiment, and that international investors recognise actual or potential policy weaknesses and adjust their portfolios accordingly, albeit sometimes with a lag. It is also clear that financial markets can serve to discipline and reinforce policy decisions in a helpful way.

Yet the IMF also notes that the markets recently have swung around remarkably, in a way economics alone cannot explain. Chartists believe their method of forecasting is better. Other analysts go for other solutions. At the end of the day, fund managers must trust their own judgement and instincts—and remember 'it's only money'.

JOHN WILEY & SONS LTD

The Reuters Guide to World Bond Markets

In order for us to send you future information about this and other Wiley publications, please complete this card. We will send you a FREE Finance, Economics and Accounting catalogue.

Name

Position

Organisation

Address

Country   Post/zip code

Telephone: Fax: e-mail:

Where did you buy this book:

❑ Bookshop _____ *(Please specify)*
❑ Direct from Wiley
❑ Other _____ *(Please specify)*

JOHN WILEY & SONS LTD

The Reuters Guide to World Bond Markets

In order for us to send you future information about this and other Wiley publications, please complete this card. We will send you a FREE Finance, Economics and Accounting catalogue.

Name

Position

Organisation

Address

Country   Post/zip code

Telephone: Fax: e-mail:

Where did you buy this book:

❑ Bookshop _____ *(Please specify)*
❑ Direct from Wiley
❑ Other _____ *(Please specify)*

REPONSE PAYEE
GRANDE-BRETAGNE

Louise Holden
John Wiley & Sons Ltd
Baffins Lane
CHICHESTER
West Sussex,
GREAT BRITAIN
PO19 1YN

**By air mail
Par avion**

IBRS/CCRI NUMBER:
PHQ-D/1204/PO

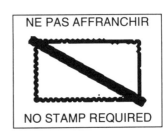

NE PAS AFFRANCHIR

NO STAMP REQUIRED

REPONSE PAYEE
GRANDE-BRETAGNE

Louise Holden
John Wiley & Sons Ltd
Baffins Lane
CHICHESTER
West Sussex,
GREAT BRITAIN
PO19 1YN